Black Bayou Lake National Wildlife Refuge

Comprehensive Conservation Plan

U.S. Department of the Interior
Fish and Wildlife Service
Southeast Region

July 2010

Submitted by: _____Signed_____   Date: 1-14-10
Brett Hortman, Refuge Manager
Black Bayou Lake NWR

Concur: _____Signed_____   Date: 1-14-10
George Chandler, Project Leader
North LA Refuges Complex

Concur: _____Signed_____   Date: 3/4/10
Ricky Ingram, Refuge Supervisor
Southeast Region

Concur: _____Signed_____   Date: 3-4-10
Jon Andrew, Regional Chief
Southeast Region

Approved by: _____Signed_____   Date: 3-10-10
Cynthia Dohner, Regional Director
Southeast Region

COMPREHENSIVE CONSERVATION PLAN

BLACK BAYOU LAKE NATIONAL WILDLIFE REFUGE

OUACHITA PARISH, LOUISIANA

**U.S. Department of the Interior
Fish and Wildlife Service**
Southeast Region
Atlanta, Georgia

July 2010

TABLE OF CONTENTS

COMPREHENSIVE CONSERVATION PLAN

LIST OF FIGURES

LIST OF TABLES

Executive Summary

The Fish and Wildlife Service (Service) has prepared this Comprehensive Conservation Plan (CCP) to guide the management of Black Bayou Lake National Wildlife Refuge (NWR) in Ouachita Parish, Louisiana. The CCP outlines programs and corresponding resource needs for the next 15 years, as mandated by the National Wildlife Refuge System Improvement Act of 1997.

Before the Service began planning, it conducted a biological review of the refuge's wildlife and habitat management program and conducted public scoping meetings to solicit public opinion of the issues the CCP should address. The biological review team was composed of biologists from federal and state agencies and non-governmental organizations that have an interest in the refuge. The refuge staff held one public scoping meeting and solicited public reaction to the proposed alternatives. Also, a 30-day public review and comment period of the Draft Comprehensive Conservation Plan and Environmental Assessment was provided.

The Service developed and analyzed three alternatives. Alternative A represented no change from current management of the refuge. Current approaches to managing wildlife and habitats, protecting resources, and allowing for public use would remain unchanged. The mix of habitats on the refuge, including bottomland hardwood and upland pine hardwood forests, would be restored and managed appropriately. Under Alternative A, the refuge would continue to work with partners to acquire lands within the current refuge boundary. The refuge would continue to benefit native wildlife species and provide habitat for wintering waterfowl and year-round habitat for nesting wood ducks. It would also maintain the current habitat mix for the benefit of other migratory birds. Staff would continue existing surveys and monitor long-term population trends and health of migratory and resident species. Existing refuge staff and volunteers would maintain the current public use and environmental education programs at the refuge. The refuge would continue to serve the public with a premier wildlife-dependent visitor services program.

Under Alternative B, the refuge would strive to optimize both its biological program and visitor services program. The refuge would continue to furnish benefits to resident wildlife species in Alternative B and would aim to increase its knowledge base about migratory birds, reptiles, amphibians, invertebrates, and species of special concern, such as the alligator snapping turtle, by developing and implementing monitoring programs, while continuing to provide habitats for the benefit of waterfowl, colonial waterbirds, and landbirds. The refuge would use its resources to create and/or maintain a variety of habitats compatible with historic habitat types. Efforts to control invasive species would increase from those under Alternative A. Under Alternative B, land acquisition, bottomland hardwood forest management, and resource protection at the refuge would be intensified from the level now maintained in the no-action alternative. In the Private Lands Program, staff would work with private landowners on adjacent tracts to manage and improve habitats.

Alternative B would provide a full-time law enforcement officer, a refuge operations specialist, a maintenance worker, and park ranger (visitor services). With regard to cultural resources, including those of an archaeological or historical nature, within 15 years of the date of this CCP, the refuge would develop and begin to implement a Cultural Resources Management Plan.

Under Alternative B, public use and environmental education would increase only slightly from the no-action alternative. The program would be enhanced and improved with the addition of two park rangers (visitor services and law enforcement). Within 3 years of the date of CCP completion, the refuge would develop a Visitor Services Plan to maintain quality public use facilities and opportunities on the refuge. This step-down management plan would provide overall, long-term direction and guidance in developing and running one of the country's premier public use programs at Black Bayou Lake NWR. Over the 15-year life of the CCP, staff would increase the emphasis on environmental education and interpretation under Alternative B to lead to increases in understanding of the importance of habitat and resources on the refuge.

Alternative C would minimize wildlife and habitat management and the public use program. Baseline inventorying and monitoring programs would be eliminated; monitoring for changes in trends would not be necessary to achieve purposes of the refuge. Public use would be maintained under this alternative and monitored for impacts to wildlife. Fishing would continue as currently managed. Environmental education, wildlife observation, and wildlife photography would be accommodated at present levels. Waterfowl hunting on the refuge would be eliminated while maintaining other current hunting practices. Staffing would remain as in the no-action alternative.

The Service selected Alternative B as its preferred alternative and is reflected in this CCP. Alternative B is selected for implementation because it directs the development of programs to best achieve the refuge purpose and goals; emphasizes management and restoration of the refuge's open wetlands and bottomland hardwood and upland forests in support of migratory and resident waterfowl and other wildlife, especially forest breeding birds, amphibians and reptiles, marsh birds, white-tailed deer, wood duck, and woodcock; collects habitat and wildlife data; and ensures long-term achievement of refuge and Service objectives. At the same time, these management actions provide balanced levels of compatible public use opportunities consistent with existing laws, Service policies, and sound biological principles. Alternative B provides the best mix of program elements to achieve desired long-term conditions.

Under this alternative, all lands under the management and direction of the refuge will be protected, managed, maintained, and enhanced and those lands within the approved acquisition boundary will be prioritized for acquisition to best achieve national, regional, ecosystem, and refuge-specific goals and objectives within anticipated funding and staffing levels. In addition, the action positively addresses significant issues and concerns expressed by the public.

I. Background

INTRODUCTION

This Comprehensive Conservation Plan (CCP) for Black Bayou Lake National Wildlife Refuge (NWR), Ouachita Parish, Louisiana, was prepared to guide management actions and direction for the refuge. Fish and wildlife conservation will receive first priority in refuge management; wildlife-dependent recreation will be allowed and encouraged as long as it is compatible with, and does not detract from, the mission of the refuge or the purposes for which it was established.

A planning team developed a range of alternatives that best met the goals and objectives of the refuge and that could be implemented within the 15-year planning period. This CCP describes the Fish and Wildlife Service's (Service) plan. The CCP was made available to state and federal government agencies, non-governmental organizations, conservation partners, and the general public for review and comment. Comments from each entity were considered in the development of this CCP.

PURPOSE AND NEED FOR THE PLAN

The purpose of the CCP is to develop an action that best achieves the refuge purpose; attains the vision and goals developed for the refuge; contributes to National Wildlife Refuge System (Refuge System) mission; addresses key problems, issues and relevant mandates; and is consistent with sound principles of fish and wildlife management.

Specifically, the CCP is needed to:

- Provide a clear statement of refuge management direction;
- Provide refuge neighbors, visitors, and government officials with an understanding of Service management actions on and around the refuge;
- Ensure that Service management actions, including land protection and recreation/education programs, are consistent with the mandates of the Refuge System; and
- Provide a basis for the development of budget requests for operations, maintenance, and capital improvement needs.

FISH AND WILDLIFE SERVICE

The Service traces its roots to 1871 and the establishment of the Commission of Fisheries involved with research and fish culture. The once independent commission was renamed the Bureau of Fisheries and placed under the Department of Commerce and Labor in 1903.

The Service also traces its roots to 1886 and the establishment of a Division of Economic Ornithology and Mammalogy in the Department of Agriculture. Research on the relationship of birds and animals to agriculture shifted to delineation of the range of plants and animals so the name was changed to the Division of the Biological Survey in 1896.

The Department of Commerce, Bureau of Fisheries, was combined with the Department of Agriculture, Bureau of Biological Survey, on June 30, 1940, and transferred to the Department of the Interior as the Fish and Wildlife Service. The name was changed to the Bureau of Sport Fisheries and Wildlife in 1956 and finally to the Fish and Wildlife Service in 1974.

The Service, working with others, is responsible for conserving, protecting, and enhancing fish and wildlife and their habitats for the continuing benefit of the American people through federal programs relating to migratory birds, endangered species, interjurisdictional fish and marine mammals, and inland sport fisheries.

As part of its mission, the Service manages more than 540 national wildlife refuges covering over 95 million acres. These areas comprise the National Wildlife Refuge System, the world's largest collection of lands set aside specifically for fish and wildlife. The majority of these lands, 77 million acres, is in Alaska. The remaining acres are spread across the other 49 states and several United States territories. In addition to refuges, the Service manages thousands of small wetlands, national fish hatcheries, 64 fishery resource offices, and 78 ecological services field stations. The Service enforces federal wildlife laws, administers the Endangered Species Act, manages migratory bird populations, restores nationally significant fisheries, conserves and restores wildlife habitat, and helps foreign governments with their conservation efforts. It also oversees the Federal Aid program that distributes hundreds of millions of dollars in excise taxes on fishing and hunting equipment to state fish and wildlife agencies.

NATIONAL WILDLIFE REFUGE SYSTEM

The mission of the National Wildlife Refuge System, as defined by the National Wildlife Refuge System Improvement Act of 1997 is:

> "...to administer a national network of lands and waters for the conservation, management, and where appropriate, restoration of the fish, wildlife and plant resources and their habitats within the United States for the benefit of present and future generations of Americans."

The National Wildlife Refuge System Improvement Act of 1997 (Improvement Act) established, for the first time, a clear legislative mission of wildlife conservation for the Refuge System. Actions were initiated in 1997 to comply with the direction of this new legislation, including an effort to complete comprehensive conservation plans for all refuges. These plans, which are completed with full public involvement, help guide the future management of refuges by establishing natural resources and recreation/education programs. Consistent with the Improvement Act, approved plans will serve as the guidelines for refuge management for the next 15 years. The Improvement Act states that each refuge shall be managed to:

- Fulfill the mission of the Refuge System;
- Fulfill the individual purposes of each refuge;
- Consider the needs of wildlife first;
- Fulfill requirements of comprehensive conservation plans that are prepared for each unit of the Refuge System;
- Maintain the biological integrity, diversity, and environmental health of the Refuge System; and

- Recognize that wildlife-dependent recreation activities including hunting, fishing, wildlife observation, wildlife photography, and environmental education and interpretation are legitimate and priority public uses; and allow refuge managers authority to determine compatible public uses.

The following are just a few examples of your national network of conservation lands. Pelican Island National Wildlife Refuge, the first refuge, was established in 1903 for the protection of colonial nesting birds in Florida, such as the snowy egret and the brown pelican. Western refuges were established for American bison (1906), elk (1912), prong-horned antelope (1931), and desert bighorn sheep (1936) after over-hunting, competition with cattle, and natural disasters decimated once-abundant herds. The drought conditions of the 1930s Dust Bowl severely depleted breeding populations of ducks and geese. Refuges established during the Great Depression focused on waterfowl production areas (i.e., protection of prairie wetlands in America's heartland). The emphasis on waterfowl continues today but also includes protection of wintering habitat in response to a dramatic loss of bottomland hardwoods. By 1973, the Service had begun to focus on establishing refuges for endangered species.

National wildlife refuges connect visitors to their natural resource heritage and provide them with an understanding and appreciation of fish and wildlife ecology to help them understand their role in the environment. Wildlife-dependent recreation on refuges also generates economic benefits to local communities. According to the report, *Banking on Nature 2006: The Economic Benefits to Local Communities of National Wildlife Refuge Visitation*, approximately 34.8 million people visited national wildlife refuges in fiscal year 2006, generating almost $1.7 billion in total economic activity and creating almost 27,000 private sector jobs producing about $542.8 million in employment income (Carver and Caudill 2007). Additionally, recreational spending on refuges generated nearly $185.3 million in tax revenue at the local, county, state, and federal levels (Carver and Caudill 2007). As the number of visitors grows, significant economic benefits are realized by local communities. In 2006, nearly 71 million people, 16 years and older, fished, hunted, or observed wildlife, spending $45.7 billion and generating $122.6 billion (Leonard 2008).

Volunteers continue to be a major contributor to the success of the Refuge System. In 2005, approximately 38,000 refuge volunteers donated more than 1.4 million hours. The value of their service was more than $25 million.

The wildlife and habitat vision for national wildlife refuges stresses that wildlife comes first; that ecosystems, biodiversity, and wilderness are vital concepts in refuge management; that refuges must be healthy and growth must be strategic; and that the Refuge System serves as a model for habitat management with broad participation from others.

The Improvement Act stipulates that comprehensive conservation plans be prepared in consultation with adjoining federal, state, and private landowners and that the Service develop and implement a process to ensure an opportunity for active public involvement in the preparation and revision (every 15 years) of the plans.

All lands of the Refuge System will be managed in accordance with an approved CCP that will guide management decisions and set forth strategies for achieving refuge unit purposes. The CCP will be consistent with sound resource management principles, practices, and legal mandates, including Service compatibility standards and other Service policies, guidelines, and planning documents.

Legal Mandates, Administrative and Policy Guidelines, and Other Special Considerations

Administration of national wildlife refuges is guided by the mission and goals of the Refuge System, congressional legislation, presidential executive orders, and international treaties. Policies for management options of refuges are further refined by administrative guidelines established by the Secretary of the Interior and by policy guidelines established by the Director of the Fish and Wildlife Service. Select legal summaries of treaties and laws relevant to administration of the National Wildlife Refuge System and management of the Black Bayou Lake NWR are provided in Appendix C.

Treaties, laws, administrative guidelines, and policy guidelines assist the refuge manager in making decisions pertaining to soil, water, air, flora, fauna, and other natural resources; historical and cultural resources; research and recreation on refuge lands; and provide a framework for cooperation between Black Bayou Lake NWR and other partners, such as the Louisiana Department of Wildlife and Fisheries, Natural Resources Conservation Service, The Nature Conservancy, Ducks Unlimited, and private landowners, etc.

Lands within the Refuge System are closed to public use unless specifically and legally opened. No refuge use may be allowed unless it is determined to be compatible. A compatible use is a use that, in the sound professional judgment of the refuge manager, will not materially interfere with or detract from the fulfillment of the mission of the Refuge System or the purposes of the refuge. All programs and uses must be evaluated based on mandates set forth in the Improvement Act. Those mandates are to:

- Contribute to ecosystem goals, as well as refuge purposes and goals;
- Conserve, manage, and restore fish, wildlife, and plant resources and their habitats;
- Monitor the trends of fish, wildlife, and plants;
- Manage and ensure appropriate visitor uses as those uses benefit the conservation of fish and wildlife resources and contribute to the enjoyment of the public; and
- Ensure that visitor activities are compatible with refuge purposes.

The Improvement Act further identifies six priority wildlife-dependent recreational uses. These uses are: hunting, fishing, wildlife observation, wildlife photography, and environmental education and interpretation. As priority public uses of the Refuge System, they receive priority consideration over other public uses in planning and management.

Biological Integrity, Diversity, and Environmental Health Policy

The Improvement Act directs the Service to ensure that the biological integrity, diversity, and environmental health of the Refuge System are maintained for the benefit of present and future generations of Americans. The policy is an additional directive for refuge managers to follow while achieving refuge purpose(s) and the Refuge System mission. It provides for the consideration and protection of the broad spectrum of fish, wildlife, and habitat resources found on refuges and associated ecosystems. When evaluating the appropriate management direction for refuges, refuge managers will use sound professional judgment to determine their refuges' contribution to biological integrity, diversity, and environmental health at multiple landscape scales. Sound professional judgment incorporates field experience, knowledge of refuge resources, knowledge of refuge role within an ecosystem, and knowledge of applicable laws and best available science, including consultation with others both inside and outside the Service.

NATIONAL AND INTERNATIONAL CONSERVATION PLANS AND INITIATIVES

Multiple partnerships have been developed among government and private entities to address the environmental problems affecting regions. There is a large amount of conservation and protection information that defines the role of the refuge at the local, national, international, and ecosystem levels. Conservation initiatives include broad-scale planning and cooperation between affected parties to address declining trends of natural, physical, social, and economic environments. The conservation guidance described below, along with issues, problems, and trends, was reviewed and integrated where appropriate into this CCP.

This CCP supports, among others, the Partners-in-Flight Plan, the North American Waterfowl Management Plan, the Western Hemisphere Shorebird Reserve Network, and the National Wetlands Priority Conservation Plan.

North American Bird Conservation Initiative. Started in 1999, the North American Bird Conservation Initiative is a coalition of government agencies, private organizations, academic institutions, and private industry leaders in the United States, Canada, and Mexico, working to ensure the long-term health of North America's native bird populations by fostering an integrated approach to bird conservation to benefit all birds in all habitats. The four international and national bird initiatives include the North American Waterfowl Management Plan, Partners-in-Flight, Waterbird Conservation for the Americas, and the U.S. Shorebird Conservation Plan.

North American Waterfowl Management Plan. The North American Waterfowl Management Plan is an international action plan to conserve migratory birds throughout the continent. The plan's goal is to return waterfowl populations to their 1970s levels by conserving wetland and upland habitat. Canada and the United States signed the plan in 1986 in reaction to critically low numbers of waterfowl. Mexico joined in 1994, making it a truly continental effort. The plan is a partnership of federal, provincial/state and municipal governments, non-governmental organizations, private companies, and many individuals, all working towards achieving better wetland habitat for the benefit of migratory birds, other wetland-associated species and people. Plan projects are international in scope, but implemented at regional levels. These projects contribute to the protection of habitat and wildlife species across the North American landscape.

Partners in Flight Bird Conservation Plan. Managed as part of the Partners in Flight Plan, the Mississippi Alluvial Valley physiographic area represents scientifically based land bird conservation planning efforts that ensures long-term maintenance of healthy populations of native land birds, primarily non-game land birds. Nongame land birds have been vastly under-represented in conservation efforts, and many are exhibiting significant declines. This plan is voluntary and non-regulatory, and focuses on relatively common species in areas where conservation actions can be most effective, rather than the frequent local emphasis on rare and peripheral populations.

Partners in Flight has formed Bird Conservation Plans by Bird Conservation Regions that set conservation priorities and habitat and population objectives. Habitats found on Black Bayou Lake NWR and associated bird species that are considered a priority in the Mississippi Alluvial Valley and West Gulf Coastal Plain include:

> 1. Loblolly/Shortleaf Pine: Henslow's sparrow, Bachman's sparrow, American kestrel, Le Conte's sparrow, chuck-will's-widow, hooded warbler, brown-headed nuthatch, prairie warbler, scissor-tailed flycatcher, red-cockaded woodpecker, and eastern wood-pewee.

2. Bottomland Hardwood Forest: swallow-tailed kite, Swainson's warbler, prothonotary warbler, white-eyed vireo, yellow-billed cuckoo, and red-headed woodpecker.

U.S. Shorebird Conservation Plan. The U.S. Shorebird Conservation Plan is a partnership effort being undertaken throughout the country to ensure that shorebird populations are restored and protected. Primary objectives of this plan are:

1. Development of a scientifically sound monitoring system to provide practical information to researchers and land managers.

2. Identify principles upon which management plans can integrate shorebird habitat conservation with multiple species strategies.

3. Design a strategy for increasing public awareness and information concerning wetlands and shorebirds.

Black Bayou Lake NWR is within the Lower Mississippi/Western Gulf Coast Shorebird Planning Region and Bird Conservation Region. This plan recommends that public lands provide as much fall shorebird habitat as possible to meet the goal of 520 ha (1,285 acres) of fall habitat in Louisiana. Although Black Bayou Lake NWR is not considered an important shorebird area, the following species are considered high priority for the region: piping plover, American golden-plover, marbled godwit, ruddy turnstone, red knot, sanderling, buff-breasted sandpiper, American woodcock, and Wilson's phalarope.

North American Waterbird Conservation Plan. A broad coalition of governmental, non-governmental, and academia organizations interested in coordinating efforts to conserve bird populations and the landscapes upon which they depend. NABCI evolved in 1998 out of recognition among conservationists of the value of coordinating and integrating planning, implementation, and evaluation efforts of NAWMP, PIF, USSCP, and colonial waterbirds. The goal is to cause the combined effectiveness of these separate programs to exceed the total of their parts.

U.S. Woodcock Plan. The U.S. Woodcock Plan was written by the Service in 1990 to "guide the conservation of woodcock in the United States." Although no stepdown plans have been written, the plan gives general guidance for habitat and population management at the national level.

RELATIONSHIP TO STATE WILDLIFE AGENCY

A provision of the Improvement Act, and subsequent agency policy, is that the Service shall ensure timely and effective cooperation and collaboration with other state fish and game agencies and tribal governments during the course of acquiring and managing refuges. State wildlife management areas and national wildlife refuges provide the foundation for the protection of species and contribute to the overall health and sustainment of fish and wildlife species in the State of Louisiana.

The Louisiana Department of Wildlife and Fisheries (LDWF) is a state-partnering agency with the Service, charged with managing state natural resources and approximately 1.4 million acres of coastal marshes and wildlife management areas. LDWF coordinates the state wildlife conservation program and provides public recreation opportunities on state wildlife management areas. The state's participation and contribution throughout the comprehensive conservation planning process provided for ongoing opportunities and open dialogue to improve the ecological health and diversity of fish and wildlife. A vital part of the comprehensive conservation planning process is integrating common mission objectives where appropriate.

In 2005, LDWF published a Comprehensive Wildlife Conservation Strategy (CWCS). The components or steps of the CWCS are:

1. Assess the distribution and abundance of wildlife species, including rare and declining species that are indicative of the diversity and health of the state's wildlife.

2. Describe the location and relative condition of key habitats and community types essential to conservation of these species.

3. Identify problems that adversely affect these species and habitats as well as research and survey efforts needed to address these problems.

4. Identify conservation actions needed to conserve these species and habitats, and priorities for implementing these actions.

5. Develop plans for monitoring these species and habitats, monitoring the effectiveness of conservation actions, and adapting conservation actions to respond to new information or changing conditions.

6. Develop procedures to review the conservation strategy at intervals not to exceed 10 years.

7. Coordinate plan development and implementation with federal, state, and local governments and other organizations that manage significant areas of the state or administer wildlife conservation programs.

8. Encourage public participation in the development, revision, and implementation of the conservation strategy.

II. Refuge Overview

INTRODUCTION

The Black Bayou Lake NWR is a unit of the North Louisiana National Wildlife Refuge Complex (Figure 1). In addition to Black Bayou Lake NWR, the Complex includes D'Arbonne, Upper Ouachita, Handy Brake, and Red River NWRs, as well as the Louisiana Farm Service Agency tracts. Each refuge has unique issues and has had separate planning efforts and public involvement.

The Black Bayou Lake NWR plays an important role regionally in fulfilling the national goals of the Refuge System. Its close proximity to a major metropolitan center gives members of the public the ability to participate in educational opportunities that promote wildlife stewardship and to learn about environmental issues/concerns that are affecting their communities.

REFUGE HISTORY AND PURPOSE

Black Bayou Lake NWR, established in 1997, is located 3 miles north of the city of Monroe, just east of Highway 165 in Ouachita Parish, Louisiana. It contains 4,522 acres of lacustrine, bottomland hardwood, and upland mixed pine/hardwood habitats (Figure 2). Although the suburban sprawl of the city of Monroe surrounds much of its boundary, the refuge itself represents many habitat types and is home to a diversity of plants and animals. Black Bayou Lake NWR is situated in the Mississippi Flyway, the Mississippi Alluvial Valley Bird Conservation Region, and the Lower Mississippi River Ecosystem.

Black Bayou Lake NWR was established for "…the conservation of the wetlands of the nation in order to maintain the public benefits they provide and to help fulfill international obligations contained in various migratory bird treaties and conventions…" 16 U.S.C. 3901 (b) (Wetlands Extension Act).

The central physical feature of the refuge is the lake itself. Black Bayou Lake, consisting of approximately 1,500 acres, is studded with baldcypress and water tupelo trees. The western half of the lake is open and deeper, unlike the eastern side which is thick with trees and emergent vegetation. This portion of the lake is naturally filling in. The lake is owned by the city of Monroe, which manages its water level as a secondary source of municipal water. The Service has a 99-year free lease on the lake and some of its surrounding land, constituting a total of 1,620 acres. The refuge owns the remaining 2,902 acres, consisting of upland pine/hardwood and bottomland hardwood forests.

On May 6, 1993, the Director of the Service approved the Preliminary Project Proposal to create Black Bayou Lake NWR. The approved acquisition boundary encompasses 6,200 acres of wetlands associated with the lake (Figure 2). Initial acquisition efforts began but soon halted when the LDWF indicated an interest in acquiring the property. Politics, escalating land values, and other factors intervened and the LDWF eventually backed out of the project. In May 1996, the Service contacted the city of Monroe about managing the area if the city purchased it. The lake serves as the city's secondary source of water, and the city had funds to protect such areas. However, the city had no interest in managing the property. Numerous meetings resulted in a plan to create an overlay refuge on the city's property via a free 99-year lease. In October, the city purchased nearly 1,700 acres of the core area for $1.725 million. On January 14, 1997, the Monroe City Council voted to lease the property to the Service for 99 years for $1 to create Black Bayou Lake NWR. The refuge was formally established on June 16, 1997, when assistant regional director Geoff Haskett signed the lease.

Figure 1. North Louisiana National Wildlife Refuge Complex

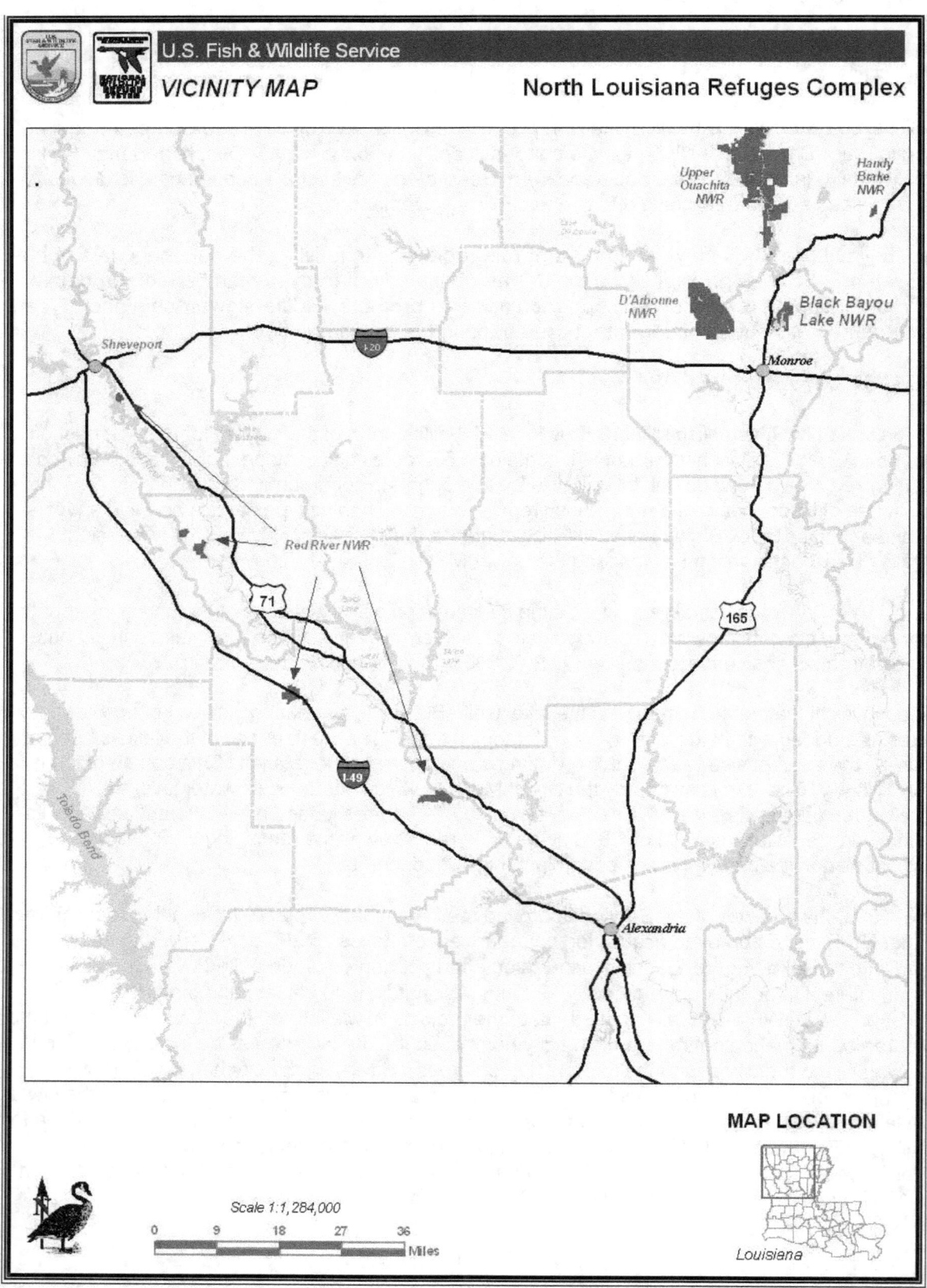

Figure 2. Black Bayou Lake National Wildlife Refuge

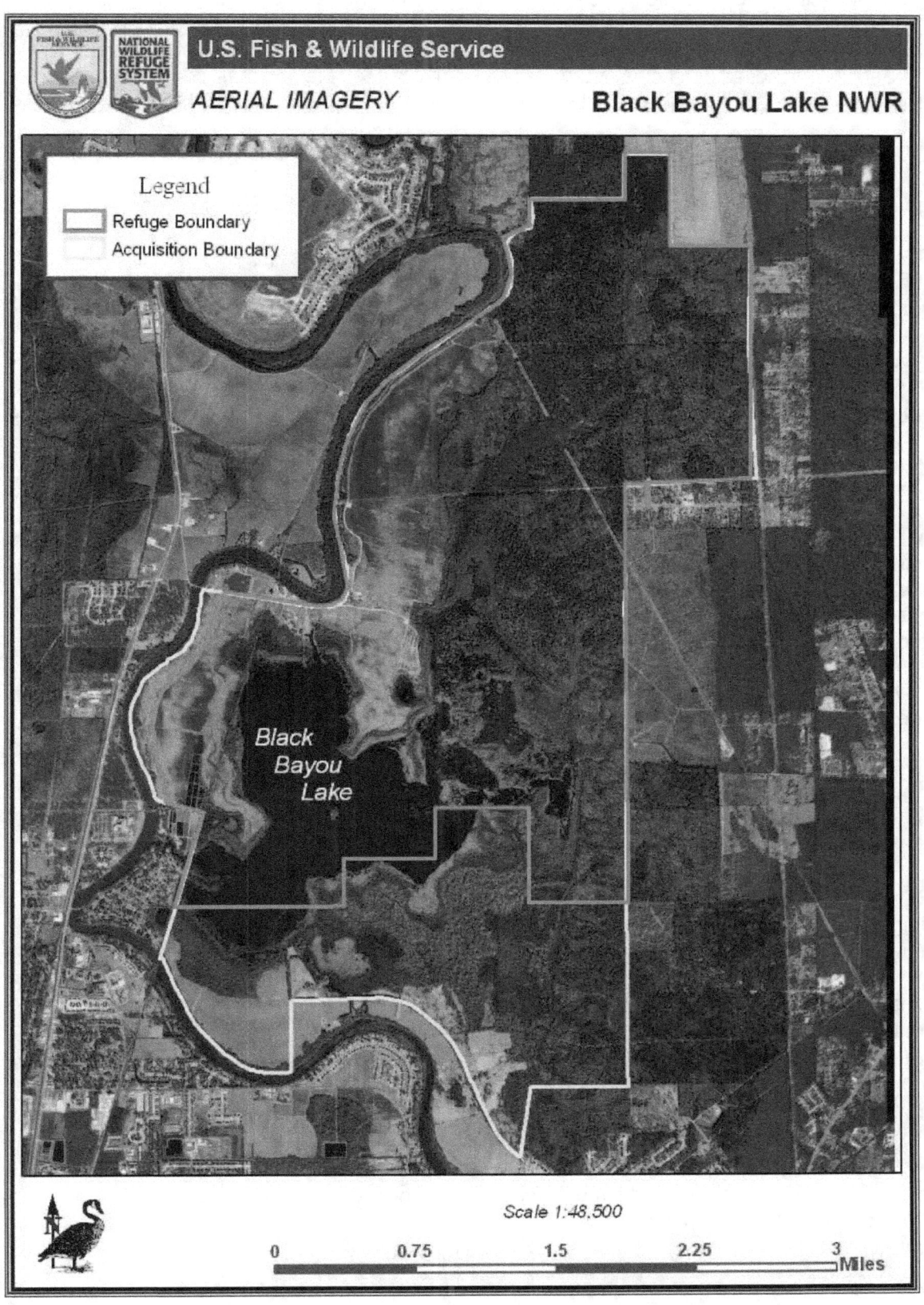

Fee title lands have been purchased since the inception of the refuge. In 1999, 41 acres were acquired from the city of Monroe. In 2000, 2,190 acres were purchased from private landowners. An additional 41 acres were acquired from the same landowner in three more purchases from 2001-02. The Service then purchased the old fish hatchery ponds and their surrounding land (15 acres) from The Nature Conservancy. In 2005, the Service purchased 615 acres of pine habitat from LDWF on the northeast corner of the refuge. This land belonged in the Cities Services Wildlife Management Area (WMA) from 1966-1985.

SPECIAL DESIGNATIONS

The refuge does not include any special designation sites such as research natural areas.

ECOSYSTEM CONTEXT

Lower Mississippi River Ecosystem (LMRE)

Black Bayou Lake NWR is situated in the Mississippi Alluvial Valley Bird Conservation Region, the LMRE, and in the Mississippi Flyway (Figure 3). The LMRE includes the alluvial plain of the Mississippi River downstream of its confluence with the Ohio River and the delta plain and associated marshes and swamps created by the meanderings of the Mississippi River and its tributaries (FWS 2002). Louisiana has twelve water quality management basins delineated on the basis of natural drainage patterns of the state's major river basins (Lester et al. 2005).

The Black Bayou Lake NWR is in the heart of protected bottomland hardwood forests and wetlands of north Louisiana. There are 5 national wildlife refuges (D'Arbonne, Upper Ouachita, Black Bayou Lake, Handy Brake and Tensas River), 36 Service easements, and 36 LDWF wildlife management areas focused on conservation, enhancement, and restoration of bottomland hardwood forests. Further, these entities also focus on moist-soil management, endangered species management, environmental education, and compatible wildlife-dependent recreation in the LMRE. The LMRE guides Service efforts to enhance, restore, and conserve the natural functional processes and habitat types of the LMRE, while maintaining the economic productivity and recreational opportunities.

The ecosystem serves as primary wintering habitat for mid-continent waterfowl populations, as well as breeding and migrating habitat for migratory songbirds. The expansive floodplain forests of the past are now fragmented bottomland hardwood patches due to conversion from agriculture and flood control projects.

The LMRE developed the following eight goals that this CCP will consider and promote when establishing refuge goals and objectives to ensure the refuge continues its contribution to ecosystem conservation and integrity.

- Conserve, enhance, protect, and monitor migratory bird populations and their habitats in the LMRE.
- Protect, restore, and manage the wetlands of the LMRE.
- Protect and/or restore imperiled habitats and viable populations of all endangered, threatened, and candidate species and species of concern in the LMRE.
- Protect, restore, and manage the fisheries and other aquatic resources historically associated with the wetlands and waters of the LMRE.
- Restore, manage, and protect national wildlife refuges and national fish hatcheries.
- Increase public awareness and support for LMRE resources and their management.
- Enforce natural resource laws.
- Protect, restore, and enhance water and air quality throughout the LMRE.

Figure 3. Lower Mississippi River Ecosystem

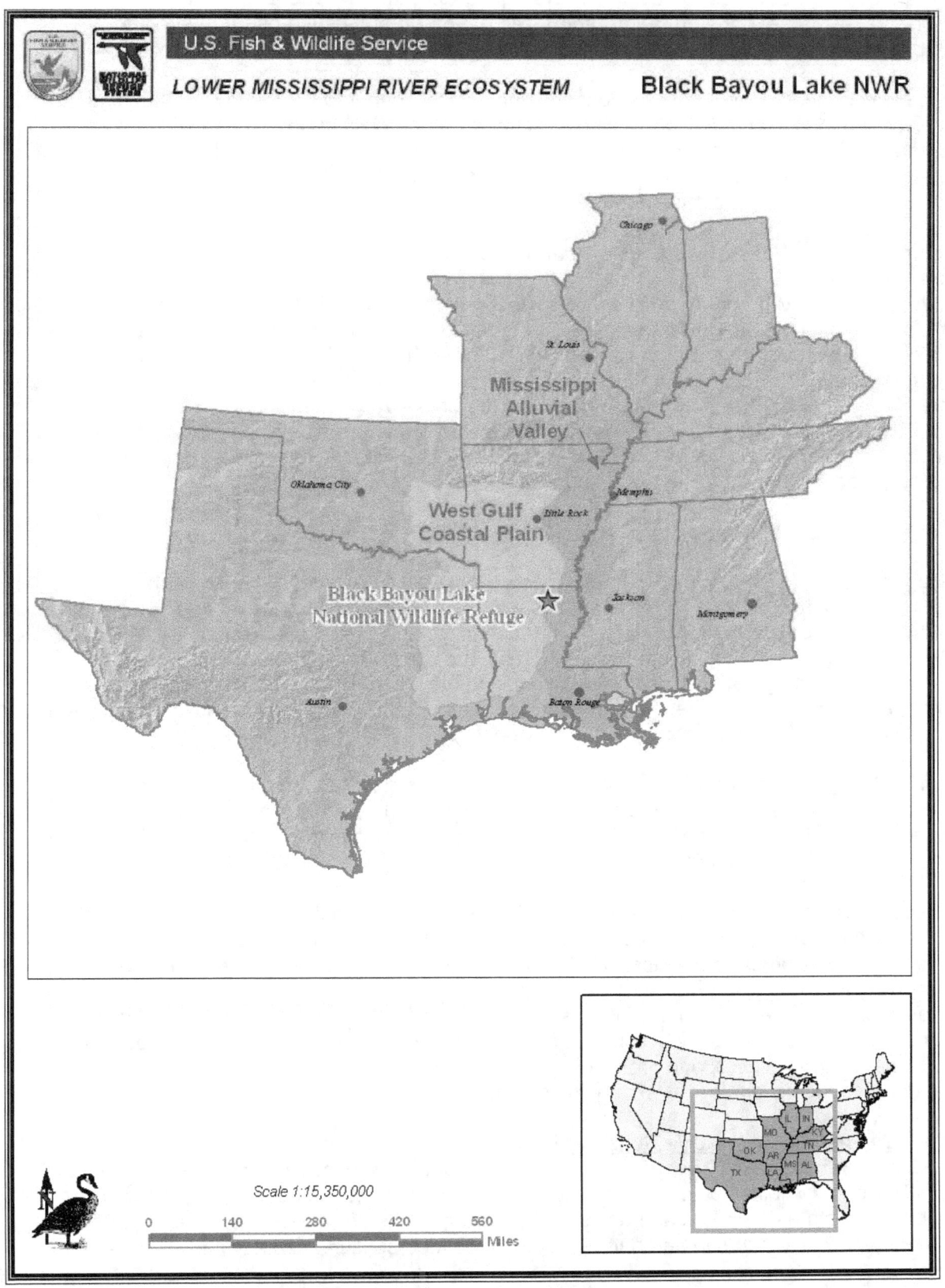

In the meantime, the expanding human population within this ecosystem is increasing demands on land and water resources to accommodate agriculture, timber production, grazing, transportation, urban expansion, and outdoor recreation pursuits such as bird watching, fishing, hiking, boating, and hunting.

Sustainable communities and species conservation and recovery require the joint efforts of private landowners and local communities, as well as state and federal governments. This synergy of federal, state, tribal, and private organizations, working together, will ensure that the Service not only protects the more important areas, but also reduces redundancy of effort, allowing precious resources to be directed where they are most needed.

Mississippi Alluvial Valley Bird Conservation Region

The LMRE is covered primarily by two bird conservation regions (BCR): Mississippi Alluvial Valley (MAV) and West Gulf Coastal Plain (WGCP) (Figure 3). The MAV includes most of Black Bayou Lake NWR, while small parts of the refuge lie within the WGCP. These forests are of high conservation priority for conserving the natural communities and the bird populations within these habitats. The primary threats to these forests include reservoir construction, stream modifications, destructive timber harvesting practices, and conversion to pine plantations, pastures, and other land uses (http://www.lmvjv.org/wgcp). The CCP will develop conservation strategies to foster support for the MAV priorities.

REGIONAL CONSERVATION PLANS AND INITIATIVES

American Woodcock Management Plan: Woodcock trends in the United States have been declining annually for the last 15 years, in spite of actions that have been taken to ensure that hunting does not substantially promote declines, such as reduced bag limits and limited season lengths. An American Woodcock Management Plan initiated in the 1990s points out the need for improved breeding, migrating, and wintering habitat to enhance population growth and survival. Much of the decline is thought to be a result of land use changes and the maturing of forest habitats resulting in less early successional scrub/shrub habitats preferred by woodcock.

Northern Bobwhite Conservation Initiative: The initiative's goal is "to restore northern bobwhite populations range wide to an average density equivalent to that which existed on improvable acres in the baseline year of 1980 [58,857,000]". The only objective that may be pertinent to habitats at Black Bayou Lake NWR is the following:

> Enhance the management practices on pinelands and mixed pine-hardwoods by thinning, controlled burning, and site preparation in a fashion that benefits bobwhites and other wildlife, and increase acreage devoted to longleaf pine where it is ecologically feasible.

The population objective for the MAV BCR is to add 66,554 new coveys and 14,584 of these in Louisiana. Habitat objectives involve improving pine/hardwood forests by conducting heavy thinnings (40-60 percent canopy cover) and prescribing frequent burning (2- 3-year rotation) sufficient to provide herbaceous nesting cover within pine stands.

Louisiana Comprehensive Wildlife Conservation Strategy: This program will direct the overall effort by the LDWF over the next 10 years in assessing the status of and managing where appropriate, the varied habitats and wildlife species in Louisiana. Conservation actions have been developed for each ecoregion in the state in order to address threats to the habitats of these areas. The state will work with a variety of partners in carrying out these recommended conservation actions. The state considers the Service an important partner in this process and the Black Bayou Lake NWR an important part of actions to be taken in this area.

Service Landscape Cooperatives: To ensure that we are "putting science in the right places," the Service determined in April 2009, that it needed a national geographic framework for implementing landscape conservation. Just as migratory bird flyways have provided an effective spatial frame of reference to build capacity and partnerships for international, national, state, and local waterfowl conservation, this geographic framework will provide a continental platform upon which the Service can work with partners to connect site-specific efforts to larger biological goals and outcomes. In its meeting on August 4-6, 2009, the Service Directorate approved a map of the geographic framework developed by a team of Service and U.S. Geological Survey experts from across the country. The map defines *Geographic Areas* that provide a spatial frame of reference for building and targeting science capacity that will support the Service and its partners in planning and designing conservation strategies at landscape scales. It also allows us to more precisely explain to partners, Congress, and the American public why, where, and how we target conservation resources and how our science-based efforts connect to a greater whole. Currently, Black Bayou Lake NWR falls into the Gulf Coast Plain and Ozarks Landscape Conservation Cooperative.

ECOLOGICAL THREATS AND PROBLEMS

In order to prepare a CCP that would establish goals and objectives on how to manage this refuge over the next 15 years, several planning steps were followed. One of those steps was an internal review of known ecological threats and problems that may hinder the ability of refuge personnel to fulfill the objectives of the refuge. That review developed the following list of concerns:

- Wildlife management in an urban environment
- Invasive and nuisance plants
- Climate change

WILDLIFE MANAGEMENT IN AN URBAN ENVIRONMENT

The 4,500-plus-acre refuge provides an opportunity for public/wildlife interaction and public education that is enhanced by its location within a suburban environment. This suburban setting also poses wildlife management problems.

As "natural" areas become reduced in size and more fragmented and isolated, urban/suburban "open space" landscapes, such as Black Bayou Lake NWR, become more important for wildlife. As urbanization increases, habitats available to wildlife become more degraded, fragmented, and isolated, and species diversity decreases. Managers of urban wildlife must understand human attitudes and social issues as well as they do ecological principles. The two species of concern here are deer and raccoons.

Raccoons (and skunks and opossums) are probably the most efficient predators of birds, bird nests, and turtle nests to the extent that many species are experiencing population declines as a result. Raccoons have been documented to depredate 100 percent of the alligator snapping turtle nests on the refuge.

Dense deer populations occur in many urban/suburban areas and the refuge is no exception. The deer herd at this unit is becoming more isolated as more of the land around the unit is being converted to housing subdivisions. Deer can rapidly change their habitat by overbrowsing vegetation and exceeding the carrying capacity. When overpopulated, deer can become susceptible to disease. White-tailed deer are important hosts of the nymphal and adult stages of the vector of Lyme disease in the eastern United States. Deer also are the cause of many auto accidents, which are exacerbated when deer herds are overpopulated.

INVASIVE AND NUISANCE PLANTS

There are two primary invasive plant species that are of concern in varying degrees throughout the refuge because of their potential negative impacts on resource management:

- Chinese tallowtree (*Triadica sebifera*)
- Water hyacinth (*Eichornia crassipes*)

Chinese Tallowtree

The Chinese tallowtree grows in abandoned fields, pastures, waste areas, and forests. It grows in a wide range of environmental conditions, from wet to dry and shade to full sun. It reproduces by seeds only, but one plant can produce hundreds of seeds, which have a tremendous ability to germinate under adverse conditions. It is a fast-growing tree and has beautiful autumn foliage, hence its popularity as an ornamental. To horticulturalists, this sounds like a dream tree, but to ecologists and land managers, it can be a nightmare, especially when it invades an area.

Over the last 30 years, the Chinese tallowtree has become common in old fields and bottomland forests in Louisiana. Several studies at the U.S. Geological Survey's National Wetlands Research Center in Lafayette are aimed at understanding the factors that contribute to Chinese tallowtree growth, spread, and management. When the tallowtree invades, it eventually monopolizes an area. This tree exhibits the classic traits of most non-native invaders: it is attractive so people want to distribute it, it grows quickly and in a variety of soils, it has incredible resiliency, and it resists pests. The tree reproduces and grows quickly and can cause large-scale ecosystem modification. For example, where it completely replaces native vegetation, it has a negative effect on birds by degrading their habitat.

Water Hyacinth

Water hyacinth is an aquatic plant native to South America, but has been naturalized in most of the southern United States. Water hyacinth plants have a tremendous growth and reproductive rate and the free-floating mats cause substantial problems. Water hyacinth can form impenetrable mats of floating vegetation. It reproduces by seeds and by daughter plants which form on rhizomes and produce dense plant beds. Individual plants break off the mat and can be dispersed by wind and water currents. As many as 5,000 seeds can be produced by a single plant, and these seeds are eaten and transported by waterfowl. Seedlings are common on mud banks exposed by low water levels. Large colonies of water hyacinth can interfere with small boat navigation and fishing, as well as provide habitat for mosquitoes. Water hyacinth in large mats blocks sunlight and keep photosynthesis from occurring, reducing oxygen in the water. Water hyacinth is controlled through a number of methods including harvesting, aquatic herbicides, and biological control agents.

Controlling these terrestrial and aquatic plant species will be an ongoing management problem at Black Bayou Lake NWR. A variety of management techniques will need to be employed on a continuing basis in order to control and mitigate impacts to resource management. Public education, particularly for residents adjacent to the refuge headquarters unit, will be an important element in this control program.

CLIMATE CHANGE

The Intergovernmental Panel on Climate Change (IPCC) has concluded that "warming of the climate system is unequivocal." Global climate change poses risks not only to human health but also to terrestrial and aquatic ecosystems. Abundance and distribution of wildlife and fish will change, particularly affecting those species already "at risk." Important economic resources such as agriculture, forestry, and water resources also can be affected. Warmer temperatures, more severe droughts and floods, and sea level rise will have a wide range of impacts. All these stresses, added to existing stresses on resources caused by other influences, such as population growth, land-use changes, and pollution, pose a significant challenge for fish and wildlife conservation.

According to NOAA and NASA data, the Earth's average surface temperature has increased by about 1.2 to 1.4°F since 1900. The ten warmest years in the 20th century have all occurred within the past 15 years. Some climate models, based on emissions of greenhouse gases, primarily carbon dioxide, methane, and nitrous oxide, predict that average surface temperatures could increase from 2.5 to 10.4°F by the end of the 21st century. The frequency of extremely hot summer days is expected to increase, along with this general warming trend. Increases in atmospheric CO_2 are attributed largely to human activities, which have grown rapidly since the 1940s. The burning of fossil fuels adds 5.6 billion tons of carbon, (and deforestation contributes another 0.4 to 2.5 billion tons of carbon) to the atmosphere each year.

The effects of climate change and global warming will be changes in weather/rainfall patterns, decreases in snow and ice cover, rising sea levels, and stressed ecosystems. For the southeastern United States and the Louisiana region, this could mean extreme precipitation events; greater likelihood of warmer/dryer summers and wetter/reduced winter cold; and alterations of ecosystems and habitats due to these changes in weather patterns. For Black Bayou Lake NWR, warmer conditions would favor increased densities of vegetation and wetter conditions would favor trees and vegetation that are better adapted to these conditions, such as bald cypress and water tupelo in freshwater areas. If conditions become drier, the current range and density of forests would be reduced and replaced by grasslands and the probability of wildfires would increase.

A recent study of the effects of climate change on eastern United States' bird species concluded that as many as 78 bird species could decrease by at least 25 percent, while as many as 33 species could increase in abundance by at least 25 percent due to climate and habitat changes (Matthews et al. 2004). In short, global warming could increase storm intensity, negatively change ecologically important plant species, alter the spread of invasive species, increase drought-induced fires, and further imperil already threatened and endangered species. Black Bayou Lake NWR will need to monitor for these changes on the refuge.

PHYSICAL RESOURCES

The climate, topography, geology, air quality, soils, and waterways form the foundation of the physical environment of the refuge.

CURRENT CLIMATE

The climate at the refuge is humid-subtropical and is primarily influenced by its subtropical latitude and proximity to the Gulf of Mexico. The climate is controlled by two principal air masses. Warm, moist air from the Gulf of Mexico generally dominates in the spring and summer, and cooler, drier air from the Central Plains prevails during the winter months. Extended, hot, sultry summers and moderately cool winters are the norm. The average annual air temperature is 65 degrees Fahrenheit. During the winter, the average temperature is 50 degrees, with an average daily minimum of 39 degrees. Average seasonal snowfall is less than 1 inch. The average temperature is 81 degrees during the summer, but temperatures above 90 degrees occur almost daily.

The mean annual precipitation is 60 inches. Half of this rainfall (30 inches) usually falls during April through September. The growing season is about 235 days, beginning in mid-March and ending in early November. Thunderstorms occur on average about 70 days each year, with most occurring during the summer months. The average relative humidity in the mid-afternoon is about 60 percent. Humidities are higher at night.

The sun shines 60 percent of the time during the summer, and 50 percent during winter. The prevailing wind is from the south. Average wind speed is highest, 9 miles per hour, during the spring months. These climatic values play an important role in influencing the area's hydrologic regime, which subsequently shapes ecosystem processes and functions.

GEOLOGY AND TOPOGRAPHY

As the climate has changed on the Earth, marine and deltaic sediments have been deposited in alternating cycles in Louisiana. The eastern half of Ouachita Parish is an alluvial floodplain except for a level, well-drained terrace standing about 20 to 30 feet above the surrounding recent floodplain area at approximately 95 feet above mean sea level (MSL) (Figure 4). This terrace begins on the east side of Black Bayou Lake and is made of materials brought in by the Ouachita River and deposited as an alluvial fan. Later this alluvial fan was partly removed by an early Arkansas River, leaving the extensive remnant known today as the Flatwoods terrace (Wang 1952).

SOILS

Nine soil types are found on the refuge (USDA 1974). Providence, Frizzell, and Muskogee represent the most acreage. The Providence soils (740 acres) are found on the northeast corner of the refuge along the lake. They are strongly acidic, moderately well-drained loamy soils. Pine forest is found on most Providence soils in the parish. Frizzell soils (700 acres), also found on the northeast corner of the refuge, are poorly drained, low in fertility, strongly acidic, and silty. These soils support mostly pine and hardwood forests. Muskogee soils (430 acres) are found on the east and southeast portions of the refuge against the lake. These soils are well-drained and loamy. They are gently sloping, acidic, and usually support second-growth pine forests and some hardwoods. The prairie demonstration area is on Rilla and Hebert soils. Rilla soils are well-drained and loamy, occurring on natural levees of the Ouachita River. They are strongly acidic and most of these soils are used for crops in the parish. Hebert soils are more poorly drained, loamy, acidic, and mostly support row crops or pasture in the parish. Soil survey maps do not indicate which soils are found beneath the lake itself; however, it would be reasonable to believe they are clays in the Alligator, Perry, and/or Litro series.

Figure 4. Elevation map of Black Bayou Lake National Wildlife Refuge

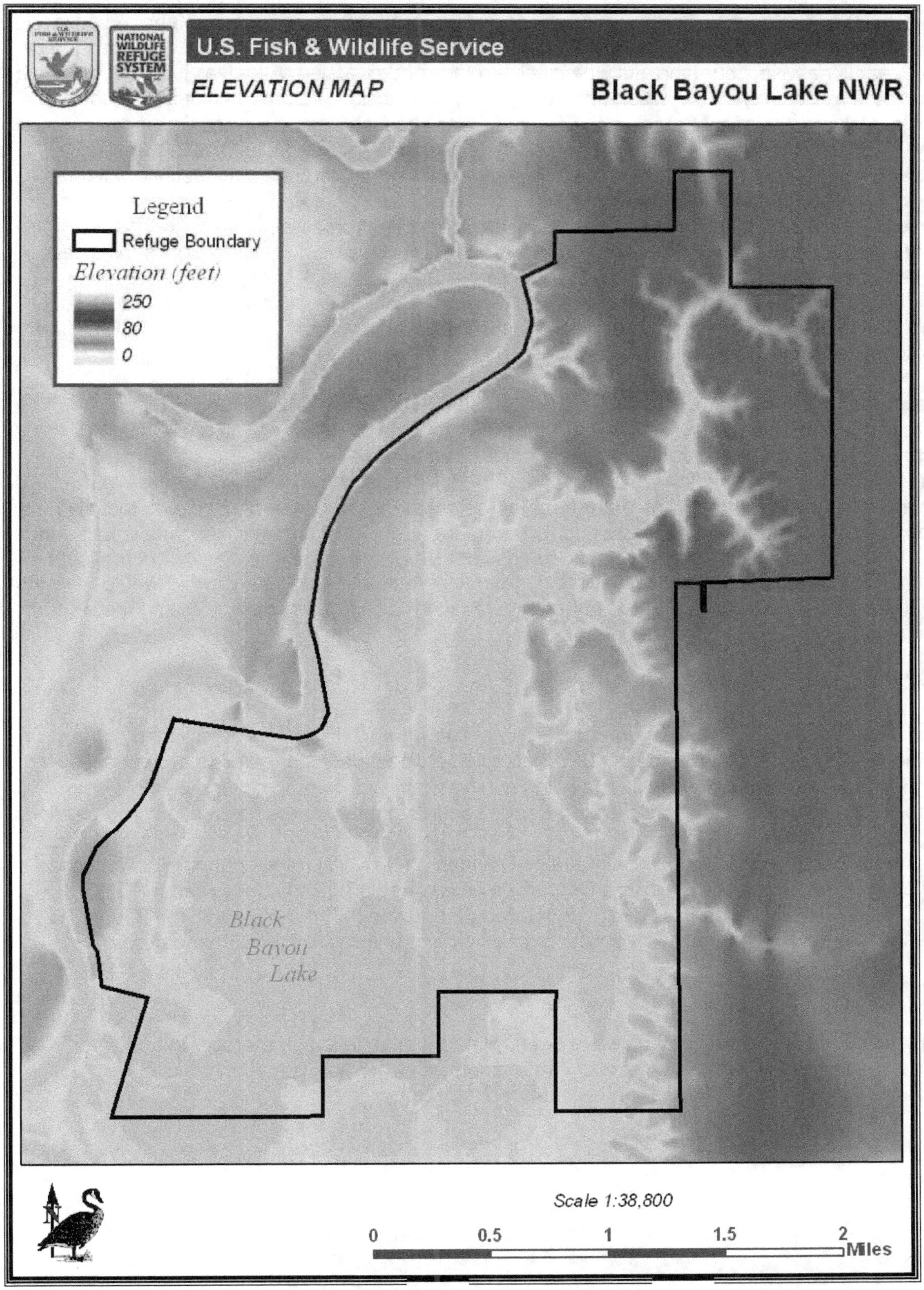

HYDROLOGY

The Ouachita River originates in northwest Arkansas in the Ouachita Mountains near Mena, Arkansas, flowing southeasterly for a distance of approximately 520 miles through Arkansas and Louisiana to the Red River near Jonesville, Louisiana. Its watershed stretches from western Arkansas to near Little Rock and south along its border with the Mississippi River basin. Cities along its path include Hot Springs, Arkadelphia, Malvern, Camden, Smackover, El Dorado, and Crossett, Arkansas; and Sterlington, Monroe, West Monroe, Columbia, and Jonesville, Louisiana. The basin may be divided into several distinctly different regions. From the headwaters, it flows as a mountain stream through the Ouachita National Forest to form Lake Ouachita, the largest lake fully within the State of Arkansas. Below Lake Ouachita, it forms Lake Hamilton and Lake Catherine and flows through a transition area near Arkadelphia and Malvern to the West Gulf Coastal Plain near Camden. Below Camden, the river gradient is much less and has been developed for commercial navigation via the Ouachita-Black Navigation Project—a distance of some 337 miles from its confluence with the Red River. Four locks and dams, H.K. Thatcher, Felsenthal, Columbia, and Jonesville, provide a 9-foot-deep, year-round channel to the lower Red River and the Atchafalaya River to the Gulf of Mexico.

Black Bayou Lake NWR is in the northern portion of the Lower Ouachita Watershed (Figure 5). Water levels at Black Bayou Lake are managed by the city of Monroe according to a water management plan to ensure a readily available drinking water source. A water control structure located near Hannah's Run on the western edge of the lake is used by the city of Monroe to manage water levels by regulating the flow of water from the adjacent Bayou DeSiard. Because the city is interested in ensuring an available water supply during the drought of summer, the lake is kept high at 72 feet. During winter and spring when flooding is possible in Monroe, the city lowers the level of the lake for flood protection to 70.5 feet. This hydrological regime is opposite of what would naturally occur, with water levels lower during the hot months of summer and higher water during the winter and spring when most rainfall occurs.

AIR QUALITY

Under the Clean Air Act, the U.S. Environmental Protection Agency (EPA) has established primary air quality standards to protect public health. EPA has also set secondary standards to protect public welfare. Secondary standards relate to protecting ecosystems, including plants and animals, from harm, as well as protecting against decreased visibility and damage to crops, vegetation, and buildings.

EPA has developed National Ambient Air Quality Standards (NAAQS) for six principal air pollutants (also called criteria pollutants). They are Ground-Level Ozone (O3), Particulate Matter (PM), Nitrogen Dioxide (NO2), Sulfur Dioxide (SO2), Carbon Monoxide (CO), and Lead (Pb). Ouachita Parish ranks high among parishes in Louisiana for all criteria pollutants (www.scorecard.org).

WATER QUALITY AND QUANTITY

Contaminant issues in the past have always been related to high levels of mercury in the water and saltwater spills at gas well sites. A mercury contaminant advisory was issued in 2003 for fish consumption. No water quality data are collected on the refuge.

Figure 5. Watershed of Black Bayou Lake National Wildlife Refuge

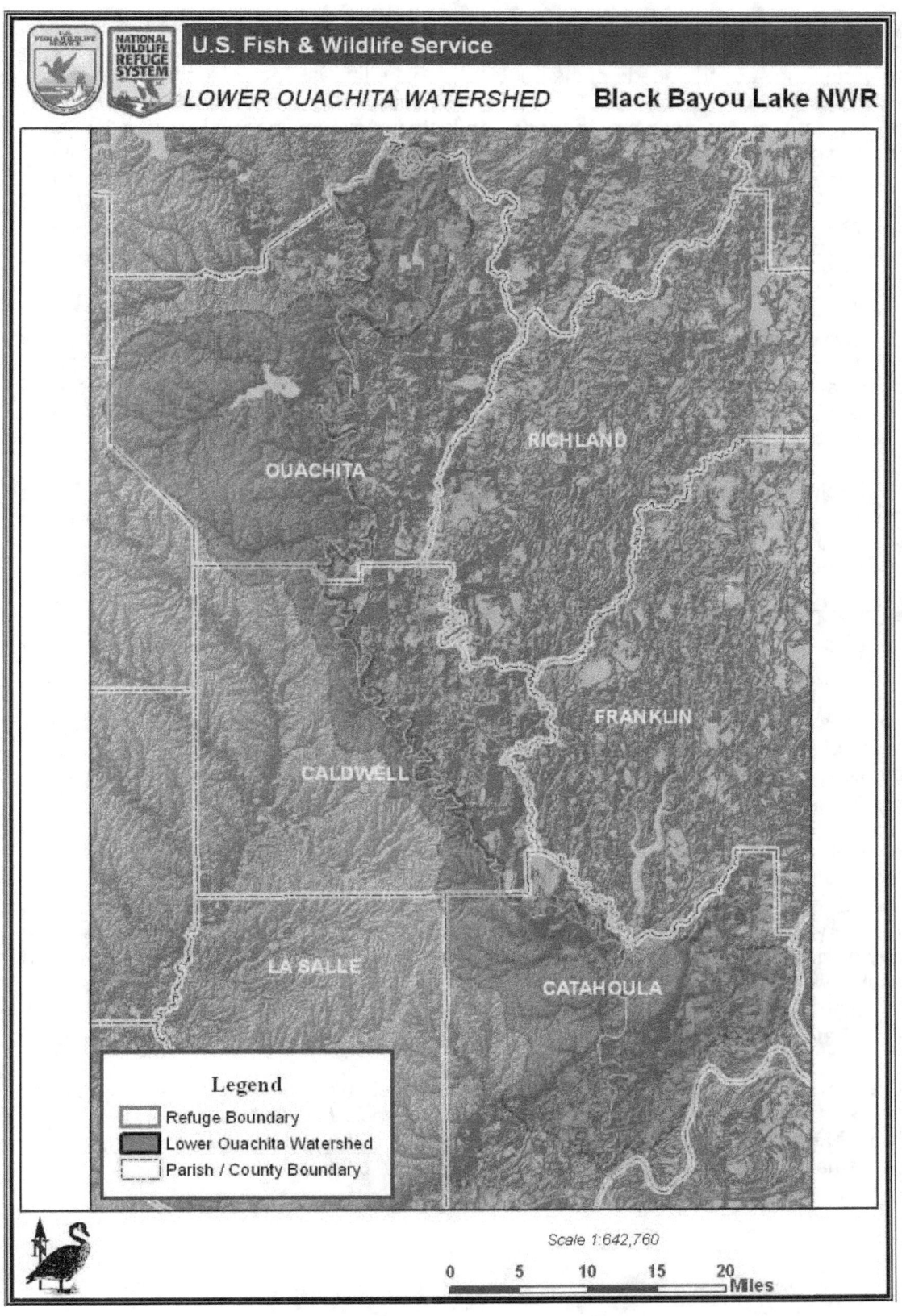

CONTAMINANTS

The Monroe Gas Field (MGF) underlies portions of Ouachita, Union, and Morehouse Parishes in northeast Louisiana, including Black Bayou Lake NWR (Figure 6). At the time of initial discovery and development, during the second decade of the 1900s, it was the largest known gas field in the country. Gas pressure initially exceeded 1,000 psi. Unlike other Louisiana gas fields, the Office of Conservation, the state regulatory agency, never promulgated minimum spacing requirements for wells in the MGF. Average well depth is around 2,300 feet and most wells could be drilled within 36 hours. The size of drilling pads varied from one company to another, but approximately 1/2-acre would be cleared for each well. This allowed room for the drilling rig, mud pits (bentonite clay/water slurry), and service vehicles. Following well completion, only a small area around the well head would be maintained by the gas company. Brine, which contains about three times as much salt as sea water, is a by-product of most gas wells.

Until the mid 1970s, economics generally restricted wells to one per 40 acres. However, tax laws and a dramatic, though short-lived, increase in natural gas prices combined to spur a rash of drilling, which lasted until about 1986. During this period, the number of wells in the MGF more than doubled. In some instances, wells were drilled within 600' of each other. These rapidly depleted gas reserves reduced the average gas pressure to about 30 psi, and caused production at many wells to cease.

Mineral rights were not obtained when the refuge was acquired. From a refuge management standpoint, the possible problems associated with natural gas production are: (1) Habitat/wildlife disturbance; (2) improperly covered mud pits; (3) abandoned/poorly maintained wells and facilities; (4) mercury contamination; and (5) brine.

BIOLOGICAL RESOURCES

HABITAT

The refuge includes 861 acres of open water, 604 acres of permanently flooded baldcypress/tupelo forest, 296 acres of bottomland hardwood forest, 1,900 acres of upland pine/hardwood forest, 856 acres of reforestation, and a 4-acre demonstration prairie and a 2-acre arboretum (Figure 7). A woody plant species list for the Complex is located in Appendix I.

Open Water

The permanent water area on the refuge consists of that portion of the lake that is not forested and the old fish hatchery ponds. Bayou DeSiard is adjacent to the western boundary of the refuge for 4.5 miles. The city of Monroe manages water levels according to a water management plan that ensures a readily available water supply.

Baldcypress/Tupelo

Black Bayou Lake is filling in naturally on the eastern and northeastern portions through sedimentation and detritus build-up from plant decomposition. Boat access is impossible in this portion of the lake for most of the year. The majority of permanently flooded tupelo and baldcypress stands is located in these areas; however, small groups of trees are scattered throughout the open lake area.

Figure 6. Natural gas wells located on Black Bayou Lake National Wildlife Refuge

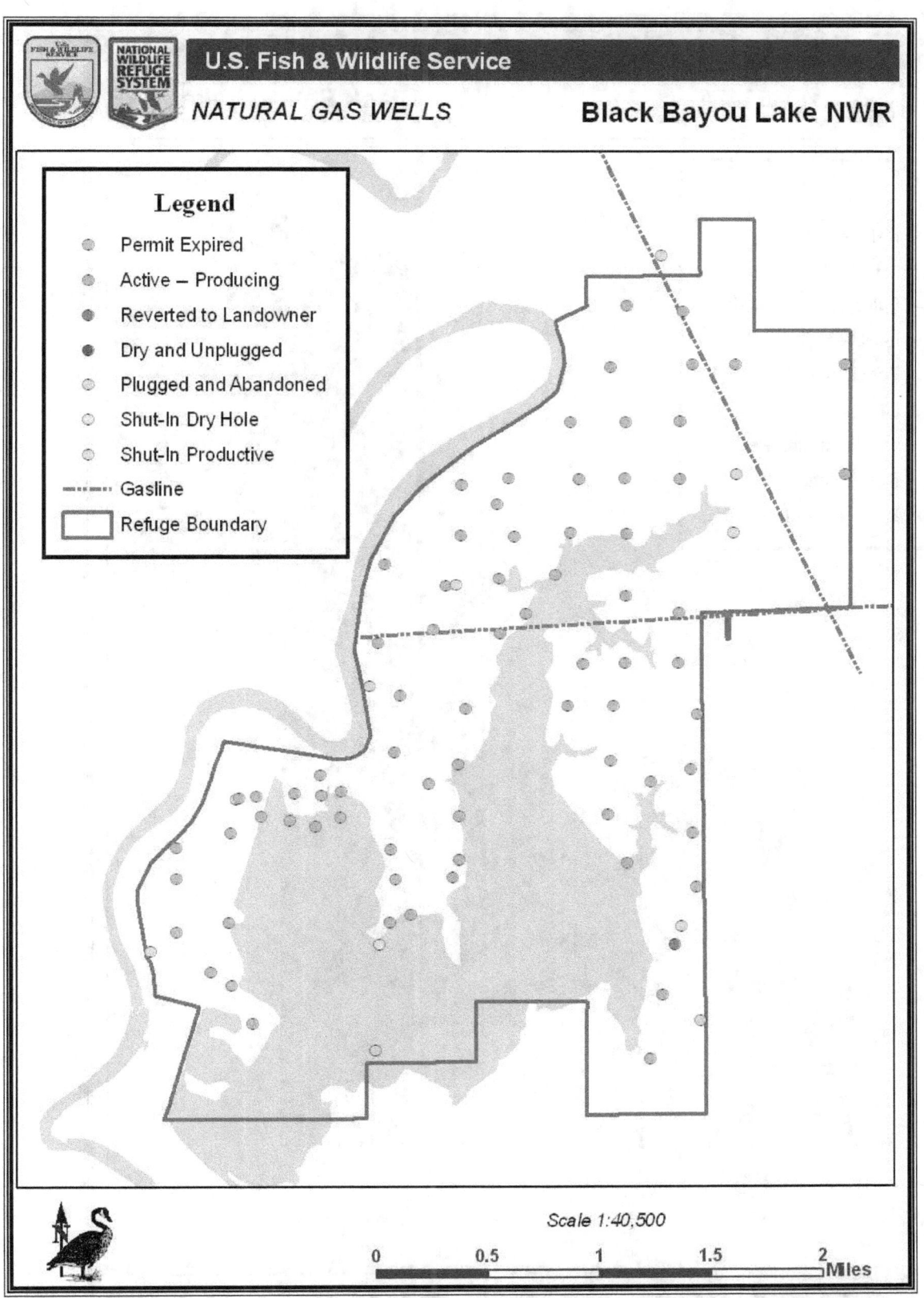

Figure 7. Vegetation map of Black Bayou Lake National Wildlife Refuge

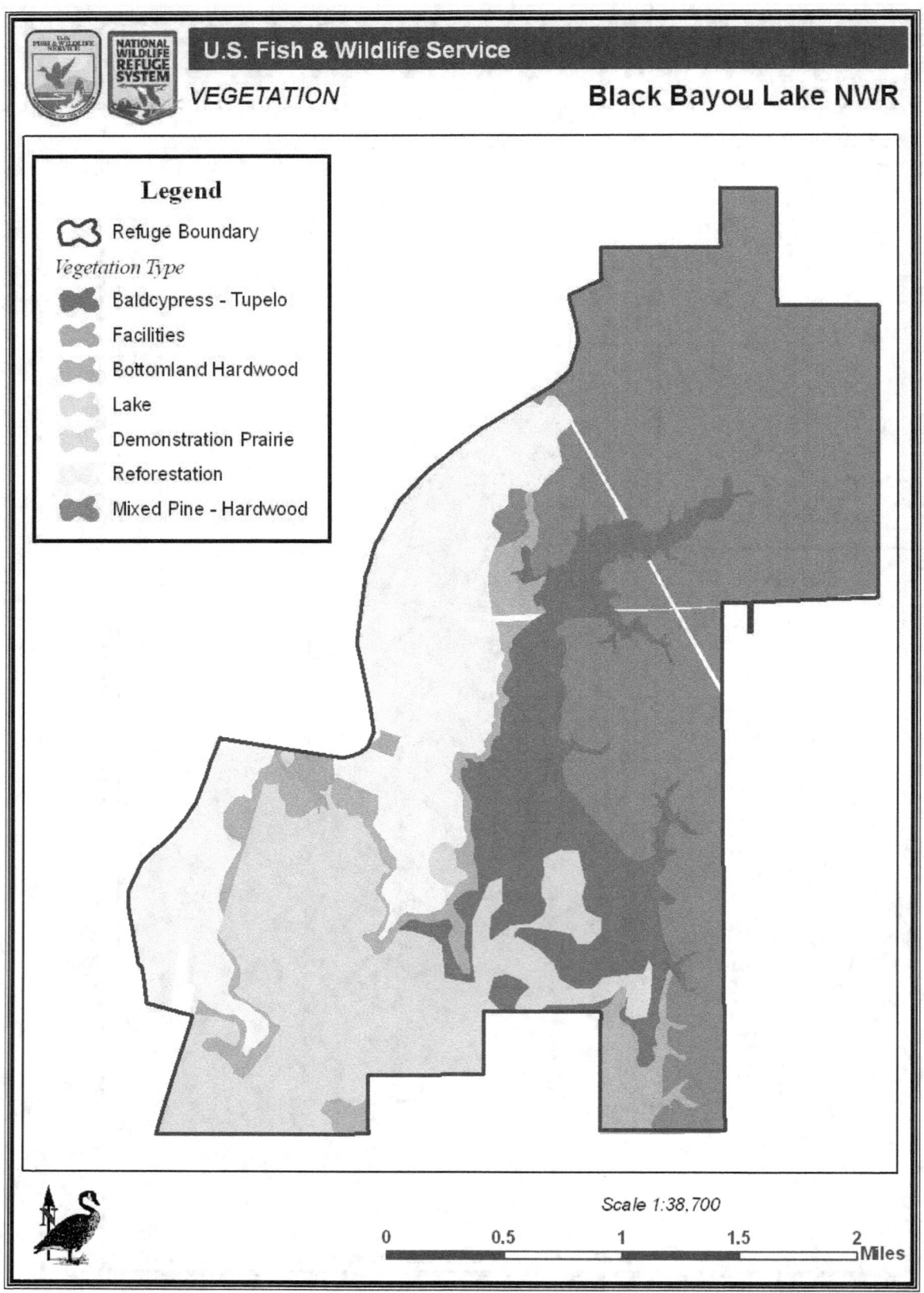

U.S. Fish & Wildlife Service

VEGETATION

Black Bayou Lake NWR

Legend

Refuge Boundary

Vegetation Type

Baldcypress - Tupelo

Facilities

Bottomland Hardwood

Lake

Demonstration Prairie

Reforestation

Mixed Pine - Hardwood

Scale 1:38,700

0   0.5   1   1.5   2
Miles

The Society of American Foresters (SAF) describes this forest type as follows:

Type 102 Baldcypress—Water Tupelo

In stands of this type, the majority of the stocking comprises baldcypress and water tupelo together. This type occurs in swamps, deep sloughs, and very low, poorly drained flats. These sites are always very wet, and surface water stands well into or throughout the growing season. Soils are generally mucks, clays, or fine sand.

Trees commonly in association are black willow, water locust, overcup oak, green ash, and persimmon. Among the shrub species are swamp privet, buttonbush, and planer tree. Woody vines include red vine. A host of herbaceous plants will be common associates and take the form of flotants, emergents, and submergents. Frequently, a variety of mosses and lichens adorn the exposed tree trunks, and the crowns may be draped with Spanish moss.

Soils in this cover type are probably clays in the series Alligator, Perry, and/or Litro.

Bottomland Hardwood Forest

The primary woody species in the lowest areas of bottomland forest are baldcypress, water tupelo, buttonbush, and swamp privet. Slightly higher on the floodplain are overcup oak, water hickory, cherrybark oak, Nuttall oak, persimmon, cedar elm, and water locust. The understory largely consists of swamp privet, greenbrier, poison ivy, and buttonbush.

The majority of bottomland forest on the refuge falls into two SAF types:

Type 91 Swamp Chestnut Oak-Cherrybark Oak

Species composition of this type may vary widely. In most stands, cherrybark oak will be much more common than swamp chestnut oak. Moreover, both oaks in total generally do not represent a majority of the species for any stand. Many other species including white oak, post oak, sweetgum, blackgum, hickory, willow oak, water oak, southern red oak, winged elm, sassafras, delta post oak, slippery elm, Shumard oak, black oak, black cherry, white ash, green ash, red maple, loblolly, and shortleaf pines are present that result in well-stocked stands. Common species in the midstory level are eastern redbud, flowering dogwood, American holly, red mulberry, American hornbeam, eastern hophornbeam, and witch-hazel. Shrub species ordinarily in association are red buckeye, devil's walkingstick, sweetleaf, and Viburnums. Grape vines, Alabama supplejack, Carolina jessamine, trumpet creeper, and greenbrier are frequent inhabitants of this forest type.

This type characteristically occurs on the best, most mature, fine sandy loam soils on the highest first bottom ridges and hammocks and on the second bottoms or terraces. These well-drained sites are seldom covered with standing water and only rarely, if ever, overflow.

Soils in this type are mostly Portland silt and Perry clay.

Type 92 Sweetgum-Willow Oak

The low ridges in the broad slackwater areas of the first bottoms are typically occupied by this forest type. Willow oak and sweetgum comprise the largest proportion of the stocking in stands of this type. These stands are strongly dominated by willow oak because of the heavy clay soils; sweetgum very often forms only a minor proportion of the stocking. A major associate on higher clay ridges and flats is Nuttall oak, which may represent 30 to 50 percent of the stocking at times. Other trees associated with this type are sugarberry, green ash, overcup oak, water oak, water hickory, cedar elm, persimmon, and sometimes baldcypress. Common shrub associates of this type include swamp privet, American snowbell, possumhaw, hawthorn, and dull-leaf indigobush. Woody vine species occasionally present are greenbrier, peppervine, and redvine.

Soils in this type are mostly Portland silt and Perry clay.

Upland Mixed-Pine/Hardwood

Upland forests on the eastern side of the refuge are mature. The primary tree species are loblolly pine, shortleaf pine, cherrybark oak, southern red oak, mockernut hickory, white oak, and sweetgum. Common understory species include French mulberry, deciduous holly, blueberry, huckleberry, greenbrier, and mayhaw.

The two SAF types represented in the uplands include:

Type 80 Loblolly—Shortleaf Pine

Loblolly and shortleaf pine together comprise a majority of the stocking. The type is usually found on sites higher and drier than those where Type 81 loblolly pine prevails because shortleaf pine does not tolerate very wet soils and loblolly pine is less thrifty on dry, thin soils. Common overstory associates are sweetgum, blackgum, southern red oak, post oak, white oak, and mockernut hickory. Tree species in the midstory include flowering dogwood, persimmon, eastern redcedar, and hawthorn. Shrub species commonly associated with this type are American beautyberry, red buckeye, rusty blackhaw, and sumac. Among the common species of woody vines are greenbrier, Carolina jessamine, blackberry, Japanese honeysuckle, and poison ivy.

Soils in this type are Muskogee, Providence, Frizzell, and Guyton.

Type 82 Loblolly Pine—Hardwood

Hardwoods are predominant in this type, with loblolly pine making up at least 20 percent of the stocking. On wet sites, loblolly pine is associated with sweetbay, blackgum, sweetgum, water oak, willow oak, red maple, and American elm. Species associated on drier sites are southern red oak, white oak, post oak, hickory, shortleaf pine, and persimmon. Generally, many of the same shrub, vine, and herb species found with the loblolly pine type are also common associates in stands of the loblolly pine/hardwood type.

Soils in this type are Muskogee, Providence, Frizzell, and Guyton.

Reforestation

All of the reforested area was farmed at some point during the past 150 years, and cotton and corn were farmed until the refuge was established. Reforestation efforts were initiated in 2000. A wide variety of tree species was planted using soil and elevation maps to determine composition. Species included baldcypress, willow oak, water oak, cow oak, southern red oak, cherrybark oak, cottonwood, green ash, American elm, sycamore, sweet pecan, plums, and many more.

Prairies

Prairie plant species, such as *Asclepias tuberosa, Liatris, Coreopsis*, and *Rudbeckia maxima*, are present within rights-of-way on the eastern edge of the refuge.

An educational demonstration prairie and arboretum are located near the Visitor's Center (Figure 8).

Farming

Farming has not occurred on the refuge since its establishment in 1997. Cotton, corn, milo, and soybeans were farmed prior to this time.

Forest Management

The refuge does not currently have a forest management plan. No timber harvest has occurred since refuge establishment. Most forest management would be confined to the eastern and northern side of the refuge within the upland pine/hardwood forest. Two parcels of land were purchased from LDWF in 2005. LDWF thinned the pines before selling the land to the Service. In the future, reforested fields will need to be managed also. Existing forest management consists of invasive plant control, which is discussed below.

Fire Management

Currently, the prairie demonstration area is to be burned on a 3-year rotation after the first good frost. After the only time it was burned, 2 years ago, many of the desired plants did not regenerate. The upland pine forest on the north and east portions of the refuge have not been burned since being purchased by the Service.

Invasive Plant Management

The two species of invasive plants that are of primary concern are Chinese tallowtree and water hyacinth. Other invasive plants that have been found on the refuge include princess tree, tree-of-heaven, Chinaberry, and mimosa (Figure 9). Salvinia spp. is an aquatic invasive plant that may likely invade Black Bayou Lake in the future. This species needs to be monitored for its presence. Chemicals such as Garlon, Rodeo, 2-4-D, and Roundup are used to kill invasives. GIS is used to map species presence and treatment type. Water hyacinth is sprayed during the growing season at varying intervals using a specially adapted boat. Monies collected from boat launch fees are used to pay for chemical and spraying equipment. The forester opportunistically hacks and squirts tallowtree with RoundUp. In addition, a commercial contractor treated 92 acres of tallowtree in September 2007.

Moist-soil Management

One 8-acre unit is located near the lake and is managed to attract a variety of wildlife for viewing opportunities. Water is drawn down in May and pumped up in the fall if necessary. There are no other managed moist soils or agriculture on Black Bayou Lake NWR.

Figure 8. Demonstration prairie and arboretum at Black Bayou Lake National Wildlife Refuge

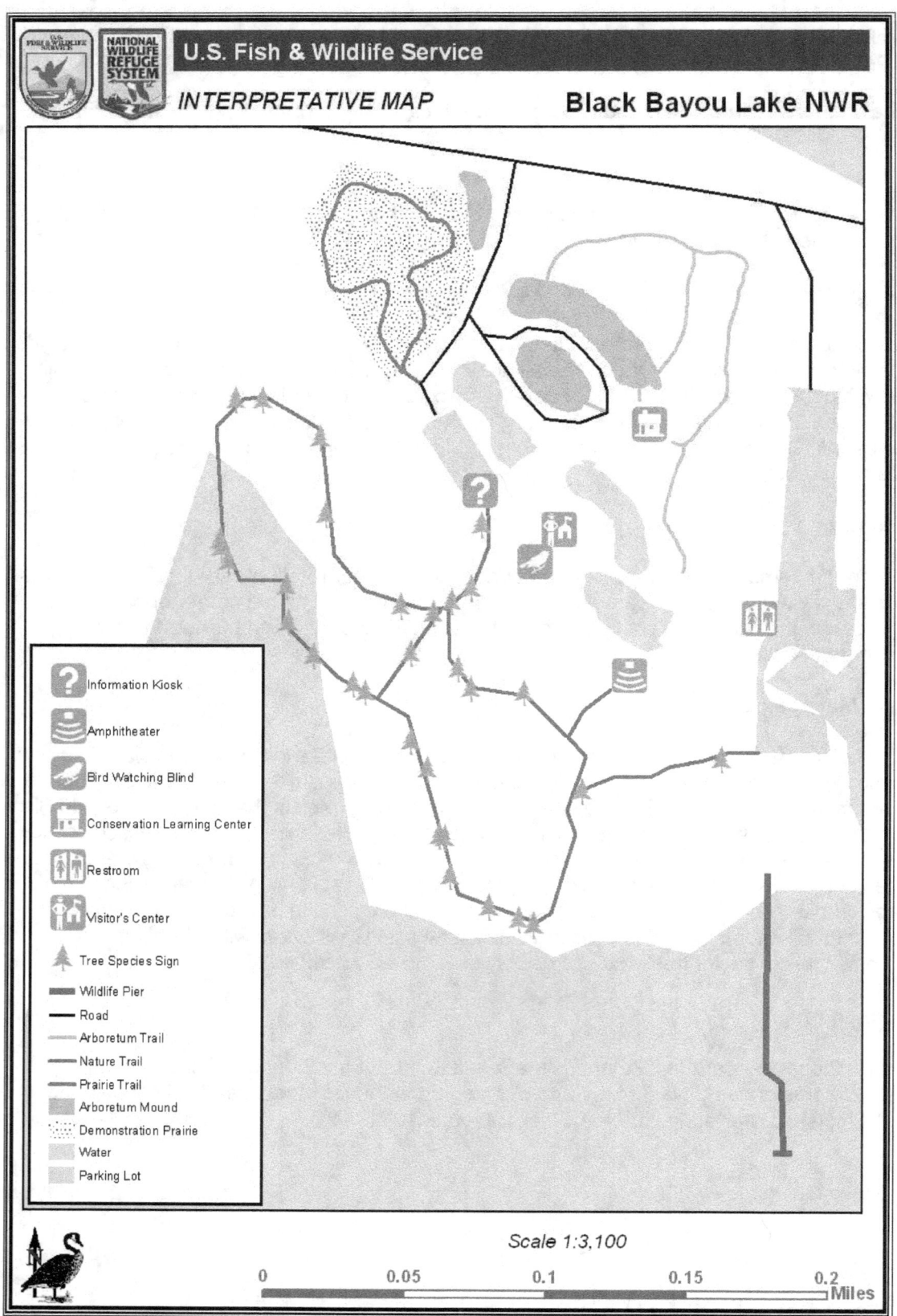

Figure 9. Mapped invasive species on Black Bayou Lake National Wildlife Refuge

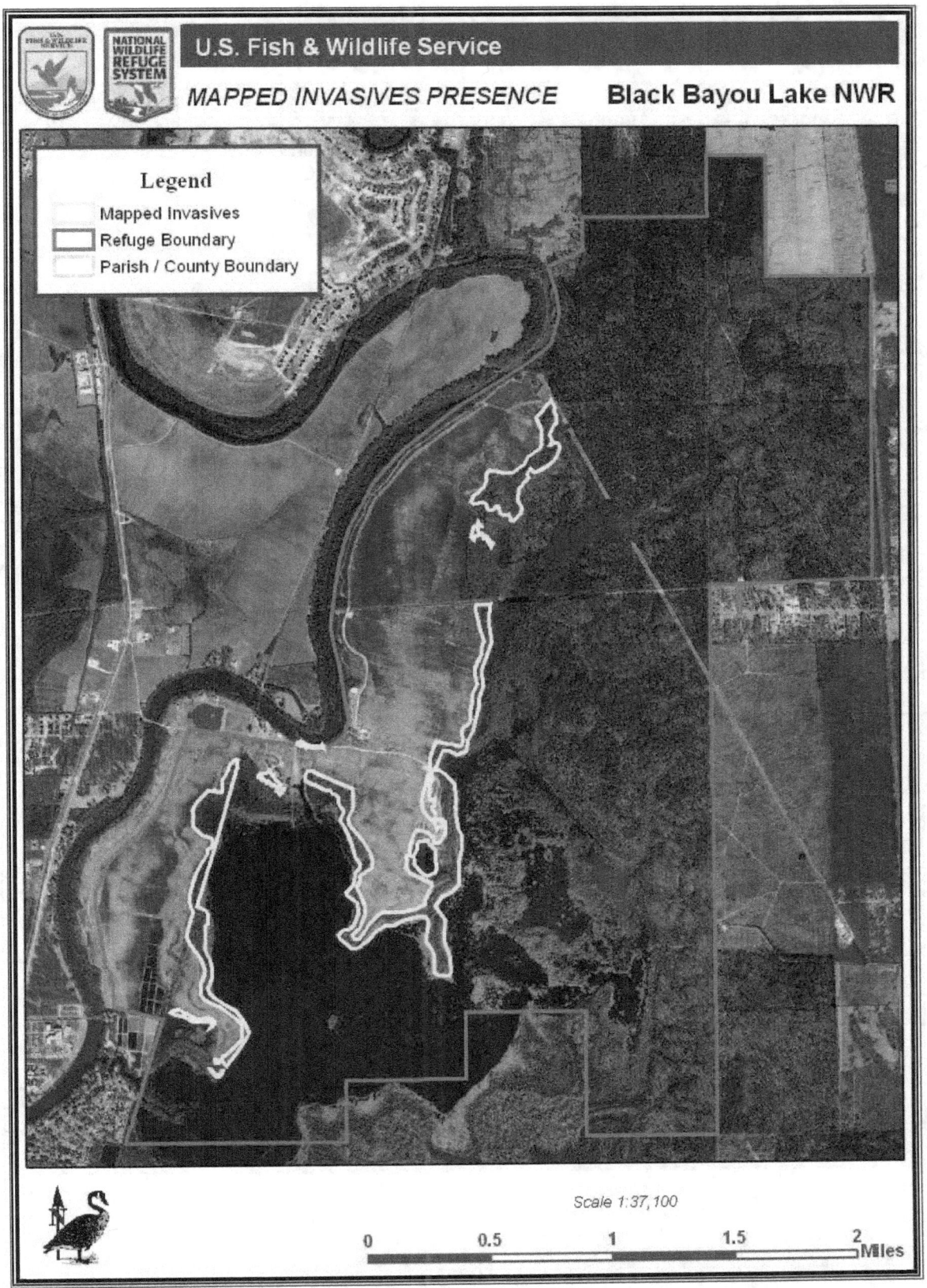

BIRDS

Wintering Waterfowl

Wood duck and hooded merganser numbers are underrepresented when using traditional waterfowl surveying methods because these species inhabit flooded timber, which is difficult to survey. Wood ducks probably are the most abundant wintering duck on the refuge. Other species utilizing the lake include mallard, gadwall, green-winged teal, wigeon, shoveler, pintail, ring-necked duck, ruddy duck, canvasback, and scaup (Table 1).

Resident Waterfowl

The refuge provides year-round habitat for wood ducks. Many natural cavities are available for nesting wood ducks. Seventeen wood duck nest boxes are located on the refuge to provide additional nesting habitat.

Wood duck nest boxes are always cleaned and repaired before January and checked at the end of the nesting season. However, boxes are usually checked more frequently to determine the number of broods, nest success, and productivity. Boxes are mapped and individually numbered. The document "Increasing Wood Duck Productivity: Guidelines for Management and Banding" are followed (USFWS 2003a).

Mergansers probably nest in natural cavities within the refuge, but they are rarely seen during summer. Black-bellied whistling ducks were seen for the first time during late summer in 2006; however, nesting in wood duck boxes has not been documented.

Table 1. Annual mid-winter waterfowl counts (first week of January) for Black Bayou Lake National Wildlife Refuge

Year	Mallard	Gadwall	Green-winged Teal	Wood Duck	Canvasback	Ring-neck	Scaup	Total Ducks
1998	75	240	0	0	0	110	0	425
1999	0	0	0	0	0	0	0	0
2000	100	300	0	0	0	0	0	400
2001*	500	600	50	200	0	50	0	1400
2002	80	0	0	20	0	0	0	100
2003	73	25	0	5	0	35	0	138
2004	25	25	0	100	0	50	0	200
2005	14	45	0	0	0	10	160	229
2006	227	302	50	5	0	60	0	644
2007	100	150	30	0	2	30	40	350

* Mid-winter waterfowl count conducted by boat instead of plane.

Water and Marsh Birds

The lake itself provides wading bird habitat at different times of the year. A major rookery was discovered on the refuge in 2000 and was active for 3 years. Small rookeries of herons still exist. Species nested include white ibis, anhinga, great blue heron, little blue heron, great egret, cattle egret, green heron, snowy egret, and night-herons. American bitterns, roseate spoonbills, and wood storks have been recorded on the refuge usually during migration or post-breeding dispersal. Large concentrations of double-crested cormorants utilize the refuge during winter. American white pelicans are sometimes seen floating on the lake.

Marsh bird habitat is not available on the refuge, but Virginia rails, clapper rails, and soras probably migrate through. King rails may breed irregularly if water levels are suitable. Coots are present year-round and are especially abundant in winter. Common moorhen and purple gallinules breed in the area.

Shorebirds

The only shorebird habitat found on the refuge would be the shorelines of the lake, hatchery ponds, and Bayou DeSiard. No impoundments are managed for shorebirds. Spotted and solitary sandpipers are seen on the edges of bayous during migration. Killdeer is the most numerous species of shorebird.

Landbirds/Neotropical Migratory Birds

Breeding land bird surveys are conducted at points chosen randomly. Points were allocated within forest compartments. Compartments are surveyed on a 3-year rotation. In 2008, 18 point counts were conducted. Totals of 31 species and 257 individuals were detected. An average of 10.9 ± 0.65 species/points ($\pm$ S.E.) and 14.3 ± 0.04 ($\pm$ S.E.) individuals/points were recorded. The most abundant species were red-eyed vireo, blue-gray gnatcatcher, and tufted titmouse. Brown-headed cowbirds were detected on 33 percent of points.

Woodcock

The 7-year-old reforestation stands and surrounding forests at Black Bayou Lake NWR may provide diurnal habitat for woodcock. No survey work has been completed to determine use by this species. Woodcock hunting is open to the public, but they are not nearly as popular to hunt as in south Louisiana. Although no woodcock surveys are conducted, hunters were asked to report any birds harvested. During the 2002-2003 hunting season, 4 woodcock were reported.

Turkey

Over-hunting in the early 1900s caused wild turkey numbers to decline precipitously in this area. During 1966-70, 25 turkeys were released onto Cities Services WMA (13,374 acres). These lands were withdrawn from the WMA in 1985; however, a portion of the historic acreage is now refuge property. Today, no turkeys utilize the refuge, except for sporadic transient birds.

Quail

When reforestation efforts in 2000 began, bobwhites were one of the more numerous species heard during breeding bird surveys. Now that trees are 7 years old, quail habitat has been greatly reduced. Quail are still heard and seen occasionally in and around the educational facilities. Bobwhites can be hunted on the refuge but very few, if any, hunters partake in the activity.

MAMMALS

Forty-four species of mammals are likely to occur on the refuge (Appendix I), although scientific studies have not been conducted.

Deer

White-tailed deer are the only big game on the refuge. Archery hunting is available throughout the state season, but few bowhunters utilize the refuge. The refuge estimates less than 10 deer are harvested annually. No formal surveys or data are collected to determine herd size; however, reforestation areas are not showing signs of overbrowsing. The refuge foresees the deer herd increasing to a level requiring management action in the future.

Furbearers

Species found on the refuge include Virginia opossum, raccoon, striped skunk, river otter, beaver, mink, nutria, and muskrat. Gray fox, red fox, coyote, and bobcats are also present. Trapping permits have not been requested by the public nor are they issued.

Rabbits

Both eastern cottontail and swamp rabbits inhabit the refuge. Rabbit hunting is available to the public, but few hunters take advantage of it.

Squirrels

Fox and gray squirrels are found on the refuge and both are hunted enthusiastically by the local public. Gray squirrels prefer dense forests with good vertical structure whereas fox squirrels inhabit more open woods. Hunters reported killing 59 squirrels during the 2002-2003 season and 115 squirrels during the 2001-2002 hunting season.

Other Mammals

No research has been conducted on small mammals such as mice, voles, and moles.

REPTILES AND AMPHIBIANS

Fifty of the seventy-nine species of reptiles and amphibians that are likely to occur on the refuge have been documented by University of Louisiana at Monroe (ULM) researchers (Appendix I). Frogs and toads have been surveyed by refuge staff and ULM using call counts fashioned after the protocol developed by the Louisiana Amphibian Monitoring Program.

In 2002, a malformed amphibian study was conducted on the refuge by ULM. Collections of Fowler's toad, bronze frog, and northern cricket frog tadpoles from two sites were made. One individual, a Fowler's toad, showed evidence of abnormality with a soft tissue covering over the entire eye.

Alligators are a common sight on the refuge and the adjacent Bayou DeSiard. Alligator surveys are conducted each summer using the same route (Table 2).

Table 2. Numbers of alligators recorded by size class from 2001-07 on Black Bayou Lake

Size Class (ft)	2001	2002	2003	2004	2005	2006	2007*
1	0	0	2	0	24	2	1
2	2	9	4	5	10	12	11
3	1	3	2	6	2	9	2
4	7	6	6	2	2	7	3
5	2	7	1	3	6	7	3
6	2	9	2	3	4	8	5
7	0	0	1	0	4	2	1
8	0	0	2	1	2	0	1
9	0	1	1	0	0	0	0
10	0	0	0	2	0	0	0
Unknown	5	8	5	11	10	7	19
Totals	19	43	26	33	64	54	46

* Incomplete count

FISHERIES

In 2000 and 2001, LDWF and ULM evaluated the sport fisheries at Black Bayou Lake (Aku and Wood 2002). They found bluegills and black crappies to represent 41 percent and 29 percent of the sample, respectively. Largemouth bass represented 18 percent. Stock density indices, condition, and growth were good for crappie, bass, and bluegill. Other species recorded during the study included brook silverside, golden shiner, spotted and longnose gar, warmouth, bantam, banded pygmy and green sunfish, white crappie, gizzard and threadfin shad, yellow and brown bullhead, mooneye, chain pickerel, and bowfin.

SPECIES OF CONCERN

Alligator Snapping Turtle

Alligator snapping turtles are the largest freshwater turtle in North America. Its native range extends from the Gulf of Mexico from Texas to Florida north to Kansas, Illinois, and Indiana. All states offer protection for snapping turtles through special designations such as threatened, endangered, or species of concern. Louisiana was the last state to protect these turtles. A moratorium on commercial harvest in Louisiana occurred in November 2004; however, recreational take is still legal in the state, but limited to one turtle per day. Commercial harvest extensively depleted populations of snapping turtles from the 1960s through the 1980s in the southern United States. Population models indicate in order to maintain a stable population, adult female survival rates must be at least 98 percent (Reed et al. 2002). This study went on to say that if adult survivorship is reduced by a quarter of one percent, the population could be reduced by half within 410 years. Another factor contributing to the decline of this species is their low reproductive success. Raccoons, skunks, opossums, and fire ants depredate nests at alarming rates. One study on the refuge indicated that

93 percent of nests found were depredated. Dr. Carr at ULM has been continually studying alligator snapping turtles on the refuge for the past several years. Presently, eggs are removed from the nest, incubated at ULM until hatched, and released into the lake. Prior to release, hatchlings are tagged and a small number are fitted with transmitters, as are adults that are captured in the lake. The researchers are studying nest-site characteristics, habitat selection, genetics, and other aspects of turtle biology (Woosley 2005).

Rafinesque's Big-eared Bat

Rafinesque's big-eared bat is the least studied bat in the eastern United States (Harvey et al. 1999) and is federally designated a species of concern. Because this bat is associated with bottomland hardwoods, many biologists are concerned about its status. Many states consider them to be endangered or threatened; however, Louisiana has no official designation for Rafinesque's big-eared bat. Forty-four roost trees of this species were found on the nearby D'Arbonne NWR inside hollow water tupelo (*Nyssa aquatica*) trees during the summer of 2000 (Gooding and Langford 2004). The roost trees found are all within the same tupelo stand. This unique stand is comprised of a high density of very large, hollow water tupelo trees, which seem to be favored by this species (Clark et al. 1998, Cochran 1999, Gooding and Langford 2004, Trousdale and Beckett 2005). Black Bayou Lake NWR has plenty of water tupelos growing in the lake; however, most of them are very difficult to access and are not of large size. More research on Rafinesque's big-eared bats is needed.

Southeastern Myotis Bat

Although southeastern myotis bats are captured more frequently in mist-nets than big-eared bats, declines are being seen in their populations in Arkansas (Harvey et al. 1999). Southeastern myotis bats, like big-eared bats, are associated with riparian areas or bottomland hardwoods and are listed federally as a species of concern. Little is known about the roosting habits of southeastern myotis bats in areas where there are no caves, such as Louisiana. Recent information shows that southeastern myotis bats also utilize water tupelo trees (Gooding and Langford 2004), at least during summer as maternity colonies. At Bayou Cocodrie NWR in Ferriday, Louisiana, several very large roosts (5,000 bats) were found in tupelo trees (personal comm. John Dickson), and on Upper Ouachita NWR, a roost of 1,000 was found in a tupelo. Again, the tupelo trees on Black Bayou Lake NWR are small, not likely hollow, and difficult to access.

ENDANGERED/THREATENED SPECIES

Red-cockaded Woodpecker (RCW)

Currently, there are no active groups of RCWs on the refuge. When the refuge was established, one male bird was present. Habitat improvement was initiated including installing inserts and mechanically removing mid-story hardwood trees. However, soon after, the bird disappeared in 2002. The RCW Recovery Plan did not list Black Bayou Lake NWR as having an RCW population nor were any population goals established for the refuge (USFWS 2003b). Consultation with the RCW Recovery Coordinator has indicated that the refuge does not have to manage for the red-cockaded woodpecker because no birds have been present for at least 5 years.

CULTURAL RESOURCES

PREHISTORIC BACKGROUND

The following is a description of the first people and settlements in north Louisiana in the refuge area:

Lithic Period (30,000-5000 B.C.)
Paleo-Indian people probably inhabited the Prairie and Deweyville Terrace zones of the refuge. The recent floodplain was probably not yet formed.

Archaic Period (5000-1500 B.C.)
Continuation of Paleo-Indian culture with beginnings of local and regional culture patterns; hunting/gathering existence; and dominant culture group inhabiting the Ouachita region, the Caddo people, were becoming defined at this time.

Late Archaic Period (1500-250 B.C.)
People of the Poverty Point culture probably had village sites along the Ouachita River near or on the present refuge. These people had rudimentary agriculture and were mound builders. Caddo Indians were developing culture patterns independently of other groups in the LMV.

Tchefuncte Period (400-150 B.C.)
The people of this period exhibited an early woodland culture. These people had simple, poorly made pottery. This culture diffused gradually up the Mississippi Valley and probably co-existed with the Poverty Point culture and Caddo in the refuge area.

Marksville Period (100-500 A.D.)
A blending of northward-moving southeastern woodland culture and the southward-moving Hopewell culture probably occurred in the refuge area. The Poverty Point culture was still in evidence, however. Fine pottery, flint artifacts, and stone projectile points first appeared at this time. Elaborate burial techniques and cults developed.

Mississippian Culture (1400-1600 A.D.)
This culture was one of the earliest recognized cultural traditions in the United States. It was widely distributed in the southeastern United States and had distinctive pottery and projectile points. Agriculture was well developed. Although Mississippian type projectile points have been found on the refuge, the area was probably on the fringe of the Mississippian culture. The Ouachita branch of the Caddo people had become the dominant group along the Ouachita River.

HISTORICAL PERIOD (EUROPEAN CONTACT)

1541 – 1542
Hernando de Soto followed the Ouachita River in his exploration of the southern United States. He found Ouachita Indians living along the river. Village site or sites may have existed on the refuge area.

1682
La Salle claims LMV area for France.

1718
Several French settlements established along the Ouachita River. Trappers, hunters, and traders probably utilized the refuge area.

1729
Natchez uprising disrupts French control of northeast Louisiana; French settlements along the Ouachita were abandoned.

1734
Most of the Ouachita Indians had been decimated by European diseases and raids by Chickasaw war parties from Mississippi.

1762
France loses French and Indian War. Louisiana Territory is ceded to Spain.

1791
Fort Miro was established at a small Spanish settlement that would eventually become the city of Monroe. European trappers and hunters lived in the refuge area.

1803
Louisiana was reacquired by France. The United States bought it from France. Choctaw Indians from Mississippi replaced the Ouachita Caddoans along the river. Congress established Territory of Orleans south of 33° N latitude.

1812
Territory of Orleans became the State of Louisiana. The county of Ouachita was established.

1839
Union Parish was established from part of the old Ouachita County. One of the Police Jury's first actions was to enact a law allowing free-ranging domestic animals in the parish.

1840-1845
This was the period of influx of settlers from Alabama, Georgia, and Mississippi. Most of these people disembarked at Alabama Landing, located on the present refuge. Towns of Marion, Haile, and Linville resulted from this wave of immigration. Most of these people were small farmers—not slaveholders. The town of Marion was named after Marion, Alabama, which was named for Francis Marion, the "Swamp Fox" of the American Revolution.

1861
Louisiana secedes from the United States. A major back-water flood occurs on the Ouachita River. The state sends aid to the victims in Union Parish. This indicates that the floodplain and refuge area were probably substantially populated at that time, probably by trappers, fishermen, and subsistence and commercial hunters.

1865-1930
Louisiana re-entered the United States. Between the Civil War and the 1940s, agriculture was the parish's major economic base. Most of the Tertiary uplands were cleared and planted in cotton and corn. By the 1930s and 1940s, much of the cropland was allowed to revert to forest. Lumber, paper, and mineral companies began buying much of the parish land. Breece Lumber Company acquired much of the refuge land prior to 1930. During this period also, natural gas was discovered in the refuge area.

1930
Breece Lumber Company sold some of the refuge land to the United Gas Company. Much of this land was subsequently sold to Union Producing Company.

1969

Union Producing Company changed its name to Pennzoil Producing Company. Pennzoil began leasing the land to private hunting clubs and continued selective harvest of overcup oak and pecan sawtimber.

About 1977, Pennzoil decided to sell its holdings in the Ouachita River Swamp. Morehouse and Union Parishes' Police Juries suggested the LWFC as a possible purchaser. Not having funds, the commission referred the Service as a possible purchaser. Numerous Service personnel worked toward culminating a purchase agreement with Pennzoil.

In 1980, a cultural resources survey of pre-selected portions of the refuge was conducted by New World Research, Inc., a private cultural resource management firm (New World Research 1981). It was an intensive survey of road easements, a pipeline corridor, and several land tracts projected as locations for various refuge support and recreational facilities. As a result of the survey, three prehistoric sites, all apparently dating to the Late Woodland (A.D. 800-1000) and Mississippian (A.D. 1000-1750) periods, were identified. Two of the sites yielded both lithic and ceramic artifacts. The third was composed solely of prehistoric lithic artifacts. One site yielded not only artifacts, but evidence of a midden and two shell concentrations. It is likely that more prehistoric sites exist on the refuge, especially on deposits of Pleistocene age.

The *National Register of Historic Places*, established by Congress in 1966, is the nation's official list of significant historic properties. The *National Register* recognizes five basic types of historic properties: historic buildings, such as plantation houses; courthouses or log cabins; historic structures, such as old bridges, lighthouses, or forts; historic districts, such as old residential or commercial neighborhoods; historic sites, such as battlefields or Indian mounds; and historic objects, such as old steamboats or fire engines. It is important to note that not every historic site or old building or neighborhood is eligible for the *National Register*. Properties must have some type of significance: properties that are closely associated with an important person, event, or development; buildings that are architecturally significant because they are important examples of a particular style or type, or a method of construction; and, properties that are archaeologically significant because the remains yield information about the nation's history or prehistory. Generally, properties are not placed on the *National Register* if they are less than 50 years old; if the period of their historical significance is less than 50 years old; or if they have been significantly altered.

Each state has a historic preservation office which is responsible for nominating buildings, sites, districts, etc., to the *National Register*. In Louisiana, this program is administered by the Division of Historic Preservation, which is part of the Office of Cultural Development, Department of Culture, Recreation, and Tourism. There are two African-American cemeteries and a barn known to be eligible for inclusion on the *National Register of Historic Places* at this time.

SOCIOECONOMIC ENVIRONMENT

The city of Monroe, Louisiana, is situated on the Ouachita River and continues to serve as the population center and distribution outlet for the surrounding farming community. Monroe is the parish seat of Ouachita Parish and the principal city of the Monroe, Louisiana, Metropolitan Statistical Area (pop. 171,188). The 2000 census shows the city had a total population of 52,027, making it the eighth largest city in Louisiana.

As of 2000, the racial makeup of the city is 36.78 percent Caucasian, 61.13 percent African-American, 0.13 percent Native-American, 1.05 percent Asian, 0.03 percent Pacific Islander, 0.25 percent from other races, and 0.63 percent from two or more races. Hispanic or Latino of any race makes up 1.01 percent of the population.

Monroe is the home of the University of Louisiana at Monroe, CenturyTel (eighth-largest telecommunications provider in the nation), a motor speedway, and a regional airport. Some of the local area attractions include: The Monroe Civic Center Complex, Northeast Louisiana Children's Museum, Biedenharn Museum and Gardens, Masur Museum of Arts, Aviation and Military Museum, Louisiana Purchase Gardens and Zoo, Louisiana Motor Speedway, and Twin City Dragway.

REFUGE ADMINISTRATION AND MANAGEMENT

LAND PROTECTION AND CONSERVATION

The refuge now owns fee title to approximately 4,522 acres within its 6,200-acre acquisition boundary. The remaining 1,678 acres consist of private lands and Black Bayou Lake itself.

VISITOR SERVICES

Black Bayou Lake is nestled in the heart of the refuge, offering visitors a wide array of outdoor opportunities. This cypress-studded lake encompasses 1,500 acres and is managed through a unique 99-year lease with the city of Monroe. Rich in significance, the lake provides not only the secondary water source to the city but also excellent habitat for wetland-dependent fish and wildlife. While many visitors come to bask in the lake's picturesque view, many locals enjoy the consumptive qualities it has to offer. Black Bayou Lake NWR provides the Service's six priority wildlife-dependent recreational opportunities to the public, which are hunting, fishing, wildlife observation, wildlife photography, and environmental education and interpretation (Figure 10).

Hunting

Black Bayou Lake NWR is open to the public for hunting. Hunters are allowed to hunt on the northern and eastern portion of the refuge. The refuge has a current and approved hunting plan. Title 50 of the Code of Federal Regulations (50 CFR) is updated to reflect the current hunting program. A compatibility determination has been completed for the hunting program.

The refuge has one large 2,000-acre designated hunting unit, with three permanent parking lots and unit entrances. Hunters can park in the lots or along the roads of the hunting area and walk or ride an all-terrain vehicle (ATV) or bicycle into the hunting unit; they may not use the public boat launch to gain entrance into the hunting unit. Hunting is not permitted from the maintained rights-of-way of roads or the ATV trails. The hunting program has no limitations on participation, but all hunters must sign and carry an annual permit obtained from the brochure. Commercial guiding is not allowed.

Waterfowl hunting is allowed within Louisiana state regulations. The refuge does not accommodate early or late season extensions. Waterfowl (duck and coot) hunters can hunt until noon and they may use retriever dogs. The refuge does not maintain any permanent blinds. Hunters are welcome to use temporary blinds that they remove at the end of each hunting day. Some hunters choose to take a small boat into the unit with their ATV from the designated parking areas.

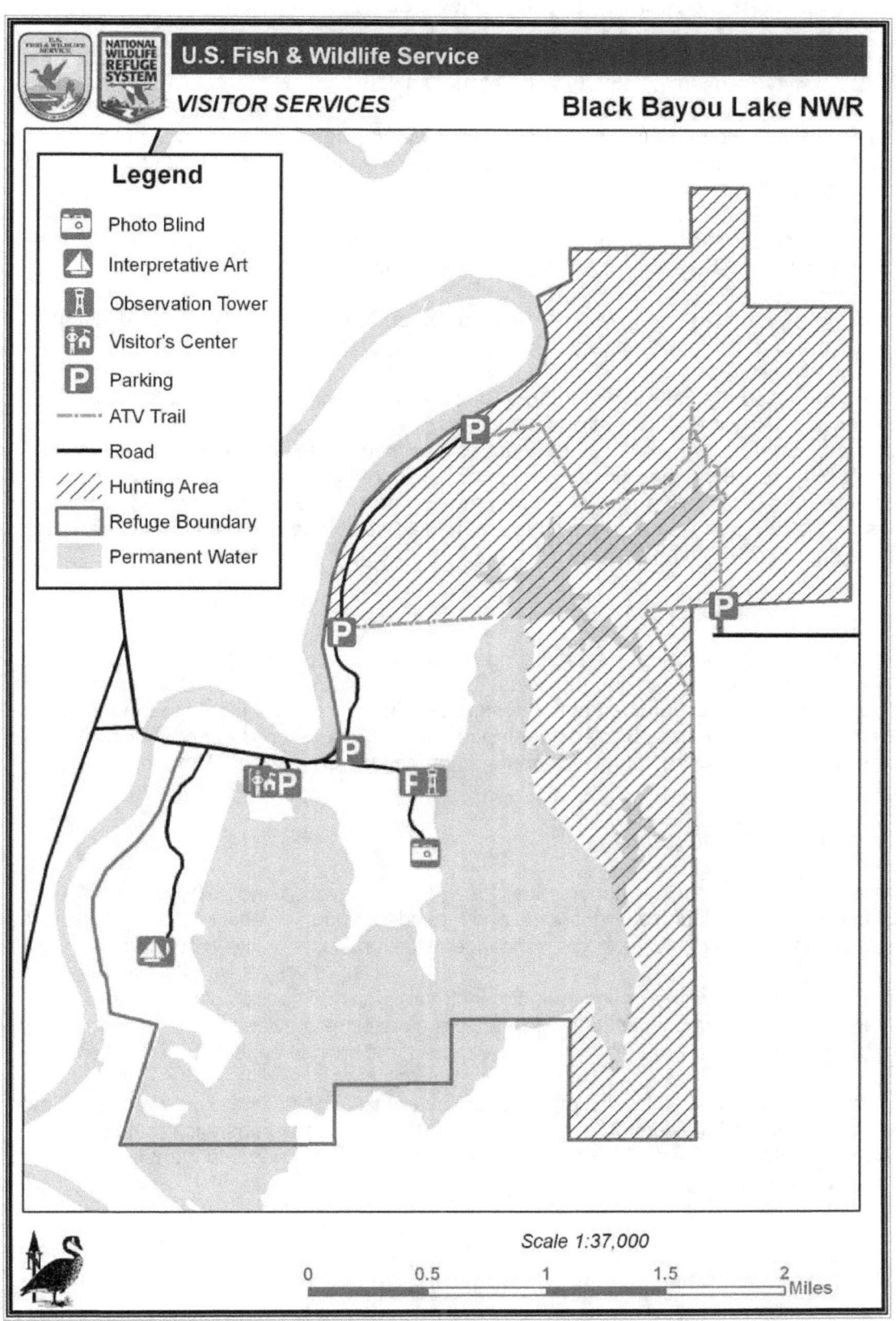

Upland bird hunting is allowed for quail and woodcock during state seasons. Louisiana state regulations apply and hunters are permitted to bring retriever dogs.

Small mammal hunting is permitted for squirrel and rabbit during the state season, except during the spring season. Dogs may be used in January and February only.

Raccoon and opossum may be hunted at night from December through January. The hunting brochure cautions that elevated mercury levels have been found and recommends that raccoons not be used for consumption.

Coyotes and beavers can be taken from the refuge during all refuge hunts, using weapons that are legal for the current season. There is no bag limit on these animals.

Archery deer hunting is permitted on the refuge. Possession and use of pods is prohibited. Hunters are permitted to take 1 deer per day – either sex.

A hunt brochure is produced annually in accordance with Service graphics standards. General prohibited activities include taking wildlife (frogs, turtles, mollusks) not specifically listed in the seasons/regulations, target practice, baiting or hunting over a baited area, possessing or using alcoholic beverages while hunting, open fires, camping or overnight parking, participating in deer drives, use or possession of lead shot, searching for or removing objects of antiquity, and using horses or mules on the refuge. Refuge regulations are made available to hunters at headquarters and kiosks before and during hunting seasons.

Fishing

A highlighted use of Black Bayou Lake is sport fishing, which is permitted year-round during daylight hours only. Common native game fish caught include bass, crappie, and sunfish. Boats with motors of 50 horsepower or less may be launched at the designated ramp located adjacent to the Visitor Center. The required launching fee is $2 per launch paid through a self-service permit located at the site. All licenses, limits, and boating safety requirements of the lake correspond with those that are regulated by LDWF.

Wildlife Observation and Photography

Black Bayou Lake NWR offers extensive opportunities for wildlife observation and photography. The refuge trails are open to visitors during daylight hours and meander through a variety of habitats, including upland forests, bottomland hardwoods, and cypress-studded lake, prairie, and dike impoundments.

The arboretum allows visitors to walk a paved path through more than 160 species of native trees, shrubs, and other vegetation. Throughout the arboretum, there are signs provided by the Friends of Black Bayou, Inc., which identify these species and interpretive panels that provide additional information.

The Prairie Demonstration Area also uses a paved pathway to take visitors into prairie habitat. Staff planted prairie grasses and wildflowers on approximately 3 acres and maintains this created prairie area by mowing in the late fall. A wayside panel discusses Louisiana prairies and identifies common butterflies found in the prairie.

From the headquarters, a raised asphalt/boardwalk nature trail winds through a wetland forest, cypress brake, and eventually out over the lake. This is considered an inspirational trail and waysides along the boardwalk are photographs with quotes to encourage visitors to make their own connections with the natural world.

The Wetlands Art Project primitive trail allows visitors to meander between impoundments where bird watching is popular. Originally planned as an outdoor art exhibit, only one piece has been installed on the trail and is an excellent place to view wildlife such as otter, raccoon, various birds, and wetland species.

In addition, a 7-mile primitive trail is maintained around the west side of the lake. This trail features distance markers and offers visitors an opportunity to get off the beaten path. The mowed trail has several available loops for those who wish to take a shorter route, but offers a more rigorous hike to those who are up to a challenge.

Near the boat launch site, visitors can walk to the 400-foot wildlife pier which traverses the lake and loops into the nature trail. Alligators, turtles, wading birds, and cypress and tupelo trees abound. Two scopes are mounted on one of two platforms and fishermen are welcome to fish anywhere along the pier.

Funds have been acquired for the development of a self-guided, 8-station, wildlife challenge trail. Trail participants will have the opportunity to record their physical abilities as compared to specific wildlife on a score card available at beginning of the trail. The trail will be located in an undeveloped area within walking distance of the refuge conservation learning center and will provide a new, physically active and fun way for families and school groups to make connections with nature. Each station will include an interpretive panel with information about and description of the behavior of some physical capability of native species of wildlife. The panels will give instructions for participants to mimic wildlife movement and/or measure their human abilities as compared to those of the wildlife.

A photography blind is open to the public via paved trail and boardwalk. The blind is large enough to accommodate several people and overlooks a wetland. The staff has installed logs and other features to attract wildlife closer to the blind. Natural snags and trees enhance the marsh for wildlife photography.

A concrete walk and sloping ramp built through a baldcypress swamp lead to a raised observation deck which is wheelchair accessible. The covered deck has a spotting scope for observing a remote part of the lake.

Near the visitor center, a birding blind has been built. To avoid bird collisions, the blind windows were installed slanted. Fences, extending from the blind, shelter feeding birds from being disturbed by approaching visitors. The blind has a solar powered fan and enough room to house 5-10 people. Outside the blind, feeding stations and water structures attract birds. Additional brush and clearings are planned to increase bird watching opportunities.

Simply driving the interior roads of the refuge offers wildlife observation and photography opportunities for visitors. Bobcats, squirrels, and small birds use the habitat alongside the roads. The refuge mows only one swath on either side for most of the year, allowing native grasses and flowers to grow up. Killdeer have been found nesting in the gravel and butterflies and dragonflies are numerous along these roads.

Annual events on the refuge include International Migratory Bird Day, the Refuge Photography Contest, and the Fall Celebration, which is hosted by the Friends of Black Bayou, Inc., during National Wildlife Refuge Week. The Friends group also hosted a native plant sale to encourage native landscaping and to educate the public about invasive species.

These events are timed with migration to provide visitors the best opportunities to observe wildlife, flowering plants in the prairie, and other refuge resources. All event attendees are given tips on wildlife observation and taught about the refuge mission. Events are available to individuals with disabilities as a large portion of the refuge facilities, trails, boardwalks, piers, and overlooks are accessible.

Partners with the refuge are numerous, including the city of Monroe, International Paper, Century Tel, Monroe Garden Study League, Monroe-West Monroe Convention Visitor's Bureau, Monroe City Schools, The Nature Conservancy of Louisiana, the Louisiana Department of Wildlife and Fisheries, the University of Louisiana at Monroe, Louisiana Purchase Gardens and Zoo, Ouachita Parish Sherrif's office, Architecture Plus, Angus Chemical Company, and various other organizations and individual volunteers.

Environmental Education

Through uniquely developed, environmentally based educational field experiences, staff and volunteers at Black Bayou Lake NWR provide quality education opportunities for more that 2,500 students annually. Correlated to national and state education standards, the curriculum-based environmental activities allow students to leave behind their normal indoor classroom and venture outdoors to discover and connect with nature.

The utilization of facilities, equipment, educational materials, teacher workshops, and several study sites provides visitors with a safe environment conducive to learning.

Currently, the education staff consists of a park ranger and wildlife refuge specialist who conduct the majority of the programs offered. The diversity of program audiences include school groups, teachers, summer camps, university classes, Girl Scouts, Boy Scouts, church groups, civic clubs, and garden clubs. Standards, regulations, and requirements have been developed by refuge staff to ensure that the quality of education delivered is one that is sustainable and does not exceed capacity. Such examples would include limited group sizes, limited days available, teacher knowledge accountability, and consolidated grade-specific activities. Such requirements were implemented in autumn 2007.

The environmental education center includes: visitor center; a 100-seat shaded amphitheater/ pavilion; nature trail and pier; arboretum with over 160 native Louisiana woody plants identified; prairie demonstration area with native grasses and wildflowers; ponds for aquatic investigations; and a conservation learning center with discovery room equipped with audio-visual equipment, 5 computers, microscopes, water and soil testing equipment, learning stations with teacher-ready activities and hands-on displays, and large aquaria exhibits of native fishes, reptiles, and amphibians.

The visitor center is a restored 1880s planter's house. It was moved about 1/4-mile to its current location and renovated by members of the nonprofit group, Friends of Black Bayou, Inc. The beautifully restored building contains interactive exhibits, which introduce visitors to the refuge's wildlife and habitats. A "Touch Me!" table filled with bones, snake skins, fur, feathers, and turtle shells provides hands-on learning for children. The center also has a meeting room and nature shop on the main floor and offices for the refuge's staff upstairs.

The Monroe City School System manages 18 primary schools, 13 elementary schools, 4 middle schools, and 3 high schools. The high schools included in the city system are Carroll High School, Neville High School, and Wossman High School. The Ouachita Parish School System is responsible for managing schools outside the Monroe city limits. Monroe is also home to River Oaks School, New Vision Learning Academy, Ouachita Christian School, St. Frederick's Catholic School, and Jesus the Good Shepard and Our Lady of Fatima Elementary Schools. Teachers and students from several surrounding parish school districts also come to the refuge for educational field experiences.

Environmental Interpretation

The exhibits at the visitor center are the main source of interpretive information for the refuge. The exhibits include the following: Black Bayou Lake panel, North Louisiana NWR Complex panel diorama, National Wildlife Refuge System and Fish and Wildlife Service panels, Wetlands, Bottomland Hardwoods, Bats, Red-cockaded woodpeckers, Upland Hardwoods, Invasive Species, Wonderful Wetlands, Bird Migration (interactive lights), Neotropical Migratory Birds (bird voice recording), Bayou Diversity (interactive backlighted pictures and voice recorded stories), Human Connection Across Time, Historic Time Line Panels, Reptile Diorama, and a "Touch Me!" table. The refuge has interpretive trail signs at major trails and prominent locations on the refuge.

Key resource issues/interpretive themes
The primary themes and messages interpreted on the refuge relate to the missions of the Service and the Refuge System and to the resource issues facing the refuge complex. The overarching interpretive theme for the refuge is "Everything in Nature is Connected," with emphasis on connecting people with nature.

Personal services interpretation
Monthly interpretive programs, including "Wild Fridays" for families and older children on the last Friday of every month, and "Tales and Trails" for younger children on the third Thursday of every month are developed and lead by refuge staff and volunteers. Interpretive programs are also offered to various groups when requested. The programs are adapted to meet individual visitor needs when necessary (e.g., the need of persons with disabilities). The park ranger has been trained and performs personal interpretation. Approximately 3,000 persons attend facilitated interpretive programs, guided hikes, etc., each year.

Visitor center/information area
Indoor space at the visitor center and conservation learning center is dedicated to resource interpretation. The space is adequate for the need and demand of groups up to 60 at the visitor center and up to 100 at the conservation learning center. Both facilities are universally accessible.

Visitor center/information area exhibits
The current exhibits are up-to-date, in good condition, and professionally designed and fabricated. There is a logical flow from one exhibit to the next, both in the information provided and in the physical layout. The text is brief, simple, and to the point, and written at an appropriate reading level for the audience. Exhibits are designed to meet the needs of a diverse audience (e.g., children and adults). Many of the exhibits are interactive.

Printed materials
The refuge Friends group is developing a series of species-related information pamphlets about wildlife, the first of which is about turtles. This publication does not comply with the Service graphics standard.

"Wetland Connections," a trail brochure developed by staff personnel with natural history information and nature trail panel and tree descriptions, is available at the visitor center.

The development of a refuge-specific brochure is being planned. This will include information on all facilities and trails at Black Bayou Lake NWR.

Large print and audio versions of publications are not available to visitors with visual disabilities.

Kiosks and wayside exhibits
Kiosks and wayside exhibits used to interpret key resources and issues are professionally designed and fabricated, and meet the visitor's various needs for information. Other kiosk signs and wayside exhibits for interpreting key resources and issues are planned by the refuge manager and staff.

Portable Exhibits
Two refuge-specific portable exhibits have been produced for interpreting key resources and issues for off-site audiences.

PERSONNEL, OPERATIONS, AND MAINTENANCE

Black Bayou Lake NWR, being one of five refuges in the North Louisiana NWR Complex, does not have its own budget. Maintenance and operation monies budgeted to the Complex are spent among all refuges within the Complex. Occasionally project specific monies are directed to only Black Bayou Lake NWR in some years. Likewise, staffing issues are complicated. Some positions are assigned to the Complex while other positions are assigned to certain refuges.

Staff Positions—FY2007 Complex Personnel

Project Leader	Refuge Manager
Refuge Operations Specialist	Forester
Biologist	Equipment Operator
Budget Administrator	Maintenance Worker
Park Ranger	

North Louisiana NWR Complex Funding—FY07

Description	Account	Amount
Refuge Operations	1261	$756,300
Refuge Maintenance	1262	$695,600
		$269,100
		$89,000
		$22,000
Total Complex Operating Budget		**$1,832,000**
Total Complex Budget (including all special project monies)		**$2,387,200**

Private Lands

Private lands work has historically been administered under the Louisiana Wetlands Management District of the North Louisiana NWR Complex. Black Bayou Lake NWR does not have a private lands biologist or private lands projects.

III. Plan Development

In accordance with Service guidelines and National Environmental Policy Act recommendations, public involvement has been a crucial factor throughout the development of the CCP for Black Bayou Lake NWR. This CCP has been written with input and assistance from interested citizens, conservation organizations, and employees of local and state agencies. The participation of these stakeholders and their ideas has been of great value in setting the management direction for Black Bayou Lake NWR. The Service, as a whole, and the refuge staff, in particular, are very grateful to each one who has contributed time, expertise, and ideas to the planning process. The staff remains impressed by the passion and commitment of so many individuals for the lands and waters administered by the refuge.

A planning team composed of refuge staff was formed to prepare the CCP. Initially, the team focused on identifying the issues and concerns pertinent to refuge management. The team met on several occasions from February 2008 to December 2008.

In preparation for developing the CCP, the refuge conducted a biological review and public use review in February 2008 and March 2008, respectively. Early in the process, the planning team identified a variety of issues, concerns, and opportunities that were provided to both review teams.

The Black Bayou Lake NWR Biological Review was held during the week of February 4, 2008. The Biological Review Team was a diverse team of experts from universities, state and federal agencies, and non-profit organizations invited to review the biological program of the refuge. The Biological Review Team conducted a critical examination of all aspects of the refuge's biological program. Members of this review team then produced a report that summarized recommendations to be used while developing the CCP.

The Public Use Review was held in March 2008. The team was comprised of Black Bayou Lake NWR staff, neighboring refuge staff, and Service Regional Office representatives from the Visitor Services and Outreach Program. The team reviewed the existing public use programs, facilities, and opportunities available. Emphasis was placed on the six priority wildlife-dependent public uses. The team prepared a Public Use Review Report that included recommendations for the short- and long-term public use program. These recommendations were taken into consideration in the development of this CCP.

A notice of intent to prepare the comprehensive conservation plan was published in the *Federal Register* on May 8, 2008 (73 FR 26139). The public was notified in the local newspapers and other media of the public meeting held May 22, 2008, in Monroe, Louisiana. In addition, information packets, including a letter of invite, public input workbook and mailing list request form, were mailed to approximately 30 different federal, state, non-governmental agencies; state and federal congressional offices; and private individuals. Approximately 10 members of the public attended the public scoping meeting. Six members of the public offered their comments at the public meeting, and two comments were mailed to the refuge.

SUMMARY OF ISSUES, CONCERNS, AND OPPORTUNITIES

The planning team identified a number of issues, concerns, and opportunities related to wildlife and habitat management, resource protection, public use and environmental education, and refuge administration. Additionally, the planning team considered federal and state mandates, as well as applicable local ordinances, regulations, and plans. The team also directed the process of obtaining public input through public scoping meetings, planning team meetings, comment packets, and personal contacts. All public and advisory team comments were considered. However, some issues important to the public fell outside the scope of the decision to be made in this planning process. The planning team developed this CCP, which attempts to balance the competing opinions regarding important issues. The team identified those issues that it felt were most significant to the refuge. A summary of these issues follows.

FISH AND WILDLIFE POPULATION MANAGEMENT

In general, although the refuge has conducted various monitoring and population surveys, complete baseline information on species abundance and distribution is needed.

Species of Concern: The alligator snapping turtle is listed as threatened or endangered by every state in its range except Louisiana, where it is considered a species of conservation concern. In 2006, it was listed on Appendix III of CITES by the United States. Black Bayou Lake NWR has a breeding population of alligator snapping turtles that has been studied by researchers for several years. Over 95 percent of alligator snapping turtle nests on the refuge are depredated. Located nests are now either protected with predator exclusion devices or the eggs are gathered, incubated in a laboratory, and hatchlings released into the lake. More information is needed on hatchling survival rates, microhabitat needs, and dispersal and age structure of the population. An excellent partnership has been established between the refuge and the University of Louisiana at Monroe to continue studying alligator snapping turtles.

The southeastern Myotis bat and Rafinesque's big-eared bat are considered federal species of concern. Although both species have been documented on Black Bayou Lake NWR, research is needed to determine their use of the refuge.

Although the Louisiana black bear has not been recorded on the refuge, concern was expressed about the encroachment of the bear into the refuge area. Black Bayou Lake NWR has the potential for establishment, yet the urban proximity and small refuge size may limit the refuge to corridor habitat only.

Resident Wildlife: To better understand the biodiversity and environmental health of refuge lands, baseline information on wildlife and their habitats must be collected. These data will document presence or absence, monitor trends, and identify the impacts of refuge programs on species. The refuge assumes responsibility for managing resident wildlife that is dependent on refuge resources.

White-tailed deer occur on the refuge and have the potential to adversely affect habitats unless their numbers are kept at or slightly below the carrying capacity of the habitat. Hunting programs also provide opportunities for the take of raccoons, rabbits, and squirrels, and the incidental take of beavers and coyotes. Raccoons, beavers, and coyotes have the potential to become overpopulated, adversely impacting other species. Raccoon and coyote predation on the nests of turkeys, wood ducks, turtles, and songbirds can limit reproductive success of those species. Raccoons also spread canine distemper, a common close-contact disease, to other species such as fox. Beavers could become pests on parts of the refuge by building dams that flood trees, which can cause die-offs of large tracts of bottomland hardwoods. American alligators can become a concern in highly developing urban areas. As urban areas develop and encroach upon the natural habitat of the alligator, human/wildlife conflicts tend to increase. Annual trends and monitoring help evaluate the need of control of this species.

Migratory Birds: Neotropical migratory birds use the Ouachita River as a primary migration corridor in north Louisiana. Black Bayou Lake NWR, being close to the river, provides important stop-over habitat for migratory birds in an increasingly urban landscape.

Specific Public Comments:

- Need a complete inventory of invertebrates prior to habitat management.
- Concerned about the encroachment of black bears into the area, how to encourage the increase of bears and also how to plan for public safety.
- Concerned about too much public access which violates the "wildlife first" mandate; suggest a moratorium on increased infrastructure.
- Concerned that there is a fine line between education, public assess, and wildlife.

HABITAT MANAGEMENT

General Concerns: One respondent is concerned about the algae growth on the lake. Another would like to see the water levels on the lake managed to mimic the historic and natural hydrological regime. One respondent would like to see certain areas always managed for early successional habitat, particularly for birds.

Mixed Pine/Hardwood Upland: Mixed pine/hardwood uplands comprise 1,900 acres on Black Bayou Lake NWR. The refuge does not currently have a forest management plan. A forest management plan would detail desired habitat conditions by taking into consideration species composition, stocking levels, proper management tools, and promotion of special microhabitats such as cane and prairie plants.

Invasive Species: Several invasive plant species are present on the refuge, including but not limited to water hyacinth, Chinese tallowtree, and Chinese privet. Water hyacinth is capable of forming dense mats over the surface of the water. It can cause dissolved oxygen levels to decrease, thereby affecting fish, mollusks, and other aquatic species. Water hyacinth also inhibits boat navigation and competes with native plant species. Chinese tallowtree and privet have the ability to become ubiquitous in distribution, outcompete native plants, and create monocultures. Invasives decrease the overall biological integrity of the refuge.

Specific Public Comments:

- Concerned about the vegetation growth on the lake.
- Want to manage water levels on the lake to mimic the historic and natural hydrological regime.
- Want to purchase land within acquisition area but only from willing landowners.
- Would like to see cooperative agreements with adjacent landowners regarding water quality and other ecological integrity issues.
- Concerned that over the next 15 years with the increased suburbanization of the surrounding area, the priority public uses will need to be re-evaluated, especially with hunting (gun safety issues).
- Would like to see that emphasis is given to birds and bird habitat.
- Would like to see certain areas always managed for early successional habitat particularly for birds

RESOURCE PROTECTION

Land Protection: The purchase of two properties within the refuge's acquisition boundary would increase core area and protect the lake's ecosystem. The Oliver Plantation consists of 1,465 acres of riparian habitat and Black Bayou Lake, the only portion of lake outside refuge management. Acquisition of this property would ensure protection of the lake and its watershed. The other property consists of a narrow strip of land between Bayou DeSiard and the refuge. Current landowners plan to subdivide the waterfront property into individual lots. Acquisition of the 75-acre Bayou DeSiard tract would protect that portion of the bayou and buffer the refuge from a residential development.

Cultural and Historic Resource Protection: There are currently two cemetery sites on the refuge and the visitor center and barn are historic resources. The Service needs to maintain protection of these important resources.

Climate Change: The refuge needs to be proactive in addressing escalating challenges such as land-use conversion, invasive species, water scarcity, and a range of other complex issues -- all of which are amplified by accelerated climate change.

VISITOR SERVICES

General Concerns: The refuge has developed community and volunteer support and built a very successful visitor services program. Because of these efforts, the refuge is considered a "Flagship Refuge" and should continue to be used as an example for other refuges building visitor services programs. The refuge is also the "Gateway" to the North Louisiana NWR Complex and offers the only visitor center facility in the Complex. All priority public uses of the Refuge System are offered at Black Bayou Lake NWR. The Complex continues to focus most of its efforts managing visitor service and volunteer programs at Black Bayou Lake NWR.

Environmental Education and Interpretation: Through uniquely developed, environmentally based, educational field experiences, staff at Black Bayou Lake NWR provide quality education opportunities for more that 2,500 students annually. Correlated to national and state education standards, the curriculum based environmental activities offered allow students to leave behind their normal indoor classroom and venture outdoors to discover and connect with nature. The utilization of facilities, equipment, educational materials, teacher workshops, and several study sites provides a safe and conducive learning environment for visitors.

Currently, a park ranger and a wildlife refuge specialist conduct the majority of the programs offered. In order to expand this program and maintain quality, supportive resources will need to be engaged, including support from a volunteer coordinator, teacher-led activities, and additional staff.

Hunting and Fishing: Hunting and fishing are integral parts of Louisiana culture. It is not surprising that there is considerable state and local interest in maintaining hunting and fishing opportunities.

If the deer herd expands beyond carrying capacity, a limited gun hunting opportunity is one management consideration for the white-tailed deer population on the refuge, but such a hunt would require careful coordination and control. There is concern that with the increased suburbanization of the surrounding area, the priority public uses will need to be re-evaluated, especially with hunting (gun safety issues).

Law Enforcement Issues: Future urban development may increase opportunities for management of public use (hunting and ATVs) and habitat programs (log trucks).

Specific Public Comments:

- Would like to see the refuge continue to be a place for people to meet and discuss refuge issues, host groups that are concerned with environmental issues and use existing facilities.
- Make the refuge a focal point for conservationists to meet and also a place to focus on education; make it a pilot for public education and awareness.
- Does not want increased access to the refuge; wants to maintain present access levels. Don't want it to become a "park."
- Concerned with litter problem on the refuge.
- Concerned with littering; need law enforcement; not enough personnel to pick up litter.
- Increase signage to discourage littering; ensure that school groups are educated on littering problem.
- Increase signage—lake high-priority area.
- Does not want the refuge open to nighttime use.
- Want to use yo-yos, juglines, and trotlines.
- May be some need for security cameras or other types of surveillance.
- Need more staff (public use and maintenance); need to educate the public about cultural resources on the refuge.
- Need more law enforcement; another law enforcement officer.
- Need the existing employees to have more law enforcement authority.
- Have signs that say "if you see someone littering, call this number" - use existing parish laws to enforce littering regulations.
- Think the refuge has a superior staff and is managed well; the community has a lot of respect for the way the refuge is managed and how much has been accomplished.
- Continue to build partnerships with the community.
- Fishing is one of the major public uses on the refuge; wants to increase partnerships with anglers on the refuge.
- Use the "free fishing" days to host an event or focus on the anglers in the community.
- Need to partner with anglers regarding subsistence fishing.
- Would like to see "clean-up" days maybe associated with Earth Day.
- Continue to educate on environmental issues that are not just refuge-specific.
- Focus education towards seniors.

REFUGE ADMINISTRATION

Specific Public Comments:

- Concerned that in the next 15 years, the refuge may not be able to support financially or logistically the existing facilities. Concerned that the refuge will "overdo" the public access.
- Want to keep in mind that the Service budget keeps getting slashed. When new facilities or uses are created, they have to be maintained and/or staffed so the refuge needs to be realistic about future capability to upkeep public use programs.
- Concerned that the refuge will have the budget necessary to maintain programs in the future.
- Concerned that the refuge somehow encourage a building of the budget to help with educational and maintenance needs. Concerned that the refuge staff is reduced— need more staff.
- Volunteers and Friends – designated volunteer to coordinate volunteer program.

- Facilities – housing and associated utilities for interns or graduate students, more facilities (washer and dryer) for resident volunteers.

WILDERNESS REVIEW

Refuge planning policy requires a wilderness review as part of the comprehensive conservation planning process that is consistent with provisions of the Wilderness Act, National Environmental Policy Act, National Historic Preservation Act, and other applicable legislation. Black Bayou Lake NWR lands were inventoried to identify whether areas met the defining wilderness criteria set forth in the Wilderness Act of 1964. Please refer to Appendix H for that determination.

IV. Management Direction

INTRODUCTION

The Service manages fish and wildlife habitats, considering the needs of all resources in decision-making. But, first and foremost, fish and wildlife conservation assumes priority in refuge management. A requirement of the Improvement Act is for the Service to maintain the ecological health, diversity, and integrity of refuges. This chapter describes the goals, objectives, and strategies that will be used to implement a science-based stewardship program for fish and wildlife resources on the refuge.

On national wildlife refuges, wildlife conservation is the first priority in refuge management. Public uses are allowed if they are appropriate and compatible with wildlife and habitat conservation. The Service has identified six priority wildlife-dependent public uses of national wildlife refuges. These uses are hunting, fishing, wildlife observation, wildlife photography, and environmental education and interpretation. These priority public uses are therefore emphasized in this CCP.

Described below is the CCP for managing the refuge over the next 15 years. This management direction contains the goals, objectives, and strategies that will be used to achieve the refuge vision.

Three alternatives for managing the refuge were considered:

A. Maintain Current Management Direction (No-Action Alternative)
B. Optimize Biological Program and Visitor Services (Preferred Alternative)
C. Minimize Management and Public Use Management

Each of these alternatives is described in the Alternatives section of the EA in the Draft CCP/EA for Black Bayou Lake NWR. The Service chose Alternative B "Optimize Biological Program and Visitor Services" as the preferred management action. This alternative best satisfies the vision of the refuge and best addresses the goals, objectives, and strategies expressed by the planning team, the refuge staff, governmental partners, and the public.

Implementing the preferred alternative will result in management based on sound science for the conservation of a structurally and species diverse bottomland hardwood habitat (along with managed wetlands and associated prairies) for migratory birds and resident wildlife. A focused effort will be put toward reducing invasive species threatening the biological integrity of the refuge. Baseline inventorying and monitoring of management actions will be completed to gain information on a variety of species from reptiles and amphibians to game animals, as well as species of concern. Several cooperative projects will be conducted with universities, LDWF, and other agencies and individuals to provide biological information to be used in management decisions. When compatible, the wildlife-dependent recreational opportunities for hunting, fishing, wildlife observation, wildlife photography, and environmental education and interpretation will be provided and enhanced, while achieving the refuge purpose.

VISION

The Black Bayou Lake National Wildlife Refuge will be managed to provide for the restoration, enhancement, and conservation of bottomland hardwood forests, wetlands, and mixed pine/hardwood uplands, as an integral component of the Black Bayou Lake ecosystem. These habitats will support a variety of migratory birds, species of special concern, and other associated wildlife and plants. This effort will be enhanced and encouraged through both strong partnerships and public support by providing opportunities for environmental education and interpretation, hunting, fishing, and wildlife observation and photography. Black Bayou Lake NWR will be the focal point for environmental education and interpretation for the entire North Louisiana National Wildlife Refuge Complex.

GOALS, OBJECTIVES, AND STRATEGIES

The goals, objectives, and strategies presented are the Service's response to the issues, concerns, and needs expressed by the planning team, the refuge staff and partners, and the public. They are presented in hierarchical format. Chapter V, Plan Implementation, identifies the projects associated with the various strategies.

These goals, objectives, and strategies reflect the Service's commitment to achieve the mandates of the Improvement Act, the mission of the Refuge System, and the purposes and vision of Black Bayou Lake NWR. With adequate resources, as outlined in Chapter V, Plan Implementation, the Service intends to accomplish these goals, objectives, and strategies within the next 15 years.

FISH AND WILDLIFE POPULATION MANAGEMENT

GOAL A: Fish and Wildlife Population Management
Promote the conservation and management of migratory bird diversity and resident wildlife in support of national, regional, and ecosystem habitat and population goals.

Discussion: Black Bayou Lake NWR is part of the LMRE and is considered to be in the MAV Bird Conservation Area. As such, Black Bayou Lake NWR is a component of many regional and ecosystem conservation planning initiatives. Wildlife species found on the refuge are typical of forested wetlands and fields. The refuge provides habitat for wintering waterfowl and year-round habitat for nesting wood ducks. Species range from diving ducks, such as scaup, ring-necked duck, redhead, and canvasback, to common puddle ducks, such as mallard and teal. More than 300 species of neotropical migratory birds use the Black Bayou Lake at various times of the year. Priority species for conservation include American woodcock, yellow-billed cuckoo, prothonotary warbler, worm-eating warbler, Louisiana waterthrush, Kentucky warbler, and hooded warbler. Other migratory birds, such wading birds and shorebirds, are numerous on shallow-flooded fields and mudflats.

Resident game and furbearer species include white-tailed deer, swamp rabbit, cottontail rabbit, gray and fox squirrels, mink, muskrat, beaver, fox, and coyote. The MAV also supports a variety of nongame mammals, amphibians, and reptiles.

The river basin supports 133 species of fish, ranging from game species such as largemouth bass, crappie, and catfish, to big river species such as shovelnose sturgeon, freshwater drum, and gar. Two species of management concern, the blue sucker and paddlefish, are also found in the Black Bayou Lake.

Objective A-1. Migratory Waterfowl: Continue to conduct mid-winter waterfowl survey on the refuge during early January in coordination with partners.

Discussion: The MAV is a critical ecoregion for migrating and wintering waterfowl in North America (Reinecke et al. 1989). Although Black Bayou Lake NWR only receives moderate use from wintering waterfowl (Table 1), the refuge still provides important foraging and resting (sanctuary) habitats within the MAV, which contributes important regional resources to an international effort known as the NAWMP that seeks to return waterfowl populations to levels that occurred during the 1970s.

Concern over waterfowl population declines in the 1980s resulted in the establishment of the NAWMP, which focused attention of federal, state, and private conservation groups on critical wintering and breeding areas. The LMVJV was organized to plan conservation efforts to provide sufficient waterfowl habitat in the MAV to ensure adequate winter survival and body condition for spring migrating and nesting. Factors limiting waterfowl populations were identified, and the LMVJV assumed foraging habitat was most likely to limit populations wintering in the MAV (Reinecke et al. 1989).

Foraging habitat objectives have not been established for Black Bayou Lake NWR, and the potential for the refuge to contribute waterfowl habitat is mainly limited to the lake itself. The flooded shrub swamps along the shallow fringes of the lake have some value as foraging habitat, but probably play a more important role by isolating birds during pair bonding and providing thermal protection on cold, windy days. Similarly, the majority of the lake provides some native wetland food plants for waterfowl, but serves a more important role as a sanctuary area, free from disturbance by hunters during the winter period. Continuing efforts by refuge staff to control water hyacinth in the lake will reduce this invasive aquatic plant's ability to compete with more preferred submerged and emergent native vegetation beneficial to wintering waterfowl.

Strategies:

- Continue conducting mid-winter waterfowl survey during early January.
- Evaluate data as appropriate.
- Continue to coordinate with partners to conduct survey efficiently.

Objective A-2. Waterfowl Sanctuary: Maintain existing waterfowl sanctuary which consists of 60 percent of the entire refuge.

Discussion: An essential component of waterfowl wintering habitat is sanctuary. Waterfowl need sanctuary from human disturbance during the winter to prepare biologically for spring migration and reproduction (Reinecke et al. 1989). Disturbance can interrupt resting and feeding bouts, resulting in a loss of energy and lowering of body weight. Paulus (1984) found in Louisiana that increased foraging time by gadwalls was insufficient to counterbalance disturbance factors. Locally, the refuge can provide sanctuary for a portion of the waterfowl population.

Sanctuary is a priority for management of wintering waterfowl to ensure that adequate and preferred feeding habitats are available. Many of the public believe that sanctuaries affect the availability of waterfowl for the hunting season. Some believe that sanctuaries hold all the ducks, or a large portion, off of public and/or private hunting areas. In contrast, it has been seen in some areas that creating sanctuary areas or areas with minimal human disturbance, among a diversity of habitat types that provide adequate food and cover resources, is probably the most effective management tool to encourage waterfowl use over time. Sanctuaries provide core use areas that enhance the use of adjacent areas by holding more birds closer to a hunting area (Bias et al. 1997).

Strategies:

- It is recommended that the "No-Hunting" area be maintained to minimize disturbance to waterfowl utilizing Black Bayou Lake NWR for feeding, resting, loafing, pair-bonding, etc.
- Post sanctuary boundary and continue to enforce no waterfowl hunting in the sanctuary.
- Monitor the sanctuary for disturbance thresholds from access during the key waterfowl wintering period of September-March.

Objective A-3. Resident/Nesting Waterfowl: Provide habitat and maintain a program of 15-20 well-monitored wood duck nest boxes to support a year-round local population.

Discussion: Wood ducks are year-round residents in the MAV and Black Bayou Lake NWR. In addition, wood ducks are probably the most abundant wintering ducks on the refuge. Preferred habitats include forested wetlands, wooded and scrub/shrub swamps, sloughs, and beaver ponds. Among the preferred foods of wood ducks are acorns, other hard and soft mast, weed seeds, and invertebrates found in shallow flooded timber, shrub swamps, sloughs, and moist-soil habitats. They loaf and roost in more secluded areas and dense shrub swamps. Fall is normally the driest time in the MAV. Wood ducks are often seeking food and cover in a greatly reduced flooded area. Any provisions to assure adequate habitat at this time is considered beneficial.

Wood ducks are cavity nesters, seeking cavities in trees, preferably within a 1/2-mile of permanent water. Brood survival is higher in situations where nests are close to water. Due to forestry practices and urban sprawl, as well as competition for nest cavities from other species, natural cavities are considered to limit reproduction in most areas. Artificial nest boxes are commonly used to supplement natural cavities and increase local production of wood ducks. Box programs are not, however, an end to all nesting problems. They require time and attention to be cleaned and repaired at least annually. Production is often increased with more frequent checks and cleaning of boxes, but this must be weighed against other time constraints. Cleaning the boxes after the initial peak of nesting activity (about mid-April) should significantly improve annual production. It is critical that boxes have functional predator guards and are located free from overhanging tree limbs to prevent predation from raccoons and snakes. In addition, boxes should be positioned so there is an unobstructed area that enables female wood ducks to fly directly into the box opening.

During the review, refuge staff indicated that box use from the refuge's 17 nest boxes has never been high. However, recommendations were to continue an active nest box program, ensuring that guidelines presented in the publication, "Increasing Wood Duck Productivity: Guidelines for Management and Banding" (USFWS 2003a) are followed.

Strategies:

- Maintain a program of 15-20 well-maintained nest boxes. Replace boxes as they deteriorate, and place them such that it is difficult to see from one box to the next, or at least 100 yards apart. Strive to check boxes at least twice annually (once pre-season and once in mid-April).
- Evaluate nest efficiency and nesting success in boxes and adjust the program accordingly.

- Maintain all current wood duck habitat, and explore opportunities to enhance these habitats when possible.
- In cooperation with partners (LDWF), contribute to the Mississippi Flyway council's Preseason Wood Duck Banding effort.

Objective A-4. Forest Breeding Birds: Continue annual breeding landbird surveys conducted at random points within forest compartments.

Discussion: Although Black Bayou NWR is relatively small (4,522 acres), it is comprised of a matrix of habitat types from open water to wet and dry bottomland hardwood forests to upland hardwoods. As such, the refuge has an opportunity to provide habitat for a multitude of avian species. To the extent possible, refuge staff should promote habitat conditions that benefit (priority) species listed in national/regional conservation plans (e.g., Partners in Flight Landbird Conservation Plan, Waterbird Conservation Plan, Shorebird Conservation Plan).

Strategies:

- Determine relative abundance of forest breeding birds over time and management regimes.
- Statistically analyze data collected to make adaptive management decisions.
- Contribute data to national database as appropriate.

Objective A-5. Forest Breeding Birds: Determine nesting success of priority neotropical migratory birds within 6 years of the date of this CCP, and use production data as a baseline for comparison in future years as surrounding land cover changes.

Strategies:

- Implement breeding bird monitoring program in conjunction with the LMVJV coordinated bird monitoring project.
- Work with partners, such as Louisiana State University and birding groups, to conduct nest searches using a statistically valid study design.
- Determine if refuge merits setting up a Monitoring Avian Production and Survivorship (MAPS) station.
- Analyze data and generate reports that management can utilize.

Objective A-6. Shorebirds and Marsh birds: Implement baseline standardized presence/absence or relative abundance surveys within the managed wetlands for shorebirds and secretive marsh birds according to approved protocol.

Discussion: The only shorebird habitat found on the refuge would be the shorelines of the lake, hatchery ponds, and Bayou DeSiard. No impoundments are managed for shorebirds.

Likewise, marsh bird habitat is not available on the refuge, but Virginia rails, clapper rails, and soras probably migrate through the refuge. King rails may breed irregularly if water levels are suitable. Coots are present year-round and are especially abundant in winter. Common moorhen and purple gallinules breed in the area.

For both sets of species, baseline, annual or time-derived surveys should be implemented to detect changes of species or relative abundance of species using the refuge.

Strategies:

- Work with city officials to pursue summer draw-down of the lake to enhance/increase foraging (habitat) opportunities.
- Record presence of shorebird species when encountered.
- Conduct secretive marsh bird surveys once every 3 years.

Objective A-7. Waterbirds: Implement baseline standardized presence/absence or relative abundance surveys within wetlands for water birds according to approved protocol. Also, continue to annually monitor habitat for rookery activity.

Discussion: Black Bayou Lake NWR provides wading bird habitat at different times of the year. A major rookery was discovered on the refuge in 2000, and was active for 3 years. Small rookeries of herons still exist. Species nested include white ibis, anhinga, great blue heron, little blue heron, great egret, cattle egret, green heron, snowy egret and night-herons. American bitterns, roseate spoonbills, and wood storks have been recorded on the refuge usually during migration or post-breeding dispersal. Large concentrations of double-crested cormorants utilize the refuge during winter. American white pelicans are sometimes seen floating on the lake.

Strategy:

- Monitor rookery activity from April to July.

Objective A-8. Scrub/Shrub Birds: Determine species presence, relative abundance, and habitat use of priority scrub/shrub species.

Discussion: While bottomland hardwood forest is the habitat type that has been most disturbed and much effort to restore such habitat will be a focus on this refuge, there will be opportunities for providing early successional habitats suitable for scrub/shrub birds. There will also be an opportunity to provide such habitat in a planed prairie demonstration area on the refuge.

Strategies:

- Working with the LMVJV, consider establishing roadside point counts along forest and field edges across the refuge to track habitat use by all priority scrub/shrub species.
- Cooperate with LDWF and a university to develop a research project with graduate students to evaluate timber management efforts on scrub/shrub birds.

Objective A-9. Mammals: Continue to record mammal species observed and add to current list. Continue to utilize graduate students to conduct research on mammals.

Discussion: Nongame mammals have been poorly understood and not well researched. On Black Bayou Lake NWR, no information exists about nongame mammal populations. Initial work should be directed towards a basic inventory to determine if any species of concern are present.

Strategies:

- Research the literature including range maps for species that should occur in northwest Louisiana.
- Review local university collections and determine if wildlife professors have species lists for the surrounding areas.
- Employ different surveying techniques such as small-mammal traps and mist-netting for bats to sample for presence of all potential species.

Objective A-10. White-tailed Deer: Monitor white-tailed deer herd health, age, and sex structure every 3 to 5 years for disease and conditions that relate to refuge habitat carrying capacity.

Discussion: Deer can reproduce quickly and should be monitored for herd health issues as well as potential impacts on available habitats. This is especially true for the isolated herd that is found at the refuge. For example, chronic wasting disease is a transmissible spongiform encephalopathy of deer and elk. It has not been found in Louisiana to date, but the high profile of this disease, combined with Service responsibilities for wildlife resources that span state and federal jurisdiction, makes it critical for the Service to continue to cooperate with the state and other federal agencies in monitoring for the disease.

Strategies:

- Continue to use hunting as the primary tool for regulating resident game mammal populations.
- Use deer herd health checks every 3 to 5 years to determine status of deer populations on the refuge.
- Conduct browse surveys annually according to standard protocol to obtain an index of deer herd size.

Objective A-11. Other Game Mammals: Maintain raccoon and beaver populations at levels consistent with carrying capacity of the habitat while providing the public with a form of wildlife-dependent recreation through hunting.

Discussion: Resident mammal species, such as white-tailed deer, raccoon, opossum, coyote, and beaver, are easily capable of overpopulation. The best management tool for maintaining healthy populations of these species is public hunting. It is imperative to particularly keep deer, raccoons, and beavers at healthy levels due to their potential to be detrimental to habitat and wildlife resources when numbers are too high. The refuge should monitor the hunting program, harvest rates, and population levels of game species annually. Adjustments to season length and bag limits should be made if monitoring data suggest population levels of game species are not within carrying capacity of the habitat. Target species or species of concern could then be focused on more intensive monitoring or research.

Strategy:

- Encourage hunting of raccoons and beavers by the public. Compile and analyze hunter harvest reports.

Objective A-12. Herpetofuana: Continue to survey the refuge for purposes of producing a complete herpetofaunal inventory and number of alligators using the refuge.

Discussion: The potential herpetofauna of the North Louisiana NWR Complex is relatively large, at least 80 species, and comparable to the 82 species of amphibians and reptiles known from Ouachita Parish (Dundee and Rossman, 1989; Jensen and George, 1993; Greenbaum, 2000; Rosenzweig et al. 2007). For most of the refuges in the Complex, the presence of relatively few of the species has been confirmed; however, that is not the case with Black Bayou Lake NWR. Since 1996, over 50 species have been recorded one or more times (Carr et al. in prep.). Only one species of Special Concern is currently known to be present on the refuge, the alligator snapping turtle (*Macrochelys temminckii*). The alligator snapping turtle is dealt with below.

Under provisions of the Improvement Act, refuges are called upon to conserve, manage, and restore wildlife populations and their habitats. When confronted with a lack of knowledge concerning the species actually resident on refuge lands, the first step in conserving them is learning of their presence, and to the extent possible, associating their presence with particular habitats. These are fundamental aspects of biodiversity knowledge recommended as priorities for helping the Department of the Interior to manage its lands (NRC 1993).

A variety of techniques has been employed in surveying the herpetofauna of the refuge since 1996, with a predominance of aquatic techniques (Carr, pers. comm.). All major habitats on the refuge should be included in the survey and up to this point less effort has been expended in the upland forest habitats on the eastern edge of the refuge. Several additional species are to be expected in that habitat, and several species that were recorded from the vicinity of the refuge in the 1950s and 1960s might yet be found in that area. Most survey work has been done incidental to other fieldwork, such as alligator snapping turtle nesting surveys, or as part of herpetology class field trips and projects (Carr).

Alligators are a common sight on the refuge and the adjacent Bayou DeSiard. Alligator surveys are conducted each summer using the same route. Surveys are being conducted in order to detect changes in alligator populations. Alligator hunting on surrounding private land is sufficient at this time to control the alligator population in the area. If our alligator surveys indicate in the future that the population is in need of control, we will consider issuing permits for alligator hunting at that time.

Strategies:

- Continue to sample anurans with the current call survey protocol at a minimum of every other year in order to monitor population trends. Explore the possibility of contributing the current Anuran Call Survey data to the Amphibian Research and Monitoring Initiative of the USGS (Corn et al. 2005). This research initiative is already gathering data from a variety of Department of Interior lands in a nationwide effort to track changes in distribution and abundance of amphibian species.
- Continue to conduct annual alligator (*Alligator mississippiensis*) surveys in order to track trends in population size within the lake.

Objective A-13. Alligator snapping turtles: Continue to conduct population dynamic research on alligator snapping turtles.

Discussion: The alligator snapping turtle (*Macrochelys temminckii*) is the largest North American freshwater turtle. As such, it is among the top tier of predators in most aquatic ecosystems that it inhabits, exceeded routinely in size only by the American alligator (*Alligator mississippiensis*). It is a characteristic component of lowland swamps, lakes, and streams in the southeastern United States;

however, it has declined in abundance to the point where it is now considered a threatened or endangered species in all range states. In Louisiana, it appears on the list of species of "conservation concern" by the Natural Heritage Program as an S3 species (rare and local throughout the state). The alligator snapping turtle has been of conservation concern for some time (Pritchard 1989; Sloan and Lovich 1995), and was recently added to Appendix III of CITES by the United States in order to monitor the growing international trade in this species.

While certain aspects of the biology of the alligator snapping turtle are slowly unfolding, population dynamics are still largely unknown (Trauth et al. 1998), yet critical to managing the species for conservation. One of the most significant features of its life history that impacts any conservation effort is delayed onset of sexual maturity; 13-21 years in females and 11-21 years in males (Tucker and Sloan 1997). Given the significance of reproductive characteristics for determining population dynamics, there are relatively few studies of reproduction in the species, and several are studies that have relied upon meat market specimens of unknown provenance (Dobie 1971; Tucker and Sloan 1997).

Maintenance of a viable population of alligator snapping turtles will involve both knowledge of the habitats used during various life stages and the species' biology and interactions with other species in an effort to enable reproduction, recruitment, and survival at a sustainable level. Several challenges to maintenance of a stable population size have been identified based on studies at the refuge (Bass 2007; Besenhofer 2006; Woosley 2005), including nesting in anthropogenic habitat, high levels of predation by a mesopredator (*Procyon lotor*), predation by an introduced predator (*Solenopsis invicta*), and hydrology management.

Black Bayou Lake NWR has proven an excellent study site for this species. There is convenient access from the University of Louisiana at Monroe (ULM) and there is a large population of alligator snapping turtles in the lake. Because of this situation, Dr. Carr, herpetology professor at ULM, and his graduate students will be able to build on the substantial base of previous studies on the species in the area (Sloan and Taylor 1987; Harrel et al. 1996), including their own (Bass 2007; Besenhofer 2006; Woosley 2005). Studies are currently underway to examine spatial ecology of adults and to focus more attention on the biology of reproduction, in particular factors that may be important to survival in the nest environment (e.g., invasion of nests by ants, nest temperature, infertility rate, timing of hatchling emergence, and soil type effects on incubation).

Strategies:

- Spatial Ecology of the Adults: Study the movements of adult males and females within the lake using radiotelemetry. This technology will address questions such as: exactly which parts of the lake are utilized, how much time is spent in various regions of the lake, are there seasonal movements within the lake, are individuals (particularly males) territorial, and do females migrate from their usual home range to specific areas to nest, or do they merely nest adjacent to their usual home range within the lake.
- Female Reproductive Cycle: Examine the reproductive state of each female whenever captured using a portable ultrasound unit capable of storing images and with measurement capabilities. Better knowledge of the annual schedule of significant reproductive events at the physiological level (i.e., activity of the ovaries and oviducts) will be tied to spatial events at those same times, and also with potential management implications for the timing of certain activities (e.g., when to apply aquatic herbicides, or change water-levels).
- Nest Site Selection, Nest Survival and Hatchling Ecology: Continue to work towards understanding nest site selection, particularly in non-anthropogenic habitats such as are found on the east side of the lake. Based on previous studies thus far (Woosley 2005),

ULM has identified two significant sources of egg/hatchling mortality that combined would appear to cause unsustainable levels of nest failure and therefore recruitment into the turtle population; i.e., raccoons (*Procyon lotor*) and red imported fire ants (*Solenopsis invicta*). Efforts should be made to expand and refine the knowledge of these two primary egg and hatchling predators. Focus should be given to monitoring the raccoon population and use of the preferred nesting areas of the alligator snapping turtles as has been done for nesting sea turtles (Engeman et al. 2005), with the intention that a raccoon management strategy will be developed. With respect to red imported fire ants, it is recommended that specific experiments be conducted involving turtle eggs and ants in differing habitats representing actual nesting sites used by turtles, and intensive nest monitoring to gather quantifiable information on the timing of nest emergence (either fall or spring).

Objective A-14. Butterflies and Moths: Inventory and create a species list and display of butterflies and moths utilizing the refuge.

Discussion: Butterflies and moths have been poorly understood and not well researched. However, recent interest has prompted studies on butterfly response to fire and forest treatments, along with studies emphasizing that butterflies and moths could be indicators of a healthy ecosystem. On Black Bayou Lake NWR, no information exists about butterfly and moth populations. Initial work should be directed towards a basic inventory to determine if any species of concern are present.

Strategy:

- Consult literature to determine best survey methods to implement. Conduct as suggested.

Objective A-15. Mussels: Inventory for mussels in refuge waters to determine whether species of concern or invasive species are present.

Discussion: Freshwater mussels are the most jeopardized animal group in North America, with 60 percent of species being classified as either threatened or endangered (Ricciardi et al. 1998). The introduction of invasive, exotic mussels, such as the zebra mussel, has threatened some species of native mussels with extinction. The Mississippi River has the largest number of endemic freshwater mussels in the world (Ricciardi et al. 1998); however, the zebra mussel has been extirpating local populations of native mussels in the basin since the early 1990s. Zebra mussels were documented in the State of Louisiana in the 1990s and survey work along the Ouachita River and on the refuge is needed to determine if species of concern are present and whether zebra mussels have encroached.

Strategy:

- Consult literature to determine best survey methods to implement. Conduct as suggested.

Objective A-16. Fisheries: Continue to conduct surveys and research studies on refuge. Increase monitoring efforts of aquatic invasive species.

Discussion: Because the western portion of the lake is open and deep, it is the most likely portion of the refuge that can provide recreational fishing opportunities. Conversely, the eastern half is densely covered with trees and emergent vegetation; it is filling in with sediment and has less recreational fisheries potential. In partnership with the city, the Service has a 99-year free lease on the lake that is owned by the city of Monroe and is managed as a secondary source of municipal water. The city of Monroe has an operating policy for flood and/or drought conditions that would take precedence over recommendations or concerns for aquatic resources. During the period of December 1 through March 31, the goal is to strive to maintain a maximum winter pool elevation of 70.50 feet MSL. From April 1 through November 30, the objective is to strive to maintain a maximum summer pool elevation of 72.00 feet MSL. The winter pool stage is maintained at a lower level for emergency floodwater retention.

The prospects for changing the current management strategies on the lake are limited because the operating policy leaves aquatic biota vulnerable to low water and poor water quality conditions. Municipal water needs are prioritized over fisheries needs. Until the risk of fisheries losses from municipal drawdown is minimized or eliminated, it would be ineffective to invest additional resources for significant changes to fisheries management.

The Baton Rouge Fisheries Resources Office (FRO) and LDWF are aware that there is an interest in the city switching to a different secondary source of water, and additional assessments and management could be derived if that transition takes place. In light of the above, the Baton Rouge FRO recommends that fisheries management in Black Bayou Lake continue to follow the regulations that LDWF has listed since the inception of the refuge.

Strategies:

- Conduct fish surveys in lake at perhaps 3- to 4-year intervals. The surveys should be for game species composition, relative abundance, size distribution, and fish body condition. Collection methods may include boat electrofishing, trap and/or fyke netting, and perhaps limited gill netting or hoop netting. The methods will depend upon the bottom topography and structure. Target species are crappie, sunfish, largemouth bass, and catfish, plus any prey species. Electrofishing is done in the spring and/or fall, whereas netting is generally done in late fall or winter.
- Conduct creel surveys periodically to monitor fishing pressure; fish catch (species, sizes); angler satisfaction; and angler biographical, geographical, and economic information (e.g., travel costs, fishing costs). Especially if the boat ramp is near the visitor center, anglers may be encouraged to voluntarily fill out angling experience/fish catch sheets.
- Based upon fish survey and fishing pressure information, it may be necessary to impose certain fishing regulations such as restrictive creel limits and/or size limits on certain species. It may be advisable to permit day only fishing, at least by boating. Effective fishing regulations require sufficient fishing pressure (which is likely here) and angler obedience; the latter is dependent upon education and enforcement. Displays and personal contact could be used for educating anglers as to the reason for the regulations.
- A map of all waterways, complete with bottom contours and bottom structure, should be made.
- Water quality should be taken initially, especially during critical times of the year. For instance, dissolved oxygen and temperature profiles in mid- to late-summer would show stratification in the lake and areas devoid of sufficient oxygen for fish life and well being.
- Determine if species of concern or invasive species are present and explore opportunities to enhance native fish habitat in these areas.

Objective A-17. Species of Concern - bats: Conduct a research project to determine roost locations, reproductive success, and wintering roost location of Rafinesque's big-eared and southeastern Myotis bats.

Discussion: The Rafinesque's big-eared bat and southeastern Myotis bat are both considered federal species of concern. The Rafinesque's bat may be listed as federally threatened in the near future. Both Rafinesque's big-eared and southeastern Myotis bats utilize Black Bayou Lake NWR to an unknown extent. Roosts of these bats are strongly associated with bottomland hardwood forests and with water tupelo trees. Little is known about location of winter roosts, relative abundance, or roosting dynamics.

Forty-four roost trees of this species were found on the nearby D'Arbonne NWR inside hollow water tupelo (*Nyssa aquatica*) trees during the summer of 2000 (Gooding and Langford 2004). Recent information shows that southeastern bats also utilize water tupelo trees (Gooding and Langford 2004), at least during summer as maternity colonies. This unique stand is comprised of a high density of very large, hollow water tupelo trees, which seem to be favored by this species (Clark et al. 1998, Cochran 1999, Gooding and Langford 2004, Trousdale and Beckett 2005). Black Bayou Lake NWR has plenty of water tupelos growing in the lake; however, most of them are very difficult to access and are not of large size.

Strategies:

- Work with partners to sample habitat biannually.
- Map any new roost or wintering locations on the refuge.

Objective A-18. Species of Special Concern - Louisiana black bear: Monitor presence and absence of Louisiana black bear.

Discussion: The Louisiana black bear is a federally threatened species that utilizes a broad spectrum of habitat types and has a large home range. Black Bayou Lake NWR is realistically too small and too close to the city of Monroe to support resident bears. However, there is always the chance of a bear utilizing the refuge during dispersal events, especially in spring when males wander over large distances in search of territories and females to breed.

Strategies:

- Document sightings of bears on Black Bayou Lake NWR and the surrounding area.
- Refuge employees maintain communication and collaboration on biological issues such as Louisiana Black bear sightings or nuisance problems.

Objective A-19. Invasive Fish and Wildlife: Monitor presence and absence of invasive wildlife and fish species.

Discussion: Invasive wildlife species on the refuge include red fire ants, nutria, Eurasian collared doves, and European starlings. Control of doves, starlings, and fire ants is practically impossible. These species will be with us always. Nutria are established throughout Louisiana and can damage levees and impact native vegetation if populations become high. Numbers can be reduced by shooting or trapping.

Strategies:

- Although wildlife, both aquatic and terrestrial, have spread over the entire refuge and do not need to be mapped, a basic species list (inventory) needs to be created.
- Develop GIS data layers depicting occurrence/abundance of invasive fish and wildlife species and management activities.

HABITAT MANAGEMENT

GOAL B. Habitat: Restore, enhance, and maintain healthy wetlands and associated bottomland hardwood and upland forests to support a natural diversity of plant and animal species and to foster the ecological integrity of Black Bayou Lake Watershed.

Objective B-1. Bottomland Hardwood Forest: Complete a forest management plan utilizing the guidelines given in the LMVJV Forest Resource Conservation Working Group publication titled, "Restoration, Management, and Monitoring of Forest Resources in Mississippi Alluvial Valley: Recommendations For Enhancing Wildlife Habitat" published in 2007 (LMVJV 2007).

Discussion: The refuge contains 604 acres of flooded bald cypress/water tupelo, 296 acres of bottomland hardwood forest, and 856 acres of reforestation. The refuge does not currently have a forest management plan. No timber harvest has occurred since refuge establishment. All of the reforested area was farmed at some point during the past 150 years, and cotton and corn were farmed until the refuge was established. Reforestation efforts were initiated in 2000. A wide variety of tree species was planted using soil and elevation maps to determine composition. Species included baldcypress, willow oak, water oak, cow oak, southern red oak, cherrybark oak, cottonwood, green ash, American elm, sycamore, sweet pecan, plums, and many more.

Strategy:

- Complete forest inventory and GIS database of refuge forest to generate baseline data for development of habitat management plan that will include a 10-year entry cycle, annual inventories by compartment, step-down prescriptions for desired conditions, and monitoring protocols such as reforestation survival surveys.

Objective B-2. Bottomland Hardwood Forest Management: Establish a multi-layered forest canopy that develops and/or maintains a diversity of plant species at various stages of development to meet the various needs of many wildlife species, including waterfowl, neotropical migratory songbirds, and resident species.

Strategies:

- Conduct a 2 percent Forest Inventory and Habitat Cruise using 1/5-acre plots. This can be accomplished by establishing a series of sample plots distributed throughout the refuge. These points can then be used to monitor habitat changes and/or breeding bird point counts.
- Pursue changes in management of Black Bayou Lake water levels to reduce stress on the bald cypress and tupelo trees within the lake.
- Use guidelines given in the LMVJV Forest Resource Conservation Working Group publication titled, "Restoration, Management, and Monitoring of Forest Resources in

Mississippi Alluvial Valley: Recommendations for Enhancing Wildlife Habitat" published in 2007 (LMVJV 2007).

- Incorporate forest management activities into environmental education programs on the refuge. The refuge is a good area to demonstrate to the public how forest management for wildlife habitat is different than forest management for profit.
- Develop a pest management plan for controlling and eliminating invasive and exotic plant species.
- Hire a forester or forestry technician to perform forest management strategies listed in this recommendation.
- Encourage buffer strips (feathered edges) along forest-field edges and riparian zones.
- Promote scrub/shrub habitats through the appropriate planting of scrub/shrub plant species (e.g., plum, swamp dogwood, devil's walking stick, deciduous holly, hawthorn species).
- Where narrower corridor linkages between forest patches are created, consider establishment of scrub/shrub habitat.

Objective B-3. Mixed Pine and Hardwood: Manage upland pine/hardwood habitat for a basal area of 80-120 square feet/acre, canopy cover of 70 to 85 percent with an emphasis on a wide variety of hardwood species, and with a diverse vertical structure of midstory and understory hardwood species to conserve the biological integrity and diversity of this habitat type on the refuge.

Discussion: Because upland hardwood tree species are being degraded and lost as a habitat type in northern Louisiana, the upland habitats will be managed to promote hardwood diversity and integrity. A vertically diverse structure will be maintained through selective thinnings. Species of hardwoods, which are found in this habitat type, include water oak, white oak, southern red oak, cherrybark oak, post oak, swamp chestnut oak, sweetgum, blackgum, hickory, eastern redbud, flowering dogwood, sweet azalea, witchhazel, sassafras, red mulberry, and American holly.

Strategies:

- Use adaptive management by conducting an inventory of current condition prior to implementing management actions to achieve desired objective outcomes.
- Forests will be thinned using silvicultural treatments (e.g., single-tree and group selection cuts) to site-specific basal area needs.
- Comply with best management practices including stream zone buffers.
- Invasive species, such as tallowtree and Japanese climbing fern, will be mapped, monitored, and treated.

Objective B-4. Invasive Plant Species: Specifically identify and geographically track locations of invasive species through monitoring and control. Annually foster opportunities for control by developing cooperative invasive control projects with other agencies, private landowners, and corporations on neighboring lands to the refuge. Ensure aquatic invasive species do not cover more than 10 percent of Black Bayou Lake. Control Chinese tallowtree and other woody invasive species such that they do not impede the growth of native species in reforested areas.

Discussion: There are numerous exotic/invasive species now on the refuge and expanding their range in the region. It is recommended that surveys be performed to inventory and monitor their presence and to determine their impacts. When deemed detrimental to the management goals of the refuge, control measures should be taken whenever possible. Control of these species should be prioritized by the refuge managers, as their levels of environmental impact are variable. The following are invasive species that are likely to or have the potential to occur on the refuge and impact native flora and fauna.

There are several species of invasive aquatic plants to be concerned with on the refuge. The majority of these are capable of forming dense mats over the surface of the water. When this occurs, dissolved oxygen levels in the water may become too low to support oxygen dependent aquatic species (fish, mollusks, etc.). These invasive aquatic plants compete with native species and can cause habitat degradation. They may also inhibit waterfowl and other animal use and boat navigation. The efficiency of water control structures may also be affected if left uncontrolled. When infestations occur, herbicidal applications are normally the most effective control measure. The following table lists invasive species known to exist in Louisiana and should be considered priorities for control.

Table 3. Invasive aquatic plant species and concerns

Alligatorweed *Alternanthera philoxercoides*	grows from shoreline, degrades and competes with shoreline species, may impede navigation, very common in area
Common salvinia *Salvinia minima*	forms dense surface mats that may deplete oxygen in water, impedes navigation, fairly common in area
Giant salvinia *Salvinia molesta*	forms dense surface mats that may deplete oxygen in water, impedes navigation, more harmful than minima, currently exists in SW and SE LA
Hydrilla *Hydrilla verticillata*	can form dense "thickets" beneath water, may impede fish movement, navigation and water flow, fairly common in area
Water hyacinth *Eichhornia crassipes*	forms dense surface mats that may deplete oxygen in water, impedes navigation and water flow, very common in area

These species may spread naturally, intentionally, or non-intentionally. The main source of non-intentional spread is by boat trailer transport. Signs should be placed at boat ramps to encourage boaters to inspect trailers for exotic plants before backing them into the water. Refuge waterbodies should be periodically checked for presence of any exotic species. If exotics are identified and serious detrimental impact is expected, a method of control should be taken immediately. Special caution should be given to *Salvinia*, which once established will completely cover a water body in a very short period of time. Little can be done once this occurs. Refuge staff should be particularly vigilant in monitoring for *Salvinia*.

Terrestrial exotic plants are a serious threat to the biological integrity of the refuge. Although many species have been recorded, such as crepe myrtle, royal palownia, mimosa, etc., the species of greatest concern are Chinese tallowtree and Japanese climbing fern. Both of these plants aggressively spread throughout the forest, with little hope of being eradicated. Refuge personnel should also aggressively treat these two species with the objective of keeping them from spreading as much as possible.

Chinese tallowtree is a small, fast growing tree with high reproductive ability. They grow in a variety of habitats, having their most detrimental impacts in marsh type areas where they have the ability to cause large-scale ecosystem modification by changing marshlands to forested communities. Chinese tallowtree would be particularly detrimental to the refuge reforestation areas. Handpulling seedlings is effective if numbers are not too high. Basal applications of triclopyr and cut-stem application of 50 percent triclopyr or 10 percent imazaypr can be effective. Fire usually will not completely kill the tree, but burning during winter followed by burning or mowing in the summer has shown some success. This species should be considered difficult to eliminate once established.

Japanese climbing fern is a fast growing woody vine which can completely shroud everything in its path. It has the ability to kill trees directly by blocking sunlight, and adds extra mass to trees acting as a sail which causes uprooting during high winds. This species is a relatively new invader (in U.S. since 1994) and is now becoming widespread throughout Louisiana and the southeast. Small patches and single plants may be hand pulled. Fire will not eliminate it, and may even promote it. No herbicides have yet been tested specifically for *L. japonicum*, but Triclopyr amine and glyphosate are effective at controlling the similar species *L. microphyllum*.

Strategies:

- Terrestrial and aquatic plants can be mapped using a GPS and entered into a GIS system.
- Establish a monitoring program of invasive plants to determine rate of spread by annually mapping areas of infestation and comparing to previous year's range.
- After comparison, calculate rate of growth (spread) by both Chinese tallowtree and Japanese fern, and any aquatic invasives.
- Treat 25 percent of invasive plants annually by hacking and squirting using chemical means such as RoundUp, Arsenal, or Garlon, for terrestrial plants.
- Treat water hyacinth in the lake at least once a week during the growing season using Rodeo or 2,4-D amine.
- Monitor boat ramp area once a week for the presence of *Salvinia*.
- Educate staff, particularly those individuals that spray for hyacinth, on identification of *Salvinia*.
- Take immediate action to treat *Salvinia*, if detected.

Objective B-5. Cane and Prairie Habitat: Map sizeable existing natural stands and research how to promote and enhance those stands.

Discussion: There are a few microhabitats within the refuge that need protection and monitoring, as some of them harbor animals that are habitat specialists. Microhabitat patches, such as remnants of prairies and cane thickets, are important for sheltering specific animals and birds. Canebrakes have declined by 98 percent in the lower MAV. Canebrakes furnish critical habitat for numerous bottomland hardwood forest species, such as the threatened Louisiana black bear (*Ursus americanus subsp. luteolus*) and several migratory birds including woodcock (*Scolopax minor*), Swainson's warbler (*Limnothlypis swainsonii*), and hooded warbler (*Wilsonia citrina*). There are at least six satyrine (*Satyrinae* sp.) and skipper butterflies that are cane obligates. Canebrakes can be excellent riparian buffers.

The remaining patches of prairies in general have the richest assemblage of insects, grasses, and wildflowers, thereby supporting a wide diversity of wildlife species. Within the refuge there is a need to restore native prairies. A great deal of scientific research proves that prairie and canebrake habitats are fire-evolved and maintained. Without fire, these habitat types decline and then are completely lost due to invasion by woody plant species. A prescribed burning program will need to be evaluated to manage these habitats on the refuge.

Strategies:

- Determine optimum growing conditions and efficient means of propagation of these canes and possibly extend the range of the patches to cover more areas within the refuge. Cane being native to the area might be able to create a more heterogeneous natural habitat for the fauna in general.
- Monitor current remnant prairies in the refuge. In areas that might sustain prairies (both edaphically and hydrologically), range extensions may be carried out.
- Explore the use of fire to maintain prairie and canebrake habitat. Conduct all prescribed burning according to an approved Fire Management Plan.

Objective B-6. Moist-soil Habitat: Provide a minimum of 8 acres of early successional, moist-soil habitat as foraging habitat for migrating and wintering waterfowl.

Discussion: The high seed production of moist-soil plants and their value as waterfowl foods has been known since at least the 1940s (Low and Bellrose 1944). However, managing seasonally flooded herbaceous wetland impoundments or "moist-soil units" only became a widely accepted practice after many years of research in southeastern Missouri (Fredrickson and Taylor 1982). Today, almost 29,500 acres of moist-soil habitat are managed in more than 400 impoundments on state and federal lands in the MAV (LMVJV Water Management System Tracking System).

Black Bayou Lake NWR is only able to provide a small amount of forage from moist-soil habitat, primarily from within the Crawfish Pond, an 8-acre moist-soil impoundment. Although the ability to manage water within the Crawfish Pond is somewhat limited, efforts should be made to maximize the acreage being managed for quality moist-soil vegetation (at least 500 pounds of moist-soil seeds/acre) within this unit.

Strategies:

- Maintain approximately 8 acres of quality moist-soil habitat (defined as 500 pounds per acre of preferred moist-soil seeds) in the Crawfish Pond.
- Strive to increase preferred moist-soil plant production by implementing good management practices, including timely and slow drawdowns, deep disking, mowing, holding shallow water through a growing season, etc.
- Monitor moist-soil impoundment unit at least weekly, throughout the growing season, keeping records of management actions, water levels, and vegetation responses.

RESOURCE PROTECTION

GOAL C. Resource Protection and Management: In collaboration with private landowners, LDWF, and other public and private organizations, the refuge will strategically plan growth by protecting lands within existing refuge acquisition boundary to provide wildlife benefits and conservation of archaeological resources and habitats where feasible for future and present generations.

Objective C-1. Land Protection: Obtain lands within current refuge acquisition boundary as opportunities arise. Work with landowners and non-governmental organizations, where appropriate, to acquire the Bayou DeSiard Tract and the Oliver Plantation within the current refuge acquisition boundary.

Discussion: The purpose of proposed land acquisition is to contribute to the goals of the Lower Mississippi River Valley Migratory Bird Conservation Initiative and the North American Waterfowl Management Plan by acquiring lands within the acquisition boundary of Black Bayou Lake NWR for incorporation into the Refuge System. Acquisition and management of privately owned properties within the acquisition boundary would protect two large areas from development. Furthermore, purchase of the Oliver Plantation would incorporate the southern end of the lake into the refuge, protecting the entire lake and its watershed. Owners of the Bayou DeSiard tract intend to subdivide the waterfront property into housing lots. Although the owners are willing to sell, the price is too high for the refuge to purchase. Acquisition of this property would protect and buffer that portion of Bayou DeSiard from development.

Strategies:

- Continue working with Realty Office and partners to find funding to purchase the Bayou DeSiard Tract.
- Continue relations with the landowner of the Oliver Plantation in the hopes that the land would come up for sale.
- Work through the Department of the Interior, Appraisal Services Directorate, and obtain approved fair market value appraisals of the properties.
- Obtain signed purchase agreements for acquisition of the properties from willing sellers.
- Work through the Realty Division of the Service, request funding from the Land and Water Conservation Fund, In-holding and Emergency Account, Migratory Bird Conservation Fund, or other source in the amount needed to acquire the properties.
- When funding is available, acquire the properties under the terms of the purchase agreements. When closing is completed, vest title in the United States and begin managing the properties as part of the refuge.

Objective C-2. Private Lands: Foster opportunities each year for developing reforestation and invasive control projects on adjacent private lands.

Discussion: Most of the land in the WGC plain and the MAV are privately owned and must play an important role in the restoration and maintenance of native biodiversity and achievement of the goals and objectives of national and regional plans, such as the NAWMP and the Partners in Flight: Mississippi River Alluvial Valley Bird Conservation Plan. In an effort to address those objectives, the Service established a private lands program known as Partners for Fish and Wildlife. Through this program, the Service provides technical assistance and delivers financial assistance programs to private landowners. The North Louisiana NWR Complex has a private lands biologist responsible for implementing the partners program in this area.

The partners program also provides financial assistance to landowners wanting to restore wetlands. Landowners are limited to $25,000 of financial assistance per year. In the MAV, most projects involve the restoration of hydrology and hardwood reforestation. Vegetation on up to 30 percent of the area can be manipulated to maintain successional stages other than what would be expected to occur naturally. For example, up to 30 percent of the area could be managed for moist-soil management. The program favors projects located adjacent to refuges and within forest bird conservation areas.

The Louisiana Waterfowl Project is a partnership with other conservation organizations to provide water control structures to private landowners who traditionally flood harvested cropland and moist-soil areas in the winter period (November 15 through February 28). The program provides significant benefits for wintering waterfowl and water quality.

Other agencies, particularly in the Department of Agriculture, such as the Farm Services Agency (FSA) and Natural Resources Conservation Service (NRCS), have large programs that will restore wetland habitats in the MAV. The NRCS administers the Wetlands Reserve Program (WRP), which is a popular program that restores croplands to wetlands by restoring hydrology and reforestation and protects these areas through the acquisition of 30-year and perpetual easements. There are over 100,000 acres of WRP easements in Louisiana. A significant acreage is manageable water for waterfowl. The Service plays an important role in developing ranking criteria, evaluating sites, and working with private landowners to manage and maximize wetland values. The FSA administers the Cropland Resource Program (CRP), which provides 50 percent cost share to reforest wetland and highly erosive sites in the MAV. The program is competitive and qualifying lands are placed under a 15-year contract. Various other programs are also available.

Strategies:

- Facilitate communications with energy companies and private landowners interested in carbon sequestration restoration on private lands.
- Private lands biologist would seek out interested landowners in areas of high priority for reforestation.
- Work through a variety of programs to provide technical and financial assistance necessary to provide additional migratory bird habitat to benefit refuge objectives.
- Work with the NRCS, FSA, private landowners, and other partners to designate conservation priority areas to provide incentives that will encourage landowners to implement practices that will benefit trust resources, refuge purposes, and MAV ecosystem goals.
- Develop cooperative invasive control projects. Communicate and meet a minimum of once a year with the Louisiana Statewide Exotic Species Task Force to identify new invaders, grant opportunities, cooperation possibilities, etc.

Objective C-3. Natural Gas Resources: Foster communication with Louisiana Department of Environmental Quality (LDEQ) and the Natural Resources Conservation Service as issues arise and information requested. Continue working with gas companies to ensure refuge resources are protected.

Discussion: The natural gas sites located within Black Bayou Lake NWR are a fact of life and although the interests of both parties clash on occasion, there should be some way for the needs of both to be met in most cases. In the event that the private entities operating within the refuge carry on activities or practices that are contrary to the mission and goals of the refuge and cooperation is not forthcoming, then regulatory and law enforcement involvement should be sought. Saltwater and oil contamination from such sites can be significant, extremely damaging, and do pose a danger to the environment in those areas. Also, the potential for devastating impact on the lake and surrounding area by a major train derailment in the area should be a possibility that is considered during planning for the refuge.

Strategies:

- Monitor gas production, storage sites, and activities on a regular basis to identify problems quickly.
- Because a railroad is adjacent to the lake, possible contingencies for diverting spilled material or shutting off flow paths should be considered. Reduce the amount of area contaminated immediately after a spill to reduce long-term damage.

Objective C-4. Water Quality: Work with local, state, and federal partners to regularly monitor databases, electronic or otherwise, which report on water quality and contaminant concentrations in fish from Bayou Desiard and Black Bayou Lake.

Discussion: The water quality in the refuge meets or exceeds water quality standards and that designated uses are unimpaired. The uses dealing with propagation of fish and wildlife and primary and secondary contact in particular are of paramount importance to the mission of the refuge.

The importance of water quality to this refuge cannot be overstressed. This refuge is primarily a lake and riparian area so water quality is probably the most important aspect of the ecosystem. The lake itself would be classified as either nearly or completely eutrophic as submergent and floating aquatic plants exist in great abundance. In addition, the killing of large mats of floating aquatics by pesticide application does result in a significant increase in biological oxygen demand that could, especially during warm weather months, adversely affect water quality. The presence of mercury in problematic concentrations occurs in primarily large bowfin (*Amia calva*), although lower levels of the metal can be found in all species. A State of Louisiana advisory against eating bowfin by sensitive groups and a reduction by non-sensitive groups is currently in place. As the city of Monroe officials maintain some control over water levels in the lake, it is important that they understand the effects of fluctuating levels on water quality and ultimately the value of the refuge to the economy of the area.

Strategies:

- Continue to monitor existing contaminants (Hg and pesticides) in fish. Requests can be made of LDEQ to periodically collect samples from the lake, or refuge personnel can collect their own samples and have them analyzed by a contract laboratory.
- Continue to work with the city of Monroe to manage water levels to maximize water quality and detritus elimination.
- Regularly monitor databases, electronic or otherwise, which report on water quality and contaminant concentrations in fish from Bayou Desiard and Black Bayou Lake.
- Conduct or request assistance in contaminant monitoring (Hg) from the LDEQ or other entities, such as local universities, for biota found in the refuge.
- Report all water quality damaging incidents dealing with oil and gas production, railroad operations, or any other activity to the LDEQ for investigation and resolution.
- Attempt to use water level management to allow accumulated organic material on the lake bottom to decompose as quickly as possible.
- Maintain a dialog with the city of Monroe about water level management and attempt to influence their activities to enhance water quality.

Objective C-5. Cultural and Historic Resources: Continue to comply with Section 106 of the National Historic Preservation Act or any other pertinent historic preservation mandate prior to the initiation of any refuge undertaking or habitat management action that will involve significant, new ground disturbance and where the land has not been substantially altered, disturbed, or created within the last 50 years. Confer with state and regional archaeologists.

Discussion: Protection and preservation of our Nation's cultural and historic resources are important parts in maintaining its heritage. This is just as true in the rural areas of our country as it is in our cities. In order to assure that no historical and/or cultural resources are ignored or inadvertently damaged on the refuge, an inventory of possible sites should be identified and evaluated. The refuge contains two African-American cemeteries and an old barn—both of which may be eligible for the National Register of Historic Places.

Strategies:

- Maintain records of refuge survey data for cultural and archaeological sites.
- Monitor for vandalism and degradation to identified sites.
- Contact Regional Archaeologist prior to construction or significant ground disturbance projects, and complete a request for cultural resources review to determine appropriate steps necessary for compliance.
- Within 5 years of the date of this CCP, refuge manager or designee will look into taking the Archaeological Resources Protection Act training course.
- Ensure that cultural resources management and protection strategies are integrated into refuge management plans, such as fire and road maintenance.
- GIS layer for archaeological and historic sites will be integrated into the refuge's GIS database.
- Maintain data as confidential per National Historic Preservation Act and Archaeological Resources Protection Act.
- Conduct detailed survey of current resources.
- As archaeological and cultural resources are discovered, coordinate with the Regional Archaeologist for cataloging and archiving as appropriate.

Objective C-6. Law Enforcement: Provide proactive law enforcement activities utilizing current two collateral duty officers among the North Louisiana NWR Complex and add full-time park ranger (law enforcement).

Discussion: Protecting the natural resources of the Complex and ensuring the safety of refuge visitors are fundamental responsibilities of the Refuge System. The North Louisiana NWR Complex is currently accomplishing this with two collateral duty officers. In addition to natural resource violations, serious felonies, including homicides, rapes, assaults, and acts of arson, are occurring on refuges every year. Littering and use of the refuge during nighttime closed hours are increasing in intensity as well.

Strategies:

- Hire a park ranger (law enforcement) to increase protection of natural resources and refuge visitors.
- Provide up-to-date training and equipment to all full-time and dual function officers.
- Develop memoranda of understanding with state and parish law enforcement agencies to facilitate cooperation and assistance in law enforcement activities. Update current law enforcement plan.

- Provide education and outreach programs in the local community as part of a preventive law enforcement effort. Focus on aquatic invasive species and littering associated with the refuge.
- Provide assistance to the Service's special agents and state conservation officers for off-refuge activities as requested.
- Establish and implement a protocol for site damage assessments and include it in the cultural resources management plan.
- Law enforcement will collaborate and coordinate with the state on regulatory issues or needs of either agency.

Objective C-7. Contaminants: Continue to be vigilant and respond to contamination on refuge as needed.

Discussion: Contaminants can affect the environment in many ways. Black Bayou Lake NWR has the potential to receive contaminants from the oil and gas industry, train derailment or leaking cars, the build-up of subdivisions around the area, agricultural drainage, and naturally occurring mercury in the soils and sediments. Contaminants such as saltwater and oil can affect water quality and may be damaging to the soil and subsequent plant diversity. None of these sources are known to be a significant problem at the current time. The manometer related mercury contamination was addressed in the early 1990s and should no longer pose much of a problem. Naturally occurring mercury in the sediment is believed to be the main source of mercury contamination found in significant and above alert levels in fish from the refuge. Historic use of chlorinated hydrocarbon pesticides in the agricultural areas around the lake may still be a source of contamination in fish from Black Bayou Lake. No recent samples have been taken to assess this possibility.

Strategies:

- Contaminants due to spillage or discharges from oil and gas sites should be scrutinized carefully and full clean up pursued vigorously. LDEQ and LDNR can assist in this when regulatory issues are involved.
- Communicate with the railroad company to learn what types of chemicals are regularly transported through or near the refuge to plan possible spill contingencies.

VISITOR SERVICES

GOAL D. Visitor Services: Provide wildlife-dependent recreation opportunities with an emphasis on environmental education and interpretation.

Objective D-1. Visitor Services Program: Develop and implement a visitor services plan that includes how Black Bayou Lake NWR will continue to serve as the focal point for the Complex's environmental education and interpretation program.

Discussion: The Improvement Act identifies six priority wildlife-dependent public use activities: hunting, fishing, wildlife observation, wildlife photography, and environmental education and interpretation. Fundamental to the provision of these uses are viable and diverse fish and wildlife populations and the habitats upon which they depend. These priority uses, along with all other proposed uses, must be compatible with the refuge purpose and the mission of the Refuge System.

A visitor services plan has not been developed. Black Bayou Lake NWR is part of the North Louisiana NWR Complex and is the focus refuge for providing environmental education and interpretation programs.

Strategies:

- Develop a Visitor Services Plan. The step-down plan should also include: messages and themes related not only to the purposes of the refuge, but to emphasize key issues of the refuge, the refuge complex, and the Refuge System; updated media or methods used to convey these messages to the public should be identified; annual funding and staffing; visitor facility maintenance, construction, and enhancement projects (including signs and exhibits); volunteer program annual work plans; potential sources of funding or partnership opportunities; recreation fee programs and business plans; and recreation carrying capacity and monitoring.
- Utilize the recreational fee program to maintain and enhance visitor facilities, (i.e., interpretive information, fishing pier, bank fishing areas, and trail access).
- Promote youth education through participation in the Youth Conservation Corp Program.
- Use consistent signage at all visitor service areas (e.g., parking, hiking, hunting, fishing, and ATVs).
- As use increases, improve parking areas (e.g., gravel and add bumpers).
- Decrease litter on the refuge by posting signs and developing approaches to address litter problems and to change user behavior over time.
- Expand the volunteer program to help implement the visitor services program.

Objective D-2. Hunting: Annually, allow deer, rabbit, squirrel, duck, coot, quail, woodcock, raccoon, opossum, coyote, and beaver hunting under LDWF and refuge-specific regulations. Increase hunting opportunities by coordinating with partners to offer a youth gun hunt and disabled only hunts.

Discussion: The Service recognizes hunting as one of the six priority public uses of the Refuge System. It is a legitimate and appropriate public use of the Refuge System that is deeply rooted in American culture. Hunting can promote a unique understanding and appreciation of wildlife, their behavior, and habitat requirements.

The refuge will monitor local, huntable populations to maintain all hunt programs in a compatible manner with the purpose of the refuge. Adaptive management will be used to modify hunting regulations if needed. In addition to having a quality hunt, overcrowding must be avoided. The refuge staff will look into providing youth and physically disabled individuals with an opportunity to hunt on the refuge. This will provide a good opportunity to introduce youth to hunting and foster a sense of appreciation and stewardship for the refuge and its mission of protecting fish, wildlife, and plants, while still providing for wildlife-dependent uses.

Strategies:

- Refuge will participate in annual state hunt coordination meetings to discuss proposed refuge hunting programs and regulations.
- Maintain communication on hunting and fishing issues that the state may have regarding opportunities or modifications to these programs.
- Update the hunt plan as needed to ensure a quality opportunity.
- Add to the hunt brochure the following wording: "This is an annual permit. To save tax dollars, please use this permit for the entire season."

- Look for an opportunity to partner with the state (or other partners) to provide a youth gun hunt.
- Partner with Wheeling Sportsmen (or other organization) to offer a disabled only hunt. (They can provide portable blinds.)

Objective D-3. Fishing: Provide quality fishing opportunities for familes visiting Black Bayou Lake by maintaining and enhancing access areas, educating the public concerning clean boats and trash pick-up, and creating handicapped accessible areas.

Discussion: The Service recognizes fishing as one of the six priority public uses of the Refuge System. It is a legitimate and appropriate public use of the Refuge System that is deeply rooted in American culture. Fishing can promote a unique understanding and appreciation of nature.

Given the delicate nature of Black Bayou Lake, educating the public about preventing the spread of invasive plants and animals and littering should be the highest priority. The addition of signs, interpretive displays, and a full-time park ranger should benefit refuge resources.

Strategies:

- Install a monofilament recycling station at the boat launch.
- Continue to limit motors to 50hp or less.
- Post signs about trash pick-up, and the importance of washing boats to prevent the spread of invasive species.
- Place small handicap accessible signs at accessible fishing areas on the pier extension.
- Continue partnering with state for youth fishing programs.
- On the map in the Hunt/Fish Brochure, indicate that all permanent water is open to fishing.
- Use the approved information collection forms or get approval for the current boat launch payment forms.
- Make sure the launch fee is listed in the general brochure.
- Consider having a kid's/family's fishing event during Boating and Fishing Week (June).
- Develop a boat tie-up pier at the boat launch.
- Place an interpretive panel about fishing/lake changes at the new boat tie-up pier.

Objective D-4. Wildlife Observation and Photography: Provide current opportunities such as photography and birding blinds, trails, observation piers with spotting scopes, and annual photo contest for wildlife observation and photography.

Discussion: Black Bayou Lake NWR offers extensive opportunities for wildlife observation and photography. The refuge trails, boardwalks, observation deck, photography blinds, visitor center, and conservation learning center are open to visitors during daylight hours and provide a top quality experience to discover a variety of habitats, including upland forests, bottomland hardwoods, bayous and open water, prairie and dike impoundments, and associated wildlife.

Strategies:

- Place an accessible symbol on the trail signs for trails that are accessible.
- Place a sign at the beginning of the photo blind boardwalk that cautions to approach quietly.
- Post information about proper etiquette in the photo blind and bird blind.
- The primitive trail needs to be a complete loop. Also cut some side trails to provide overlooks of the water/bayou.
- Place mileposts along the primitive trail.
- Consider ways to make the bird feeding area look more natural (similar to the way the water is hidden in the hollow log).
- In the bird blind keep a white board to list "today's sightings," wasp spray, and check-out binoculars and field guides. Consider putting framed bird ID posters on the walls. Also consider putting fan on a motion detector.
- Continue to work with birders and photographers to make improvements to blinds as needed.
- If use increases and it becomes necessary, consider posting a "in use/not in use" sign at photo blind boardwalk.
- Develop trailhead kiosks for the primitive trail at the boat launch entrance, and the observation deck entrance. Include information about how long the trail is, what visitors might see, and any precautions.
- Develop a trailhead kiosk at the parking area for the Art Trail.
- Develop opportunities for adults to learn about wildlife (e.g., birding clinics, nature walks, and photography clinics.)
- If needed, allow vegetative screening on each side of photo blind to help prevent birds from flying away when someone walks up to the blind.
- Add benches/seats to Art Trail and Arboretum Trail
- Use vegetation to create screening and viewing windows along sections of the Art Trail.
- Develop a webcam viewing opportunity. (Explore putting a webcam on an alligator nest.)

Objective D-5. Environmental Interpretation: Maintain interpretive panels and kiosks on refuge with the addition of a wildlife challenge trail as an element of the Connecting People with Nature Initiative.

Discussion: The refuge has done an outstanding job of developing interpretive trail signs at major trails and prominent locations on the refuge, interpretive programs, interpretive displays on the refuge and in the visitor center and conservation learning center, exhibits, and printed material. The primary interpretive themes and messages on the refuge relate to the purposes and resource issues, and these themes and messages help visitors understand the key resource issues related to the Service, the Refuge System, and the refuge.

Strategies:

- As part of the visitor services step-down plan, develop a basic interpretive plan that identifies: interpretive themes for the refuge; methods to deliver messages (e.g., talks, panels); and locations. Avoid information overload and focus on key messages that tie to the purpose of the refuge and the Refuge System, but also engage people and generate interest in and support for the refuge.
- Develop an interpretive panel about the "green" strategies used at the refuge (e.g., solar panels, recycling)

- Develop an interpretive panel about the historical/cultural heritage of the area. Could put it at one of the cemetery sites.
- Interpret succession – tie in invasive species management (e.g., water hyacinth, Chinese tallowtree).
- Develop a Podcast version of Nature Trail brochure. (Could have MP3 players to checkout from visitor center).
- Explore the possibility of developing a cell phone interpretive trail.
- Develop a web-based virtual geocache. Could have loaner GPS available.

Objective D-6. Environmental Education: With the addition of a park ranger (visitor services) permanent staff position and development of an intern/teacher program to support environmental education in coordination with partners, maintain a quality environmental education program with hands-on activities and outdoor experiences. Continue conducting teacher workshops and providing outreach programs at schools.

Discussion: Through uniquely developed, environmentally based, educational field experiences, staff at Black Bayou Lake NWR provide quality education opportunities for more that 2,500 students annually. Correlated to national and state education standards, the curriculum-based environmental activities offered allows students to leave behind their normal indoor classroom and venture outdoors to discover and connect with nature.

The utilization of facilities, equipment, educational materials, teacher workshops, and several study sites provides a safe environment conducive to learning.

Strategies:

- Consolidate the number and type of programs offered to each grade level. Offer different programs to each grade level to prevent too much repetition.
- Continue to evaluate programs to increase percentage of outdoor activities. Always ask "can this activity can be done outside?" If not, "how could I modify it so it could be done outside?"
- Develop a "Free Discovery Time" option as one activity choice during field trips. (Establish guidelines/rules without establishing pre-determined outcome.)
- Develop an intern program to support environmental education.
- Develop a discovery backpack type of program for teachers to use for self-guided visits to the refuge.
- Partner with friends group to provide financial and staff (volunteers) support for environmental education program.
- Develop intern/volunteer housing.
- Develop a cadre of volunteers to assist with environmental education program.
- Have the friends group fund a position to support the environmental education program.
- Develop a series of activity kits or trunks to provide to teachers who cannot schedule a time to come to the refuge for programs.
- Gradually transition environmental education to the program delivery model that uses trained teachers and parents to lead the activities instead of staff. (Use videos or trainings to train teachers and parents to lead the programs.)
- Replace amphitheatre with a more site-appropriate structure which would be rainproof.

Objective D-7. Refuge Volunteers: Increase the number of volunteers that assist with enivronmental education and interpretation programs, facility maintenance, and staffing the visitor center.

Discussion: The refuge staff explores the use of volunteers and provides volunteer opportunities for the public according to need. Although volunteer programs require an intense amount of staff time initially, once they are operating, the staff time is substantially reduced and supported by volunteers, and the benefits of volunteer support is substantial.

Approximately $5,000 funding is needed to run the volunteer program. Specific training for heavy equipment operation, etc., conducting interpretive tours, and providing environmental education is needed. Volunteers are recognized for their efforts at annual volunteer recognition dinners and regional and national awards ceremonies. The park ranger is responsible for managing the volunteer program and this is a collateral duty. The bulk of volunteer management is to manage volunteers at the visitor center and to coordinate with the friends group for any other needs for the refuge. This person has not yet gone to NCTC for volunteer training.

Volunteers and paid visitor services staff are integrated and generally included in decisions that affect them. Volunteers are given meaningful duties and specific responsibilities within the visitor services program. The volunteer program is evaluated each year by preparing an annual report and through awards recognition.

Additional support needed by the refuge staff from the regional volunteer coordinator could include funding, recruitment, and providing specific examples or guidance regarding position descriptions, refuge orientation manuals, etc.

Strategies:

- Develop standard position descriptions for on-going volunteer opportunities (i.e., maintenance, bookstore, conducting environmental education programs). Review http://www.volunteer.gov/gov/ for a list of position descriptions.
- Volunteers that work the visitor center should have a uniform that identifies them as visitor center staff
- Keep the volunteer manual updated.
- Hire a volunteer coordinator.
- Volunteer coordinator should review the Volunteer Handbook.
- Make sure that all volunteers receive appropriate training.
- Develop a written policy on resident volunteer retention/length of stay.
- Review, http://www.friendsofthesmokies.org/, and other websites, such as Neil Smith NWR, Friends of the Prairie Learning Center (http://www.tallgrass.org/) to get ideas for future design and program management. For instance, the Smokey Mountain website has a list of projects for 2008 to which people can make donations. It also has a merchandise category with lots of good ideas and "How You Can Help" category for making donations. It also describes pod cast downloads. The Neil Smith website lists Intern Opportunity information and bookstore items for sale, including wildlife photographs and other ideas.
- Work with staff to identify any jobs they have for volunteers and develop a job description for each (contact regional volunteer coordinator for examples).
- Explore options for diversifying the demographics of the volunteers.
- Keep a current list of projects to better respond when someone offers to volunteer.
- Develop a residential area with shared facilities (i.e., picnic shelter, evaluate need for laundry facility). Consider privacy options for volunteer pads.

- Develop a Frequently Asked Questions notebook for volunteers in case they don't have the information and staff is not available.

Objective D-8. Friends Group: Maintain very successful partnership with Friends of Black Bayou Lake, Inc., to address refuge needs, with an emphasis on additional support of the environmental education programs.

Discussion: A refuge that is well used by the public for a variety of interests will generate support from the public for the refuge. Supporting a variety of public involvement activities requires personnel, equipment, training, and a well-designed public outreach program.

Strategies:

- Refuge manager should continue to attend friends group monthly meetings.
- Work with friends group to focus its efforts on supporting program development.
- If friends group is looking at providing Complex assistance, other managers of refuges in the Complex should make efforts to periodically attend monthly meetings.
- Make sure friends group brochure/information is readily available.
- Inform friends group that it can use volunteer.gov to recruit new members.
- Provide training opportunities for staff and friends group members.

REFUGE ADMINISTRATION

Goal E. Refuge Administration: Secure and enhance staffing, funding, and facilities to maintain the integrity of habitats, wildlife resources, and wildlife-dependent recreation of the Black Bayou Lake National Wildlife Refuge in support of the National Wildlife Refuge System mission.

Discussion: The administrative functions include a wide array of activities that are critical to the mission of the Refuge System and the purpose of each refuge. Refuges must have appropriate staff, facilities, and equipment in order to accomplish their goals and objectives and conserve the integrity of the refuge.

Many of the proposed objectives and strategies cannot be implemented without the addition of personnel. Some work may be taken on by volunteers or interns, but generally still requires staff oversight to ensure accomplishment of objectives. There is a need to add one park ranger (visitor services), one park ranger (law enforcement), one refuge operations specialist, and one maintenance worker.

The first priority would be the positions dealing with visitors. Nationally, visitation is increasing at an annual average of 6.6 percent. Protecting the natural resources and ensuring the safety of refuge visitors are fundamental responsibilities of the refuge. Currently, the refuge has two collateral duty officers who have Complex-wide responsibilities. The addition of one law enforcement position is critical with the increasing visitation and increasing public use activities.

Objective E-1. Refuge Administration: Increase base funding of the Complex by 6 percent as well as add 4 additional staff positions to support Black Bayou Lake NWR.

Discussion: Sufficient personnel permanently assigned to the refuge are needed to provide the level of services necessary to support the achievement of the Refuge System's mission.

Strategy:

- Add 4 full-time positions, including 1 refuge operation specialist, 1 park ranger (outdoor recreation specialist), 1 park ranger (law enforcement officer), and 1 maintenance worker.

Objective E-2. Facilities: Repair and maintain existing facilities, building, and roads at high standards to enhance refuge programs that can provide safe and efficient operations.

Discussion: Adequate facilities have been developed to allow visitors opportunities to participate in all activities in a safe manner and to minimize disturbance to critical wildlife areas. All facilities are for the most part universally accessible to meet the needs of all visitors. Some of the boardwalks may need to have toe rails added to make them safer for wheelchairs, strollers, and sight-impaired visitors.

Strategies:

- Place a handicapped accessible sign at the Art Trail parking lot.
- When a group or an individual requires special accommodations, keep a log of how that request was met to ensure consistence for future requests.
- All of the boardwalks should have toe-guards.

If hunting and trail use increases, consider options to prevent user conflict. Some ideas to consider include placing signage to inform visitors when hunts are in progress; closing trails during hunts.

- Partner with a university to develop a study on visitor carrying capacity as it relates to protection of the resource and to quality of experience.

V. Plan Implementation

INTRODUCTION

Refuge lands are managed as defined under the Improvement Act. Congress has distinguished a clear legislative mission of wildlife conservation for all national wildlife refuges. National wildlife refuges, unlike other public lands, are dedicated to the conservation of the Nation's fish and wildlife resources and wildlife-dependent recreational uses. Priority projects emphasize the protection and enhancement of fish and wildlife species first and foremost, but considerable emphasis is placed on balancing the needs and demands for wildlife-dependent recreation and environmental education.

To accomplish the purpose, vision, goals, and objectives contained in this CCP for Black Bayou Lake NWR, this chapter identifies projects, funding and personnel needs, volunteers, partnership opportunities, and step-down management plans. This chapter also covers the need for monitoring to determine management effects on wildlife populations, and the need for plan review and revision.

PROPOSED PROJECTS

Listed below are the proposed project summaries and their associated costs for fish and wildlife population management, habitat management, resource protection, visitor services, and refuge administration over the next 15 years. This proposed project list reflects the priority needs identified by the public, planning team, and refuge staff based upon available information. These projects were generated for the purpose of achieving the refuge's objectives and strategies. The primary linkages of these projects to those planning elements are identified in each summary.

FISH AND WILDLIFE POPULATION MANAGEMENT

Science-based inventorying and monitoring of wildlife populations – Science-based inventorying and monitoring of wildlife populations are critical to ensuring the biological integrity of the refuge. Information collected will serve as the basis for developing habitat management plans and will influence all refuge management activities. A systematic inventorying and monitoring program will enable the refuge to make informed management decisions and valuable long-term contributions to national and regional objectives for waterfowl, shorebirds, forest breeding birds, and wintering forest and scrub/shrub birds, among others.

Standardized census and survey techniques will be employed and all data compiled into databases, including GIS, for spatial analysis. This information is critical to formulating management actions and evaluating bottomland hardwood reforestation, moist-soil unit manipulation, and other refuge programs. All data will be shared with appropriate state and federal partners in an effort to further ecosystem management. *(Linkages: Goal A, Objectives A-1-19.)*

Recurring Costs: $40,000   Special Project Cost: $154,000

Determine Nesting Success of Priority Neotropical Migratory Songbirds – Improve Black Bayou Lake NWR's ability to manage bottomland hardwood forests to increase the biological potential for nesting habitat of hooded warbler, Kentucky warbler, northern parula, Swainson's warbler, wood thrush, and prothonotary warbler species. Management practice impacts should be incorporated into the research design to determine the bird response so that adaptive management decisions can be made. The research project should be explored for cooperation with the LDWF and a university.

Point count surveys, nest searches, and vegetation and landscape analyses will be conducted for a minimum of 3 years. *(Linkages: Goal A, Objectives A-4-5; and Goal B, Objectives B-1-2.)*

Recurring Costs: $50,000   Special Project Cost: $300,000

Population Status and Management Impacts with Reptiles and Amphibians – Although the prospective herpetofauna of the refuge is large, at least 80 species, the presence of relatively few of the species has been confirmed and associated with particular refuges or their habitats. When confronted with a lack of knowledge concerning the species actually residing on refuge lands, the first step in conserving them is learning of their presence, and to the extent possible, associating their presence with particular habitats and how forest management activities are impacting their populations. The refuge will cooperate with a university or organization to design and implement the project and collaborate with the USGS for cooperative funding possibilities through the Amphibian and Reptile Monitoring Initiative. While certain aspects of the biology of the alligator snapping turtle are slowly unfolding, population dynamics are still largely unknown. In cooperation with the University of Louisiana and its herpetologist, J.Carr, the refuge provides a good opportunity to further our understanding of alligator snapping turtle nesting requirements and components of successful nesting. These data are crucial in furthering our conservation efforts of this declining species. *(Linkages: Goal A, Objective A-12-13; and Goal B, Objective B-5).*

Recurring Costs: $90,000   Special Project Cost: $108,000

HABITAT MANAGEMENT

Bottomland Hardwood Forest Health – Continual management of existing forested wetlands for forest health and wildlife habitat. This includes maintenance of the arboretum trail which consists of 160 labeled Louisiana native tree and woody shrub species and prairie demonstration area. Both require repeated planting and watering and monitoring. The prairie demonstration area also requires mowing or burning to promote growth and sustainability. In addition, 800 acres of former agricultural fields have been reforested with eleven bottomland hardwood tree species and need to be monitored on a continual basis. An additional 900 acres of bottomland forest needs silvicultural treatments to promote a diverse, healthy forest. This includes the need for conducting forest inventories, writing prescriptions, and marking timber. *(Linkages: Goal B, Objectives B-1-6).*

Recurring Costs: $15,000   Special Project Cost: $40,000

Invasive Species Control – Control invasive, exotic water hyacinth infesting Black Bayou Lake NWR. The invasive, non-native plant is degrading aquatic habitats and causing access problems for fishermen, university researchers, refuge biologists, and law enforcement officers. Water hyacinth grows very fast, doubling in size every 7 to 10 days during the growing season. Approximately 50 percent of the lake is covered with this exotic plant. Control of the water hyacinth will greatly increase public use opportunities such as fishing, canoeing, wildlife observation, and photography on this semi-urban refuge, while promoting our partnerships with the city of Monroe and the Friends of Black Bayou, Inc. Further, Black Bayou Lake is a secondary water source for the city of Monroe and control of this invasive aquatic plant is imperative to the management of this system. *(Linkages: Goal B, Objective B-1-6).*

Recurring Costs: $35,000   Special Project Cost: $45,000

Land Protection – Purchase of the Oliver Plantation would incorporate the southern end of the lake into the refuge, protecting the entire lake and its watershed. Owners of the Bayou DeSiard tract intend to subdivide the waterfront property into housing lots. Although the owners are willing to sell, the price is too high for the refuge to purchase. Acquisition of this property would protect and buffer that portion of Bayou DeSiard from development. *(Linkages: Goal C, Objective C-1-2).*

The estimated cost to acquire the remaining 1,678 acres within the current acquisition boundary $1,200 per acre is $2,013,600.

Watershed Protection and Water Quality – The importance of water quality to this refuge cannot be overstressed. This refuge is primarily a lake and riparian area so water quality is probably the most important aspect of the ecosystem. The lake itself would be classified as either nearly or completely eutrophic as submergent and floating aquatic plants exist in great abundance. Conduct water resources inventory and assessment in coordination with partners. *(Linkages: Goal C, Objectives C-3-4).*

Recurring cost: $10,000   Project cost: $10,000

Safety and Resource Protection – Black Bayou Lake NWR relies on one collateral duty law enforcement officer whose time is split among all the refuges within the Complex. Public use has continued to increase with hunting and fishing pressure on the refuge along with other issues requiring law enforcement, such as vandalism, littering, compliance with access, and public use regulations. The refuge is currently unable to adequately address safety and resource protection issues. The refuge needs to hire one full-time park ranger (GS-0025-7/9) ($140,000), to just begin to keep up with a growing population utilizing the refuge from public use to access issues to gas lease compliance. *(Linkages: Goals A, B, C, D, and E.)*

Recurring cost: $115,000   Special project cost: $150,000

Cultural and Historical Resource Interpretation Overview of the Refuge – Using available scientific and historic information, the selected contractor will author an interdisciplinary overview of the refuge's cultural landscape as it has changed over the past 15-20,000 years. The final technical report will include, at a minimum, sections about the area's geomorphology and hydrological regime, paleoenvironmental reconstruction, the area's cultural history, the scope and scale of past archaeological investigations on and near the refuge, a detailed list of the refuge's historic properties, and future research questions. Submission of the overview report will satisfy the cultural resource objectives listed in the CCP, as well as those listed in other Service documents. Using the information generated from the overview, as well as on-going scientific archaeological investigations of the area, the selected contractor will inventory and then evaluate the National Register's eligibility of historic properties located on the refuges. Recurring costs include conservation and protection of sites and administrative needs for existing or new sites that are found. This project would also include interpretation and display of pertinent information for the visiting public. *(Linkages: Goal C, Objective C-5.)*

Recurring Costs: $10,000   Special Project Cost: $75,000

Black Bayou Lake NWR – A focal point of Environmental Education for North Louisiana NWR Complex – Black Bayou Lake NWR is a 4,600-acre semi-urban refuge that is now serving 38,000 visitors annually with a potential to serve over 100,000. There are currently 1.5 full-time positions that assist with maintenance projects at Black Bayou Lake NWR. Facilities include a conservation learning center, visitor center, wildlife pier, boat launch site, raised observation deck, photo blind, bird blind, nature trails, and arboretum. There is regular maintenance that is required on the refuge facilities and lands, such as mowing around facilities and primitive trails, grading roads, trash collection, vehicle maintenance, and ordering/stocking supplies for the refuge. Given the upkeep on existing facilities, another full-time maintenance worker is needed to keep up with day-to-day operations of the refuge. Environmental education and interpretation programs at Black Bayou Lake NWR are excellent and serve to exemplify all other units in the North Louisiana NWR Complex. Increasing visitation and interpretation of environmental educational facilities and programs also justifies the addition of another full-time park ranger (visitor services). *(Linkages: Goal D, Objectives D-1-8.)*

Recurring Costs: 100,000   Special Project Cost: 160,000

Wildlife Refuge Specialist (GS-4085-7/9) – Black Bayou Lake NWR is a 4,600-acre semi-urban refuge that is now serving 38,000 visitors annually, with a potential to serve over 100,000. The refuge has established several partnerships with the local community and is very active in community events. In addition, Black Bayou Lake NWR has an excellent environmental education program and is increasing in public use opportunities. There are currently two management positions at Black Bayou Lake NWR--a refuge manager and a wildlife refuge specialist. However, due to the extreme growth of the public use program, there will be a need to create another wildlife refuge specialist position to help with day-to-day management issues, assist with refuge activities, support the environmental education program, and represent the Service within the community. *(Linkages: Goal D, Objectives D-1-8.)*

Recurring Costs: $80,000   Special Project Cost: $90,000

Black Bayou Lake NWR Cell Phone Tour – Implement a cell phone tour on Black Bayou Lake NWR. This will provide an additional public use opportunity on the refuge and does not require staff to be present to conduct a program or provide information. There will be signs with call-in information and instructions strategically placed throughout the refuge. Each stop will provide different information on the refuge and the facilities. This project promotes the Service's "Let's Go Outside" Initiative and the priority to Connect People with Nature. *(Linkages: Goal D, Objectives D-1-8.)*

Recurring Costs: $8,000   Special Project Cost: $10,000

Technology Projects (Podcast tour of refuge, virtual geo-caching) – Implement new technology projects such as a podcast tour of the refuge and virtual geo-caching on the refuge. School groups and youth organizations consist of a large percentage of visitations to the refuge. The younger generation is very fascinated by technology and these projects will help to relate to these individuals, as well as incorporate our message of conservation. The podcast can be toured on-line as a pre-visit activity and will provide information about the refuge and the facilities. This will increase awareness of the refuge to students and adults. Virtual geo-caching will provide an additional public use opportunity on the refuge and can be conducted by teachers and other facilitators. The virtual geo-caching project promotes the Service's "Let's Go Outside" Initiative and the priority to Connect People with Nature. *(Linkages: Goal D, Objectives D-1-8.)*

Recurring Costs: $8,000   Special Project Cost: $25,000

Black Bayou Lake NWR Informational Video – Develop an informative audio visual video about the refuge. This would include history of refuge, objectives, management practices, things to do on the refuge, facilities, and local partnerships. Since Black Bayou Lake NWR is also responsible for interpretation/education for all the other refuges in the Complex, a brief description of other refuges will be included in video. The video will provide visitors with an excellent orientation of the refuge and will answer any basic questions they may have. This video can be shown by volunteers/interns and will not require staff to be present during busiest times of the year. *(Linkages: Goal D, Objectives D-1-8.)*

Recurring Costs: $5,000   Special Project Cost: $40,000

REFUGE ADMINISTRATION

Expand the Ability to Maintain Quality Refuge Programs – The maintenance staff is challenged to adequately provide for existing needs. To adequately maintain existing infrastructure for public use activities and habitat management, and to comply with SAMMS database requirements, additional staff, equipment, office space, and funding are needed. Additional funding and personnel would be used to maintain existing roads and trails, maintain observation platforms, maintain water control structures, levees and refuge facilities, maintain equipment and vehicles, input and manage information in SAMMS, and other refuge maintenance needs. This project supports the addition of a permanent maintenance worker (1 FTE, WG-4749-9). *(Linkages: Goals A, B, C, D, and E.)*

Recurring Costs: $90,000   Special Project Cost: $110,000

PARTNERSHIP/VOLUNTEERS OPPORTUNITIES

VOLUNTEERS

The refuge currently has an excellent partnership with the volunteer group, "Friends of Black Bayou Lake, Inc.," and will use this as a model for other partnerships. This group of volunteers is actively involved in helping make the refuge a part of the surrounding community. The refuge will continue to use this group of volunteers as well as recruit others to assist in such activities as wood duck and blue bird box management, environmental education, staffing of the visitor's center, grounds maintenance, etc.

PARTNERSHIP OPPORTUNITIES

A major objective of this CCP is to establish partnerships with local volunteers, landowners, private organizations, and state and federal natural resource agencies. In the immediate vicinity of the refuge, opportunities exist to establish partnerships with sporting clubs, elementary and secondary schools, universities, and community organizations. At the regional and state level, partnerships might be established with organizations such as LDWF, Ducks Unlimited, The Nature Conservancy, Audubon Society, etc.

FUNDING AND PERSONNEL

Table 4. Summary of projects

PROJECT NUMBER	PROJECT TITLE	FIRST YEAR COST ($)	RECURRING ANNUAL COST ($)	STAFF (FTE'S)
1	Science-Based Inventory And Monitoring Of Fish And Wildlife Populations	154,000	40,000	
2	Determine Nesting Success of Priority Neotropical Migratory Songbirds	300,000	50,000	
3	Population Status and Management Impacts with Reptiles and Amphibians	108,000	90,000	
4	Bottomland Hardwood Forest Health	40,000	15,000	
5	Control Of Invasive Plants	45,000	35,000	
6	Land Protection	2,013,600	Unknown	
7	Watershed Protection and Water Quality	10,000	10,000	
8	Safety and Resource Protection	150,000	115,000	1
9	Cultural and Historical Resource Interpretation Overview of the Refuge	75,000	10,000	
10	Black Bayou Lake NWR – A focal point of Environmental Education for North Louisiana NWR Complex	100,000	160,000	1
11	Wildlife Refuge Specialist (GS-4085-7/9)	90,000	80,000	1
12	Black Bayou Lake NWR Cell Phone Tour	10,000	8,000	

13	Technology Projects (Podcast tour of refuge, virtual geo-caching)	25,000	8,000	
14	Black Bayou Lake NWR Informational Video	40,000	5,000	
15	Expand the Ability to Maintain Quality Refuge Programs	90,000	110,000	1

The refuge volunteer program and other partnerships generated will depend upon the number of staff positions the Service provides the refuge. As staff and resources are committed to the refuge, opportunities to expand the volunteer program and to develop partnerships will be enhanced.

If staff can be expanded to allow time for additional outreach to local communities, there may be opportunities to expand existing volunteer opportunities on the refuge. The refuge already has an active and growing volunteer program, managed by the refuge manager and the volunteer coordinator. Properly supervised and directed, these volunteers could make even more valuable contributions to the refuge by assisting future staff with any number of activities, including projects to monitor habitat and wildlife populations and environmental education both on and off the refuge.

The goals and objectives outlined in this CCP need the support and the partnerships of federal, state, and local agencies, non-governmental organizations, and private citizens. This broad-based approach to managing fish and wildlife resources extends beyond social and political boundaries and requires a foundation of support from many stakeholders. The refuge will continue to seek creative partnership opportunities to achieve its vision for the future.

STEP-DOWN MANAGEMENT PLANS

A CCP is a strategic plan that guides the direction of the refuge. A step-down management plan provides specific guidance on activities, such as habitat, prescribed burning, and visitor services. These plans (Table 5) are also developed in accordance with NEPA.

MONITORING AND ADAPTIVE MANAGEMENT

Adaptive management is a flexible approach to long-term management of biotic resources that is directed over time by the results of ongoing monitoring activities and other information. More specifically, adaptive management is a process by which projects are implemented within a framework of scientifically driven experiments to test the predictions and assumptions outlined within a plan.

To apply adaptive management, specific surveying, inventorying, and monitoring protocols will be adopted for the refuge. The habitat management strategies will be systematically evaluated to determine management effects on wildlife populations. This information will be used to refine approaches and determine how effectively the objectives are being accomplished. Evaluations will include ecosystem team and other appropriate partner participation. If monitoring and evaluating indicate undesirable effects for target and non-target species and/or communities, then alterations to the management projects will be made. Subsequently, the CCP will be revised. Specific monitoring and evaluating activities will be described in the step-down management plans.

Table 5. Step-down management plans for Black Bayou Lake National Wildlife Refuge

Step-down Plan	Completion Date
Station Safety Plan	2017
Law Enforcement Plan	2019
Fishery Management Plan	2018
Fire Management Plan	2015
Animal Control Plan	2018
Biological Inventorying and Monitoring Plan	2010
Trapping Plan	2018
Hunt Plan (update)	2022
Cultural Resource Protection Plan	2015
Habitat Management Plan	2012
Visitor Services Management Plan	2013
Invasive Management Plan	2011

PLAN REVIEW AND REVISION

This CCP will be reviewed annually as the refuge's annual work plans and budgets are developed. It will also be reviewed to determine the need for revision. A revision will occur if and when conditions change or significant information becomes available, such as a change in ecological conditions or a major refuge expansion. This final CCP will be augmented by detailed step-down management plans to address the completion of specific strategies in support of the refuge's goals and objectives. Revisions to the CCP and the step-down management plans will be subject to NEPA compliance.

Appendix A. Glossary

Adaptive Management: Refers to a process in which policy decisions are implemented within a framework of scientifically driven experiments to test predictions and assumptions inherent in management plan. Analysis of results help managers determine whether current management should continue as is or whether it should be modified to achieve desired conditions.

Alluvial: Sediment transported and deposited in a delta or riverbed by flowing water.

Alternative: 1. A reasonable way to fix the identified problem or satisfy the stated need (40 CFR 1500.2). 2. Alternatives are different sets of objectives and strategies or means of achieving refuge purposes and goals, helping fulfill the Refuge System mission, and resolving issues (Service Manual 602 FW 1.6B).

Anadromous: Migratory fishes that spend most of their lives in the sea and migrate to fresh water to breed.

Approved Acquisition Boundary: A project boundary that the Director of the United States Fish and Wildlife Service approves upon completion of the detailed planning and environmental compliance process for establishment of a refuge.

Biological Diversity: The variety of life and its processes, including the variety of living organisms, the genetic differences among them, and the communities and ecosystems in which they occur (USFWS Manual 052 FW 1. 12B). The System's focus is on indigenous species, biotic communities, and ecological processes. Also referred to as Biodiversity.

Biological Integrity: Composition, structure, and function at the genetic, organism, and community levels consistent with natural conditions, and the biological processes that shape genomes, organisms, and communities.

Canopy: A layer of foliage, generally the upper-most layer, in a forest stand. It can be used to refer to mid or understory vegetation in multi-layered stands. Canopy closure is an estimate of the amount of overhead tree cover.

Carrying Capacity:	The maximum population of a species able to be supported by a habitat or area.
Categorical Exclusion (CE,CX, CATEX, CATX):	A category of actions that do not individually or cumulatively have a significant effect on the human environment and have been found to have no such effect in procedures adopted by a Federal agency pursuant to the National Environmental Policy Act (40 CFR 1508.4).
Community:	A distinct assemblage of plants that develops on sites characterized by particular climates and soils, and the species and populations of wild animals that depend on the plants for food, cover and/or nesting.
Compatible Use:	A proposed or existing wildlife-dependent recreational use or any other use of a national wildlife refuge that, based on sound professional judgment, will not materially interfere with or detract from the fulfillment of the National Wildlife Refuge System mission or the purpose(s) of the national wildlife refuge [50 CFR 25.12 (a)]. A compatibility determination supports the selection of compatible uses and identifies stipulations or limits necessary to ensure compatibility.
Comprehensive Conservation Plan (CCP):	A document that describes the desired future conditions of a refuge or planning unit and provides long-range guidance and management direction to achieve the purposes of the refuge; helps fulfill the mission of the Refuge System; maintains and, where appropriate, restores the ecological integrity of each refuge and the Refuge System; helps achieve the goals of the National Wilderness Preservation System; and meets other mandates (Service Manual 602 FW 1.6 E).
Concern:	See Issue.
Cover Type:	The present vegetation of an area.
Cultural Resource Inventory:	A professionally conducted study designed to locate and evaluate evidence of cultural resources present within a defined geographic area. Inventories may involve various levels, including background literature search, comprehensive field examination to identify all exposed physical manifestations of cultural resources, or sample inventory to project site distribution and density over a larger area. Evaluation of identified cultural resources to determine eligibility for the National Register follows the criteria found in 36 CFR 60.4 (Service Manual 614 FW 1.7).

Cultural Resource Overview:	A comprehensive document prepared for a field office that discusses, among other things, its prehistory and cultural history, the nature and extent of known cultural resources, previous research, management objectives, resource management conflicts or issues, and a general statement on how program objectives should be met and conflicts resolved. An overview should reference or incorporate information from a field offices background or literature search described in Section VIII of the Cultural Resource Management Handbook (Service Manual 614 FW 1.7).
Cultural Resources:	The remains of sites, structures, or objects used by people in the past.
Designated Wilderness Area:	An area designated by the United States Congress to be managed as part of the National Wilderness Preservation System (Draft Service Manual 610 FW 1.5).
Disturbance:	Significant alteration of habitat structure or composition. May be natural (e.g., fire) or human-caused events (e.g., aircraft overflight).
Ecosystem:	A dynamic and interrelating complex of plant and animal communities and their associated non-living environment.
Ecosystem Management:	Management of natural resources using system-wide concepts to ensure that all plants and animals in ecosystems are maintained at viable levels in native habitats and basic ecosystem processes are perpetuated indefinitely.
Ecotone:	Edge or transition zone between two or more adjacent but different plant communities, ecosystems, or biomes.
Endangered Species (Federal):	A plant or animal species listed under the Endangered Species Act that is in danger of extinction throughout all or a significant portion of its range.
Endangered Species (State):	A plant or animal species in danger of becoming extinct or extirpated in the state within the near future if factors contributing to its decline continue. Populations of these species are at critically low levels or their habitats have been degraded or depleted to a significant degree.

Environmental Assessment (EA):	A concise public document, prepared in compliance with the National Environmental Policy Act, that briefly discusses the purpose and need for an action, alternatives to such action, and provides sufficient evidence and analysis of impacts to determine whether to prepare an environmental impact statement or finding of no significant impact (40 CFR 1508.9).
Environmental Impact Statement (EIS):	A detailed written statement required by section 102(2) of the National Environmental Policy Act, analyzing the environmental impacts of a proposed action, adverse effects of the project that cannot be avoided, alternative courses of action, short-term uses of the environment versus the maintenance and enhancement of long-term productivity, and any irreversible and irretrievable commitment of resources (40 CFR 1508.11).
Estuary:	The wide lower course of a river into which the tides flow. The area where the tide meets a river current.
Exotic:	A species that does not normally live and thrive in a particular ecosystem.
Extirpation:	The localized extinction of a species that is no longer found in a locality or country, but still exists elsewhere in the world.
Fauna:	All the vertebrate and invertebrate animals of an area.
Flora:	All the plants of an area.
Fragmentation:	The process of reducing the size and connectivity of habitat patches. The disruption of extensive habitats into isolated and small patches.
Finding of No Significant Impact (FONSI):	A document prepared in compliance with the National Environmental Policy Act, supported by an environmental assessment, that briefly presents why a Federal action will have no significant effect on the human environment and for which an environmental impact statement, therefore, will not be prepared (40 CFR 1508.13).
Goal:	Descriptive, open-ended, and often broad statement of desired future conditions that conveys a purpose but does not define measurable units (Service Manual 620 FW 1.6J).

Habitat:	Suite of existing environmental conditions required by an organism for survival and reproduction. The place where an organism typically lives.
Habitat Restoration:	Management emphasis designed to move ecosystems to desired conditions and processes, and/or to healthy ecosystems.
Habitat Type:	See Vegetation Type.
Herbicide:	A chemical agent used to kill plants or inhibit plant growth.
Historic Conditions:	Composition, structure, and functioning of ecosystems resulting from natural processes that we believe, based on sound professional judgment, were present prior to substantial human-related changes to the landscape.
Hydrology:	The properties, distribution, and effects of water in the atmosphere, on the earth's surface and in soil and rocks. The movement of water and how it changes in depth, timing, flow, or location of surface water.
Kiosk:	A small structure with one or more open sides that is used to display or provide information.
Improvement Act:	The National Wildlife Refuge System Improvement Act of 1997.
Indicator Species:	A species of plant or animals that is assumed to be sensitive to habitat changes and represents the needs of a larger group of species.
Invasive Species:	A species of plant or animal that is non-native and whose establishment does, or is likely to, cause economic or environmental harm.
Inventory:	A point-in-time measurement of the resource to determine location or condition.
Issue:	Any unsettled matter that requires a management decision, e.g., an initiative, opportunity, resource management problem, threat to the resources of the unit, conflict in uses, public concern, or other presence of an undesirable resource condition (Service Manual 602 FW 1.6K).
Littoral Zone:	The area from high water mark to low water mark or the intertidal zone.

Management Alternative:	See Alternative.
Management Concern:	See Issue.
Management Opportunity:	See Issue.
Migration:	The seasonal movement from one area to another and back.
Mission Statement:	Succinct statement of the unit's purpose and reason for being.
Monitoring:	The process of collecting information to track changes of selected parameters over time.
Monoculture:	When the plant life in an area comprises of only one species.
National Environmental Policy Act of 1969 (NEPA):	Requires all agencies, including the Service, to examine the environmental impacts of their actions, incorporate environmental information, and use public participation in the planning and implementation of all actions. Federal agencies must integrate NEPA with other planning requirements, and prepare appropriate NEPA documents to facilitate better environmental decision making (40 CFR 1500).
National Wildlife Refuge System Improvement Act of 1997 (Public Law 105-57):	Under the Refuge Improvement Act, the U.S. Fish and Wildlife Service is required to develop 15-year comprehensive conservation plans for all national wildlife refuges outside Alaska. The Act also describes the six public uses given priority status within the Refuge System (e.g., hunting, fishing, wildlife observation, wildlife photography, and environmental education and interpretation).
National Wildlife Refuge System Mission:	The mission is to administer a national network of lands and waters for the conservation, management, and where appropriate, restoration of the fish, wildlife, and plant resources and their habitats within the United States for the benefit of present and future generations of Americans.

National Wildlife Refuge System:	Various categories of areas administered by the Secretary of the Interior for the conservation of fish and wildlife, including species threatened with extinction; all lands, waters, and interests therein administered by the Secretary as wildlife refuges; areas for the protection and conservation of fish and wildlife that are threatened with extinction; wildlife ranges; games ranges; wildlife management areas; or waterfowl production areas.
National Wildlife Refuge:	A designated area of land, water, or an interest in land or water within the Refuge System.
Native Species:	Species that normally live and thrive in a particular ecosystem.
Neo-tropical Song Birds:	A bird species that breeds north of the United States/Mexico border and winters primarily south of that border, which includes Mexico, West Indies, Central America, and part of South America.
Notice of Intent (NOI):	A notice that an environmental impact statement will be prepared and considered (40 CFR 1508.22). Published in the Federal Register.
Noxious Weed:	A plant species designated by Federal or State law as generally possessing one or more of the following characteristics: aggressive or difficult to manage; parasitic; a carrier or host of serious insect or disease; or non-native, new, or not common to the United States, according to the Federal Noxious Weed Act (PL 93-639), a noxious weed is one that causes disease or had adverse effects on man or his environment and therefore is detrimental to the agriculture and commerce of the Untied States and to the public health.
Nuisance Species:	A plant or animal for economic or environmental reason causes problems. A native species can be a nuisance species.
Objective:	A concise statement of what we want to achieve, how much we want to achieve, when and where we want to achieve it, and who is responsible for the work. Objectives derive from goals and provide the basis for determining strategies, monitoring refuge accomplishments, and evaluating the success of strategies. Making objectives attainable, time-specific, and measurable (Service Manual 602 FW 1.6N).
Plant Association:	A classification of plant communities based on the similarity in dominants of all layers of vascular species in a climax community.

Plant Community: An assemblage of plant species unique in its composition; occurs in particular locations under particular influences; a reflection or integration of the environmental influences on the site such as soils, temperature, elevation, solar radiation, slope, aspect, and rainfall; denotes a general kind of climax plant community.

Preferred Alternative: This is the alternative determined [by the decision-maker] to best achieve the refuge purpose, vision, and goals; contributes to the Refuge System mission; addresses the significant issues; and is consistent with principles of sound fish and wildlife management.

Prescribed Fire: The application of fire to wildland fuels to achieve identified land use objectives (Service Manual 621 FW 1.7). May be from natural ignition or intentional ignition.

Priority Species: Fish and wildlife species that the Service believes require protective measures and/or management guidelines to ensure their perpetuation. Priority species include the following: (1) State-listed and candidate species; (2) species or groups of animals susceptible to significant population declines within a specific area or statewide by virtue of their inclination to aggregate (e.g., seabird colonies); and (3) species of recreation, commercial, and/or tribal importance.

Public Involvement Plan: Broad long-term guidance for involving the public in the comprehensive planning process.

Public Involvement: A process that offers impacted and interested individuals and organizations an opportunity to become informed about, and to express their opinions on Service actions and policies. In the process, these views are studied thoroughly and thoughtful consideration of public views is given in shaping decisions for refuge management.

Public: Individuals, organizations, and groups; officials of Federal, State, and local government agencies; Indian tribes; and foreign nations. It may include anyone outside the core planning team. It includes those who may or may not have indicated an interest in service issues and those who do or do not realize that Service decisions may affect them.

Purposes of the Refuge: "The purposes specified in or derived from the law, proclamation, executive order, agreement, public land order, donation document, or administrative memorandum establishing, authorizing, or expanding a refuge, refuge unit, or refuge sub-unit." For refuges that encompass congressionally designated wilderness, the purposes of the Wilderness Act are additional purposes of the refuge (Service Manual 602 FW 106 S).

Recommended Wilderness:	Areas studied and found suitable for wilderness designation by both the Director and Secretary, and recommended for designation by the President to Congress. These areas await only legislative action by congress in order to become part of the Wilderness System. Such areas are also referred to as "pending in Congress" (Draft Service Manual 610 FW 1.5).
Record of Decision (ROD):	A concise public record of decision prepared by the Federal agency, pursuant to NEPA, that contains a statement of the decision, identification of all alternatives considered, identification of the environmentally preferable alternative, a statement as to whether all practical means to avoid or minimize environmental harm from the alternative selected have been adopted (and if not, why they were not), and a summary of monitoring and enforcement where applicable for any mitigation (40 CFR 1505.2).
Refuge Goal:	See Goal.
Refuge Purposes:	See Purposes of the Refuge.
Riparian:	Relating to the banks of a water body.
Scoping:	A process for determining the scope of issues to be addressed by a comprehensive conservation plan and for identifying the significant issues. Involved in the scoping process are Federal, Tribal, State and local agencies; private organizations (businesses and non-profit); and individuals.
Songbirds: (Also Passerines)	A category of birds that are medium to small, perching landbirds. Most are territorial singers and migratory.
Species:	A distinctive kind of plant or animal having distinguishable characteristics, and that can interbreed and produce young. In taxonomy, a category of biological classification that refers to one or more populations of similar organisms that can reproduce with each other but is reproductively isolated from – that is, incapable of interbreeding with – all other kinds of organisms.
Species of Management Concern:	This is a category assigned to species for which information in the of the Service indicated that proposing to list as threatened or endangered was possibly appropriate, but for which sufficient data were not available to support proposed rules.

Step-down Management Plan:	A plan that provides specific guidance on management subjects (e.g., habitat, public use, fire, safety) or groups of related subjects. It describes strategies and implementation schedules for meeting CCP goals and objectives (Service Manual 602 FW 1.6 U).
Strategy:	A specific action, tool, technique, or combination of actions, tools, and techniques used to meet unit objectives (Service Manual 602 FW 1.6 U).
Study Area:	The area reviewed in detail for wildlife, habitat, and public use potential. For purposes of the CCP, the study area includes the lands within the currently approved refuge boundary and potential refuge expansion areas.
Threatened Species (Federal):	Species listed under the Endangered Species Act that are likely to become endangered within the foreseeable future throughout all or a significant portion of their range.
Threatened Species (State):	A plant or animal species likely to become endangered in the state within the near future if factors contributing to population decline or habitat degradation or loss continue.
Tiering:	The coverage of general matters in broader environmental impact statements with subsequent narrower statements of environmental analysis, incorporating by reference, the general discussions and concentrating on specific issues (40 CFR 1508.28).
U.S. Fish and Wildlife Service Mission:	The mission of the U.S. Fish and Wildlife Service is working with others to conserve, protect, and enhance fish and wildlife and their habitats for the continuing benefit of the American people.
Unit Objective:	See Objective.
Vegetation Type, Habitat Type, Forest Cover Type:	A land classification system based upon the concept of distinct plant associations.

Vision Statement: A concise statement of what the planning unit should be, or what we hope to do, based primarily upon the Refuge System Mission and specific refuge purposes, and other mandates. We will tie the vision statement for the refuge to the mission of the Refuge System; the purpose(s) of the refuge; the maintenance or restoration of the ecological integrity of each refuge and the Refuge System; and other mandates (Service Manual 602 FW 1.6 Z).

Watershed: The entire land area that collects and drains water into a stream or stream system.

Wetland: Areas such as lakes, marshes, bogs, and streams that are inundated by surface or ground water for a long enough period of time each year to support, and that do support under natural conditions, plants and animals that require saturated or seasonally saturated soils.

Wilderness Study Areas: Lands and waters identified through inventory as meeting the definition of wilderness and undergoing evaluation for recommendation for inclusion in the Wilderness System. A study area must meet the following criteria:

- Generally appears to have been affected primarily by the forces of nature, with the imprint of man's work substantially unnoticeable

- Has outstanding opportunities for solitude or a primitive and unconfined type of recreation

- Has at least 5,000 contiguous roadless acres or is sufficient in size as to make practicable its preservation and use in an unimpaired condition (Draft Service Manual 610 FW 1.5).

Wilderness: See Designated Wilderness.

Wildfire: A free-burning fire requiring a suppression response; all fire other than prescribed fire that occurs on wildlands (Service Manual 621 FW 1.7).

Wildland Fire: Every wildland fire is either a wildfire or a prescribed fire (Service Manual 621 FW 1.3.

Wildlife Corridor: A landscape feature that facilitates the biologically effective transport of animals between larger patches of habitat dedicated to conservation functions. Such corridors may facilitate several kinds of traffic, including frequent foraging movement, seasonal migration, or the once in a lifetime dispersal of juvenile animals. These are transitional habitats and need not contain all habitat elements required by migrants for long-term survival or reproduction.

Wildlife Dependent Recreational Use: A use (activity) on a refuge that involves hunting, fishing, wildlife observation and photography, or environmental education and interpretation, as identified in the National Wildlife Refuge System Improvement Act of 1997.

Wildlife Diversity: A measure of the number of wildlife species in an area and their relative abundance.

ACRONYMS AND ABBREVIATIONS

U.S. Fish and Wildlife Service

ACRONYM	DESCRIPTION
ATV	All-terrain vehicle
BCC	Birds of Conservation Concern
BCR	Bird Conservation Region
BRT	Biological Review Team
CATX	Categorical Exclusion
CCP	Comprehensive Conservation Plan
CFR	Code of Federal Regulations
CRP	Conservation Reserve Program
CWCS	Comprehensive Wildlife Conservation Strategy
DNR	Department of Natural Resources
DOI	Department of the Interior
DED	Duck-energy days
EA	Environmental Assessment
EE	Environmental Education
EIS	Environmental Impact Statement
EPA	U.S. Environmental Protection Agency
ESA	Endangered Species Act
FONSI	Finding of No Significant Impact
FR	Federal Register
FTE	Full-time equivalent
FWS	Fish and Wildlife Service
FY	Fiscal Year
GIS	Global Information System
HQ	Headquarters
LDEQ	Louisiana Department of Environmental Quality
LDWF	Louisiana Department of Wildlife and Fisheries
LMVJV	Lower Mississippi Valley Joint Venture
MAV	Mississippi Alluvial Valley
MMS	Maintenance Management System

NAAQS	National Ambient Air Quality Standars
NABCI	North American Bird Conservation Initiative
NAWMP	North American Waterfowl Management Plan
NEPA	National Environmental Policy Act
NGO	Non-governmental organizations
NHPA	National Historic Preservation Act
NRCS	National Resources Conservation Service
NRHP	National Register of Historic Places
NWR	National Wildlife Refuge
NWRS	National Wildlife Refuge System
PFT	Permanent Full Time
PIF	Partners In Flight
RHPO	Regional Historic Preservation Officer
ROD	Record of Decision
RONS	Refuge Operating Needs System
RRP	Refuge Roads Program
Service	U.S. Fish and Wildlife Service (also, FWS or USFWS)
SHPO	State Historic Preservation Officer
T&E	Threatened and Endangered Species
TFT	Temporary Full Time
USC	United States Code
USFWS	U.S. Fish and Wildlife Service
VC	Visitor Center
WGCP	West Gulf Coastal Plain
WRP	Wetlands Reserve Program

Appendix B. References and Literature Citations

Aku, P. and M. Wood. 2002. Evaluation of the status of sport fishes of the Black Bayou Lake National Refuge. Technical Report, Challenge Cost-Share Agreement 42651, University of Louisiana at Monroe and Louisiana Dept. of Wildlife and Fisheries, 20 pp.

Bass, A.A. 2007. Habitat use and movements of Alligator Snapping Turtle (Macrochelys temminckii) hatchlings [Master of Science thesis]. Monroe, LA: University of Louisiana at Monroe. 56 p.

Besenhofer, L. 2006. Assessment of paternity in Alligator Snapping Turtle (Macrochelys temminckii) clutches [Master of Science thesis]. Monroe, LA: University of Louisiana at Monroe. 69 p.

Bias, M.A., M.A. Wolder, and P.E. Schmidt. 1997. Disturbance as a component of waterfowl habitat quality. Ducks Unlimited, Inc., Valley Habitats: a technical guidance series for private land managers in California's Central Valley. Number 17. 12pp.

Braun, C.E., K.W. Harmon, J.A. Jackson, and C.D. Littlefield. 1978. Management of National Wildlife Refuges in the United States: its impacts on birds. Wilson Bull. 90:309-321.

Brauning, D. W., editor. 1992. Atlas of breeding birds in Pennsylvania. University of Pittsburgh Press, Pittsburgh, Pennsylvania. 484 pp.

Brush, T. 1991. Nesting ecology of Prothonotary Warblers in eastern Iowa: 1988-1991. Report submitted to the Iowa Department of Natural Resources. Unpublished.

Bushman, E. S., and G. D. Therres. 1988. Habitat management guidelines for forest interior breeding birds of coastal Maryland. Maryland Dept. Natural Resources, Wildlife Tech. Publ. 88-1. 50 pp.

Carr, J.L., A.A. Bass, and L.B. White. In preparation. Herpetofauna of Black Bayou Lake National Wildlife Refuge.

Carver, Erin and James Caudill. 2007. Banking on Nature 2006: The Economic Benefits to Local Communities of National Wildlife Refuge Visitation. Division of Economics, U.S. Fish and Wildlife Service. Washington, DC.

Chambers, A., D.M. Kline, L. Vimmerstedt, A. Diem, D. Dismukes, and D. Mesyanzhinov. 2005. Comparison of Methods for Estimating the Nitros Oxide Emission Impacts of Energy Efficiency and Renewable Energy Projects: Shreveport, Louisiana Case Study., Technical Report NREL/TP-710-37721, Revised July 2005., National Renewable Energy Laboratory.

Charlebois, P. 2002. Non-native aquatic and wetland plants in the United States. National Invasive Aquatic Plant Outreach and Research Initiative. Sea Grant Program.

Clark, M.K. 1990. Roosting ecology of the eastern big-eared, Plecotus rafinesquii, in North Carolina. Unpublished M.S. Thesis. North Carolina State University, Raleigh, North Carolina.

Clark, M.K., A. Black, M. Kiser. 1998. Draft Report C7745.11: Roosting and Foraging Activities of Corynorhinus rafinesquii and Myotis austroriparius within the Francis Beidler Forest, South Carolina. North Carolina State Museum of Natural Sciences, Raleigh, North Carolina, 10 pp.

Conservation Commission of Missouri. February 2002. Managing Wetlands: Moist-Soil Management (Seasonally Flooded Impoundments). Missouri Department of Conservation. 2pp.

Cochran, S.M. 1999. Roosting and habitat use by Rafinesque's big-eared bat and other species in a bottomland hardwood forest ecosystem. M.S. Thesis. Arkansas State Univ., 50 pp.

Corn, P.S., M.J. Adams, W.A. Battaglin, A.L. Gallant, D.L. James, M. Knutson, C.A. Langtimm, J.R. Sauer. 2005. Amphibian Research and Monitoring Initiative--Concepts and Implementation. U.S. Geological Survey Scientific Investigations Report 2005–5015, 23 p.

Davis, J.B. 2001. Survival, recruitment, and management of box-nesting wood ducks in Mississippi and Alabama. PhD Dissertation. Mississippi State University. 185pp.

Dobie, J.L. 1971. Reproduction and growth in the Alligator Snapping Turtle, Macroclemys temminckii (Troost). Copeia 1971:645-658.

Dundee, H.A. and D.A. Rossman. 1989. The Amphibians and Reptiles of Louisiana. Baton Rouge: Louisiana State University Press, xi + 300 pp.

Engeman, R.M., R.E. Martin, H.T. Smith, J. Woolard, C.K. Crady, S.A. Shwiff, B. Constantin, M. Stahl and J. Griner. 2005. Dramatic reduction in predation on marine turtle nests through improved predator monitoring and management. Oryx 39:318-326.

Fredrickson, L.H. 1996. Moist-soil management, 30 years of field experimentation. International Waterfowl Symposium. 7:168-177.

Fredrickson, L.H., and T.S. Taylor. 1982. Management of seasonally flooded impoundments for wildlife., U.S. Fish and Wildlife Service Resource Publication 148, Washington, D.C. USA.

Gabrielson, G.W., and E.N. Smith. 1995. "Physiological responses of wildlife to disturbance." Pages 95-107 in R.L. Knight and K.J. Gutzwiller, ed. Wildlife and Recreationists: coexistence through management and research. Island Press, Washington, D.C. 372pp.

Greenbaum, E. 2000. Geographic distribution: Hyla avivoca (Bird-voiced treefrog). Herpetological Review 31:251.

Guillory, H. D. 1987. "Cavity competition and suspected predation on Prothonotary Warberls by PEROMYSCUS spp." Journal of Field Ornithology 58:425-7.

Gooding, G. and R. Langford. 2004. Characteristics of tree roosts of Rafinesque's big-eared bat and southeastern bat in Northeastern Louisiana. Southwestern Naturalist 49(1):61-67

Harrel, J.B., C.M. Allen, and S.J. Hebert. 1996. Movements and habitat use of subadult Alligator Snapping Turtles (Macroclemys temminckii) in Louisiana. Amer. Midl. Nat. 135:60-67.

Harvey, M.J. 1992. Bats of the eastern United States. Arkansas Game & Fish Commission and U.S. Fish & Wildlife Service, 64pp.

Harvey, M.J., J.S. Altenbach, and T.L. Best. 1999. Bats of the United States. Arkansas Game & Fish Commission and U.S. Fish & Wildlife Service, 64pp.

Heitmeyer, M.E., and D.G. Raveling. 1988 . Winter resource use by three species of dabbling ducks in Calofornia. Dept. Wildlife and Fisheries Biology, Univ. of Calif., Davis. Final Report to Delta Waterfowl and Wetlands Research Center, Portage La Prairie, Manitoba, Canada. 200 pp.

Hunter, B.E. 2000. Wood duck use rates of small versus large nest boxes. MS Thesis. Louisiana State University.

Jenson, S.L. and S.G. George. 1993. Geographic distribution: Hemidactylus turcicus (Mediterranean Gecko). Herpetological Review 24:154.

Johnson, R.E. 1964. Fish and fowl. Pages 453-458 in J.P. Linduska, editor. Waterfowl tomorrow. U.S. Dept. of Interior, Fish & Wildlife Service. U.S. Govt. Printing Office, Washington D.C.

Kaminski, R. and B. Davis. 2002. Wood Duck Broods in Dixie: Striving to Survive Early Life. Research Advances, Vol. 7, No. 2, Mississippi State University, Forest and Wildlife Research Center, Mississippi State, MS. 4pp.

Keppie, D.M. and R.M. Whiting Jr. 1994. American Woodcock; The Birds of North America. Vol. 3, No. 100. American Orinithologists' Union. The Academy of Natural Sciences of Philadelphia.

Kilgore, K.J., E.D. Dibble, and J.J. Hoover. 1993. Relationships between fish and aquatic plants: A plan of study. Misc. Paper A 93-1. U.S. Army Corps of Engineers, Waterways Experimental Station. Vicksburg, MS.

Kross, J. 2006. Conservation of waste rice and estimates of moist-soil seed abundance for wintering waterfowl in the Mississippi Alluvial Valley, Thesis, Mississippi State University, Mississippi State, MS. 56 pp.

Leberman, R. C. 1992. Prothonotary Warbler. Pages 334-5 in D. W. Brauning (editor). Atlas of breeding birds in Pennsylvania. University of Pittsburgh Press, Pittsburgh, Pennsylvania.

Leonard, Jerry. 2008. Wildlife Watching in the U.S.: The Economic Impacts on National and State Economies in 2006 – Addendum to the 2006 National Survey of Fishing, Hunting, and Wildlife-Associated Recreation. Report 2006-1. Wildlife and Sport Fish Restoration Programs. U.S. Fish and Wildlife Service. Arlington, VA.

Lester, Gary D., Stephen G. Sorensen, Patricia L. Faulkner, Christopher S. Reid, and Ines E. Maxit. 2005. Louisaina Comprhensive Wildlife Conservation Strategy. Louisiana Department of Wildlife and Fisheries. Baton Rouge, LA.

LMVJV Forest Resource Conservation Working Group. 2007. Restoration, Management, and Monitoring of Forest Resources in the Mississippi Alluvial Valley: Recommendations for Enhancing Wildlife Habitat. Edited by R. Wilson, K. Ribbeck, S. King, and D. Twedt, 88 pp.

Loesch, C.R., K.J. Reinecke, and C.K. Baxter. 1944. Lower Mississippi Valley Joint Venture Evaluation Plan. U.S. Fish and Wildlife Service, Lower Mississippi Valley Joint Venture, Vicksburg, Mississippi, USA.

Louisiana Department of Environmental Quality. 1998. Water Quality Inventory, Section 305b Report. Water Quality Management Division, Non-point Source Unit. Baton Rouge, LA.

Louisiana Geologic Survey. 1990. Generalized geology of Louisiana. Information obtained from the website http://www.lgs.lsu.edu/lgs/gengeo.html.

Low, J.B. and F.C. Bellrose, Jr. 1944. The seed and vegetable yield of waterfowl food plants in the Illinois River Valley. Journal of Wildlife Management. 8: 7-22.

Mayer, J. L. and Brisbin, L. Jr. 1991. Wild pigs in the United States: Their history, comparative morphology, and current status. The University of Georgia Press, 314pp.

Meyer, Kenneth D. 1995. American Swallow-Tailed Kite; The Birds of North America. Vol. 4, No. 138. American Orinithologists' Union. The Academy of Natural Sciences of Philadelphia.

Mississippi Alluvial Valley. Pages 203-247 in L.M. Smith, R.L. Pederson, and R.M. Kaminski, eds. Habitat management for migrating and wintering waterfowl in North America. Texas Tech. Univ. Press, Lubbock 560 pp.

New Employee Handbook. U.S. Fish and Wildlife Service

New World Research , Inco. 1981. A cultural resources survey of pre-selected portions of the Upper Ouachita National Wildlife Refuge, Union and Morehouse Parishes, LA. Project Report. 65pp.

NRC (National Research Council). 1993. A Biological Survey for the Nation. Washington, DC: National Academy Press, xv + 205 pp.

Oliarnyk, C.J. and R.J. Robertson. 1996. Breeding behaviour and reproductive success of Cerulean Warblers in southeastern Ontario. Wilson Bull., 108(4):673-684.

Paulus, S.L. 1984. Activity budgets of nonbreeding gadwalls in Louisiana. J. Wildlife Management 48:371-380

Pease, M.L., R.K. Rose, and M.J. Butler. 2005. Effects of human disturbances on the behavior of wintering ducks. Wild. Soc. Bull. 33(1):103-112.

Petit, L. J. 1991. Adaptive tolerance of cowbird parasitism by Prothonotary Warblers: a consequence of nest-site limitation? Animal Behavior 41:425-32.

Pritchard, P.C.H. 1980. The Alligator Snapping Turtle: Biology and Conservation. Milwaukee Public Museum, 104 pp.

Prosser, D. J., and R. P. Brooks. 1998. A verified Habitat Suitability Index for the Louisiana Waterthrush. Journal of Field Ornithology 69(2):288-298.

Reed, R. N., J. Congdon, and J.W. Gibbons. 2002. The alligator snapping turtle (Macrochelys [Macroclemys] temminckii): A review of ecology, life history, and conservation, with demographic analyses of the sustainability of take from wild populations. Savannah River Ecology Laboratory, University of Georgia, 16 pp.

Reinecke, K.J. and C.K. Baxter. 1996. Waterfowl Habitat Management in the Mississippi Alluvial Valley. Pages 159-167 in 7th International Waterfowl Symposium. J.T. Ratti, Editor.

Reinecke, K.J. and C.R. Loesch. 1996. Integrating research and management to conserve wildfowl (Anatidae) and wetlands in the Mississippi Alluvial Valley, USA. Gibier Faune Sauvage, Game and Wildlife. 13: 927-940.

Reinecke, K.J., R.M. Kaminski, D.J. Moorehead, J.D. Hodges, and J.R. Nassar. 1989. Mississippi Alluvial Valley. Pp. 203-247, Habitat Management for Migrating and Wintering Waterfowl in North America, eds. L.M. Smith, R.L. Pederson, and R.M. Kaminski. 1989. Texas Tech University Press. 506pp.

Robbins, C.S., J.W. Fitzpatrick, and P.B. Hamel. 1992. A warbler in trouble: DENDROICA CERULEA. Pages 549-562 IN J.M. Hagan III, and D.W. Johnson, editors. 1992. Ecology and conservation of neotropical migrant landbirds. Smithsonian Institution Press, Washington, D.C. xiii + 609 pp.

Robinson, S.K. 1993. Trans. North Am. Wildlife Natural Resources Conference Vol. 58. p. 379.

Rosenzweig, A. H., J. Hatfield, S. Trichell, M. Rachel, M. Antwine, B. Lynch. 2007. New distributional records for amphibians and reptiles in northeastern Louisiana. Herpetological Review 38:243-244.

Shea D., C.S. Hofeltet, D.R. Luellen, A.Huysman, P.R. Lazaro, R. Zarzecki, and J.R. Kelly. 2001. Chemical contamination at National Wildlife Refuges in the Lower Mississippi River Ecosystem. Report by NC State University to the US Fish and Wildlife Service, Atlanta, GA. 40pp.

Sloan, K.N. and J.E. Lovich. 1995. Exploitation of Alligator Snapping Turtle, Macroclemys temminckii, in Louisiana: a case study. Chelonian Conserv. Biol. 1:221-222.

Sloan, K.N. and D. Taylor. 1987. Habitats and movements of adult alligator snapping turtles in northeast Louisiana. Proc. Ann. Conf. Southeast. Assoc. Fish Wildl. Agencies 41:343-348.

Strader, R.W., and P.H. Stinson. 2005. Moist Soil Guidelines for the U.S. Fish and Wildlife Service, Southeast Region. Division of Migratory Birds, U.S. Fish and Wildlife Service. Jackson, MS.

Trauth, S.E., J.D. Wilhide and A. Holt. 1998. Population structure and movement patterns of Alligator Snapping Turtles (Macroclemys temminckii) in northeastern Arkansas. Chelonian Conserv. Biol. 3:64-70.

Trousdale, A.W. and D.C. Beckett. 2005. Characteristics of tree roosts of Rafinesque's Big-eared Bat (*Corynorthinus rafinesquii*) in Southeastern Mississippi. American Midland Naturalist 154: 442-449.

Tucker, A.D. and K.N. Sloan. 1997. Growth and reproductive estimates from Alligator Snapping Turtles, Macroclemys temminckii, taken by commercial harvest in Louisiana. Chelonian Conserv. Biol. 2:587-592.

U.S. Department of Agriculture, Soil Conservation Service. 1974. Soil Survey of Ouachita Parish, Louisiana. U.S. Government Printing Office, Washington D.C., 80 pp.

U.S. Fish and Wildlife Service, Division of Migratory Birds. 2003a. Increasing Wood Duck
Productivity: Guidelines for Management and Banding,
USFWS Lands (Southeast Region). 16 pp.

U.S. Fish and Wildlife Service. 2003b. Recovery plan for the red-cockaded woodpecker (*Picoides
borealis*): second revision. U.S. Fish and Wildlife Service, Atlanta, GA. 296 pp.

U.S. Department of Interior. 2003. U.S. Fish and Wildlife Service and U.S. Department of Commerce,
U.S. Census Bureau. "2001 National Survey of Fishing, Hunting, and
Wildlife-Associated Recreation – Louisiana."

U.S. Fish and Wildlife Service. 1990. American woodcock management plan. USFWS,
Office of Migratory Bird Management. 11 pp.

U.S. Fish and Wildlife Service. 1999. Species of Special Management Concern List, December, 1999.

Wang, K.K. 1952. Geology of Ouachita Parish. Department of Conservation Louisiana Geological
Survey, Baton Rouge, LA, 126 pp.

Wolder, M. 1993. Disturbance of wintering northern pintails at Sacramento National Wildlife Refuge,
California. M.S. Thesis, Humbolt State Univ., Arcata. 62pp.

Wood, G. W. and Roark, D. N. 1980. Food habits of feral hogs in Coastal South Carolina. J.
Wildlife Management, 44(2): 506-511.

Woosley, L.B. 2005. Population structure and reproduction of Alligator Snapping Turtles, Macrochelys
temminckii, at Black Bayou Lake National Wildlife Refuge [Master of Science thesis].
Monroe, LA: University of Louisiana at Monroe. 59 p.

Yarrow, G. K. 1988. The potential for inter-specific resource competition between white-tailed deer
and feral hogs in the Post Oak Savannah Region of Texas.
Diss. Abstr. Int. B. Sci. Eng., 48(10): 283737.

Appendix C. Relevant Legal Mandates and Executive Orders

STATUTE	DESCRIPTION
Administrative Procedures Act (1946)	Outlines administrative procedures to be followed by federal agencies with respect to identification of information to be made public; publication of material in the Federal Register; maintenance of records; attendance and notification requirements for specific meetings and hearings; issuance of licenses; and review of agency actions.
American Antiquities Act of 1906	Provides penalties for unauthorized collection, excavation, or destruction of historic or prehistoric ruins, monuments, or objects of antiquity on lands owned or controlled by the United States. The Act authorizes the President to designate as national monuments objects or areas of historic or scientific interest on lands owned or controlled by the Unites States.
American Indian Religious Freedom Act of 1978	Protects the inherent right of Native Americans to believe, express, and exercise their traditional religions, including access to important sites, use and possession of sacred objects, and the freedom to worship through ceremonial and traditional rites.
Americans With Disabilities Act of 1990	Intended to prevent discrimination of and make American society more accessible to people with disabilities. The Act requires reasonable accommodations to be made in employment, public services, public accommodations, and telecommunications for persons with disabilities.
Anadromous Fish Conservation Act of 1965, as amended	Authorizes the Secretaries of Interior and Commerce to enter into cooperative agreements with states and other non-federal interests for conservation, development, and enhancement of anadromous fish and contribute up to 50 percent as the federal share of the cost of carrying out such agreements. Reclamation construction programs for water resource projects needed solely for such fish are also authorized.
Archaeological Resources Protection Act of 1979, as amended.	This Act strengthens and expands the protective provisions of the Antiquities Act of 1906 regarding archaeological resources. It also revised the permitting process for archaeological research.
Architectural Barriers Act of 1968	Requires that buildings and facilities designed, constructed, or altered with federal funds, or leased by a federal agency, must comply with standards for physical accessibility.
Bald and Golden Eagle Protection Act of 1940, as amended	Prohibits the possession, sale or transport of any bald or golden eagle, alive or dead, or part, nest, or egg except as permitted by the Secretary of the Interior for scientific or exhibition purposes, or for the religious purposes of Indians.

STATUTE	DESCRIPTION
Bankhead-Jones Farm Tenant Act of 1937	Directs the Secretary of Agriculture to develop a program of land conservation and utilization in order to correct maladjustments in land use and thus assist in such things as control of soil erosion, reforestation, conservation of natural resources and protection of fish and wildlife. Some early refuges and hatcheries were established under authority of this Act.
Cave Resources Protection Act of 1988	Established requirements for the management and protection of caves and their resources on federal lands, including allowing the land managing agencies to withhold the location of caves from the public, and requiring permits for any removal or collecting activities in caves on federal lands.
Clean Air Act of 1970	Regulates air emissions from area, stationary, and mobile sources. This Act and its amendments charge federal land managers with direct responsibility to protect the "air quality and related values" of land under their control. These values include fish, wildlife, and their habitats.
Clean Water Act of 1974, as amended	This Act and its amendments have as its objective the restoration and maintenance of the chemical, physical, and biological integrity of the Nation's waters. Section 401 of the Act requires that federally permitted activities comply with the Clean Water Act standards, state water quality laws, and any other appropriate state laws. Section 404 charges the U.S. Army Corps of Engineers with regulating discharge of dredge or fill materials into waters of the United States, including wetlands.
Coastal Barrier Resources Act of 1982 (CBRA)	Identifies undeveloped coastal barriers along the Atlantic and Gulf Coasts and included them in the John H. Chafee Coastal Barrier Resources System (CBRS). The objectives of the act are to minimize loss of human life, reduce wasteful federal expenditures, and minimize the damage to natural resources by restricting most federal expenditures that encourage development within the CBRS.
Coastal Barrier Improvement Act of 1990	Reauthorized the Coastal Barrier Resources Act (CBRA), expanded the CBRS to include undeveloped coastal barriers along the Great Lakes and in the Caribbean, and established "Otherwise Protected Areas (OPAs)." The Service is responsible for maintaining official maps, consulting with federal agencies that propose spending federal funds within the CBRS and OPAs, and making recommendations to Congress about proposed boundary revisions.
Coastal Wetlands Planning, Protection, and Restoration (1990)	Authorizes the Director of the Fish and Wildlife Service to participate in the development of a Louisiana coastal wetlands restoration program, participate in the development and oversight of a coastal wetlands conservation program, and lead in the implementation and administration of a national coastal wetlands grant program.

STATUTE	DESCRIPTION
Coastal Zone Management Act of 1972, as amended	Established a voluntary national program within the Department of Commerce to encourage coastal states to develop and implement coastal zone management plans and requires that "any federal activity within or outside of the coastal zone that affects any land or water use or natural resource of the coastal zone" shall be "consistent to the maximum extent practicable with the enforceable policies" of a state's coastal zone management plan. The law includes an Enhancement Grants Program for protecting, restoring, or enhancing existing coastal wetlands or creating new coastal wetlands. It also established the National Estuarine Research Reserve System, guidelines for estuarine research, and financial assistance for land acquisition.
Emergency Wetlands Resources Act of 1986	This Act authorized the purchase of wetlands from Land and Water Conservation Fund moneys, removing a prior prohibition on such acquisitions. The Act requires the Secretary to establish a National Wetlands Priority Conservation Plan, required the states to include wetlands in their Comprehensive Outdoor Recreation Plans, and transfers to the Migratory Bird Conservation Fund amounts equal to import duties on arms and ammunition. It also established entrance fees at national wildlife refuges.
Endangered Species Act of 1973, as amended	Provides for the conservation of threatened and endangered species of fish, wildlife, and plants by federal action and by encouraging the establishment of state programs. It provides for the determination and listing of threatened and endangered species and the designation of critical habitats. Section 7 requires refuge managers to perform internal consultation before initiating projects that affect or may affect endangered species.
Environmental Education Act of 1990	This Act established the Office of Environmental Education within the U.S. Environmental Protection Agency to develop and administer a federal environmental education program in consultation with other federal natural resource management agencies, including the Fish and Wildlife Service.
Estuary Protection Act of 1968	Authorized the Secretary of the Interior, in cooperation with other federal agencies and the states, to study and inventory estuaries of the United States, including land and water of the Great Lakes, and to determine whether such areas should be acquired for protection. The Secretary is also required to encourage state and local governments to consider the importance of estuaries in their planning activities relative to federal natural resource grants. In approving any state grants for acquisition of estuaries, the Secretary was required to establish conditions to ensure the permanent protection of estuaries.

STATUTE	DESCRIPTION
Estuaries and Clean Waters Act of 2000	This law creates a federal interagency council that includes the Director of the Fish and Wildlife Service, the Secretary of the Army for Civil Works, the Secretary of Agriculture, the Administrator of the Environmental Protection Agency and the Administrator for the National Oceanic and Atmospheric Administration. The council is charged with developing a national estuary habitat restoration strategy and providing grants to entities to restore and protect estuary habitat to promote the strategy.
Food Security Act of 1985, as amended (Farm Bill)	The Act contains several provisions that contribute to wetland conservation. The Swampbuster provisions state that farmers who convert wetlands for the purpose of planting after enactment of the law are ineligible for most farmer program subsidies. It also established the Wetland Reserve Program to restore and protect wetlands through easements and restoration of the functions and values of wetlands on such easement areas.
Farmland Protection Policy Act of 1981, as amended	The purpose of this law is to minimize the extent to which federal programs contribute to the unnecessary conversion of farmland to nonagricultural uses. Federal programs include construction projects and the management of federal lands.
Federal Advisory Committee Act (1972), as amended	Governs the establishment of and procedures for committees that provide advice to the federal government. Advisory committees may be established only if they will serve a necessary, nonduplicative function. Committees must be strictly advisory unless otherwise specified and meetings must be open to the public.
Federal Coal Leasing Amendment Act of 1976	Provided that nothing in the Mining Act, the Mineral Leasing Act, or the Mineral Leasing Act for Acquired Lands authorized mining coal on refuges.
Federal-Aid Highways Act of 1968	Established requirements for approval of federal highways through national wildlife refuges and other designated areas to preserve the natural beauty of such areas. The Secretary of Transportation is directed to consult with the Secretary of the Interior and other federal agencies before approving any program or project requiring the use of land under their jurisdiction.
Federal Noxious Weed Act of 1990, as amended	The Secretary of Agriculture was given the authority to designate plants as noxious weeds and to cooperate with other federal, State and local agencies, farmers' associations, and private individuals in measures to control, eradicate, prevent, or retard the spread of such weeds. The Act requires each Federal land-managing agency, including the Fish and Wildlife Service, to designate an office or person to coordinate a program to control such plants on the agency's land and implement cooperative agreements with the states, including integrated management systems to control undesirable plants.

STATUTE	DESCRIPTION
Fish and Wildlife Act of 1956	Establishes a comprehensive national fish, shellfish, and wildlife resources policy with emphasis on the commercial fishing industry but also includes the inherent right of every citizen and resident to fish for pleasure, enjoyment, and betterment and to maintain and increase public opportunities for recreational use of fish and wildlife resources. Among other things, it authorizes the Secretary of the Interior to take such steps as may be required for the development, advancement, management, conservation, and protection of fish and wildlife resources including, but not limited to, research, development of existing facilities, and acquisition by purchase or exchange of land and water or interests therein.
Fish and Wildlife Conservation Act of 1980, as amended	Requires the Service to monitor non-gamebird species, identify species of management concern, and implement conservation measures to preclude the need for listing under the Endangered Species Act.
Fish and Wildlife Coordination Act of 1958	Promotes equal consideration and coordination of wildlife conservation with other water resource development programs by requiring consultation with the Fish and Wildlife Service and the state fish and wildlife agencies where the "waters of a stream or other body of water are proposed or authorized, permitted or licensed to be impounded, diverted…or otherwise controlled or modified" by any agency under federal permit or license.
Improvement Act of 1978	This act was passed to improve the administration of fish and wildlife programs and amends several earlier laws, including the Refuge Recreation Act, the National Wildlife Refuge System Administration Act, and the Fish and Wildlife Act of 1956. It authorizes the Secretary to accept gifts and bequests of real and personal property on behalf of the United States. It also authorizes the use of volunteers on Service projects and appropriations to carry out volunteer programs.
Fishery (Magnuson) Conservation and Management Act of 1976	Established Regional Fishery Management Councils comprised of federal and state officials, including the Fish and Wildlife Service. It provides for regulation of foreign fishing and vessel fishing permits.
Freedom of Information Act, 1966	Requires all federal agencies to make available to the public for inspection and copying administrative staff manuals and staff instructions; official, published and unpublished policy statements; final orders deciding case adjudication; and other documents. Special exemptions have been reserved for nine categories of privileged material. The Act requires the party seeking the information to pay reasonable search and duplication costs.
Geothermal Steam Act of 1970, as amended	Authorizes and governs the lease of geothermal steam and related resources on public lands. Section 15 c of the Act prohibits issuing geothermal leases on virtually all Service-administrative lands.

STATUTE	DESCRIPTION
Lacey Act of 1900, as amended	Originally designed to help states protect their native game animals and to safeguard U.S. crop production from harmful foreign species, this Act prohibits interstate and international transport and commerce of fish, wildlife or plants taken in violation of domestic or foreign laws. It regulates the introduction to America of foreign species.
Land and Water Conservation Fund Act of 1948	This Act provides funding through receipts from the sale of surplus federal land, appropriations from oil and gas receipts from the outer continental shelf, and other sources for land acquisition under several authorities. Appropriations from the fund may be used for matching grants to states for outdoor recreation projects and for land acquisition by various federal agencies, including the Fish and Wildlife Service.
Marine Mammal Protection Act of 1972, as amended	The 1972 Marine Mammal Protection Act established a federal responsibility to conserve marine mammals with management vested in the Department of the Interior for sea otter, walrus, polar bear, dugong, and manatee. The Department of Commerce is responsible for cetaceans and pinnipeds, other than the walrus. With certain specified exceptions, the Act establishes a moratorium on the taking and importation of marine mammals, as well as products taken from them.
Migratory Bird Conservation Act of 1929	Established a Migratory Bird Conservation Commission to approve areas recommended by the Secretary of the Interior for acquisition with Migratory Bird Conservation Funds. The role of the commission was expanded by the North American Wetland Conservation Act to include approving wetlands acquisition, restoration, and enhancement proposals recommended by the North American Wetlands Conservation Council.
Migratory Bird Hunting and Conservation Stamp Act of 1934	Also commonly referred to as the "Duck Stamp Act," requires waterfowl hunters 16 years of age or older to possess a valid federal hunting stamp. Receipts from the sale of the stamp are deposited into the Migratory Bird Conservation Fund for the acquisition of migratory bird refuges.
Migratory Bird Treaty Act of 1918, as amended	This Act implements various treaties and conventions between the United States and Canada, Japan, Mexico, and the former Soviet Union for the protection of migratory birds. Except as allowed by special regulations, this Act makes it unlawful to pursue, hunt, kill, capture, possess, buy, sell, purchase, barter, export or import any migratory bird, part, nest, egg, or product.
Mineral Leasing Act for Acquired Lands (1947), as amended	Authorizes and governs mineral leasing on acquired public lands.

STATUTE	DESCRIPTION
Minerals Leasing Act of 1920, as amended	Authorizes and governs leasing of public lands for development of deposits of coal, oil, gas, and other hydrocarbons; sulphur; phosphate; potassium; and sodium. Section 185 of this title contains provisions relating to granting rights-of-way over federal lands for pipelines.
Mining Act of 1872, as amended	Authorizes and governs prospecting and mining for the so-called "hardrock" minerals (i.e., gold and silver) on public lands.
National and Community Service Act of 1990	Authorizes several programs to engage citizens of the U.S. in full- and/or part-time projects designed to combat illiteracy and poverty, provide job skills, enhance educational skills, and fulfill environmental needs. Among other things, this law establishes the American Conservation and Youth Service Corps to engage young adults in approved human and natural resource projects, which will benefit the public or are carried out on federal or Indian lands.
National Environmental Policy Act of 1969	Requires analysis, public comment, and reporting for environmental impacts of federal actions. It stipulates the factors to be considered in environmental impact statements, and requires that federal agencies employ an interdisciplinary approach in related decision-making and develop means to ensure that unqualified environmental values are given appropriate consideration, along with economic and technical considerations.
National Historic Preservation Act of 1966, as amended	It establishes a National Register of Historic Places and a program of matching grants for preservation of significant historical features. Federal agencies are directed to take into account the effects of their actions on items or sites listed or eligible for listing in the National Register.
National Trails System Act (1968), as amended	Established the National Trails System to protect the recreational, scenic, and historic values of some important trails. National recreation trails may be established by the Secretaries of Interior or Agriculture on land wholly or partly within their jurisdiction, with the consent of the involved state(s), and other land managing agencies, if any. National scenic and national historic trails may only be designated by Congress. Several national trails cross units of the National Wildlife Refuge System.
National Wildlife Refuge System Administration Act of 1966	Prior to 1966, there was no single federal law that governed the administration of the various national wildlife refuges that had been established. This Act defines the National Wildlife Refuge System and authorizes the Secretary of the Interior to permit any use of a refuge provided such use is compatible with the major purposes(s) for which the refuge was established.

STATUTE	DESCRIPTION
National Wildlife Refuge System Improvement Act of 1997	This Act amends the National Wildlife Refuge System Administration Act of 1966. This Act defines the mission of the National Wildlife Refuge System, establishes the legitimacy and appropriateness of six priority wildlife-dependent public uses, establishes a formal process for determining compatible uses of Refuge System lands, identifies the Secretary of the Interior as responsible for managing and protecting the Refuge System, and requires the development of a comprehensive conservation plan for all refuges outside of Alaska.
Native American Graves Protection and Repatriation Act of 1990	Requires federal agencies and museums to inventory, determine ownership of, and repatriate certain cultural items and human remains under their control or possession. The Act also addresses the repatriation of cultural items inadvertently discovered by construction activities on lands managed by the agency.
Neotropical Migratory Bird Conservation Act of 2000	Establishes a matching grant program to fund projects that promote the conservation of neotropical migratory birds in the united States, Latin America, and the Caribbean.
North American Wetlands Conservation Act of 1989	Provides funding and administrative direction for implementation of the North American Waterfowl Management Plan and the Tripartite Agreement on wetlands between Canada, the United States, and Mexico. The North American Wetlands Conservation Council was created to recommend projects to be funded under the Act to the Migratory Bird Conservation Commission. Available funds may be expended for up to 50 percent of the United States' share cost of wetlands conservation projects in Canada, Mexico, or the United States (or 100 percent of the cost of projects on federal lands).
Refuge Recreation Act of 1962, as amended	This Act authorizes the Secretary of the Interior to administer refuges, hatcheries, and other conservation areas for recreational use, when such uses do not interfere with the area's primary purposes. It authorizes construction and maintenance of recreational facilities and the acquisition of land for incidental fish and wildlife-oriented recreational development or protection of natural resources. It also authorizes the charging of fees for public uses.
Partnerships for Wildlife Act of 1992	Establishes a Wildlife Conservation and Appreciation Fund to receive appropriated funds and donations from the National Fish and Wildlife Foundation and other private sources to assist the state fish and game agencies in carrying out their responsibilities for conservation of non-game species. The funding formula is no more that 1/3 federal funds, at least 1/3 foundation funds, and at least 1/3 state funds.
Refuge Revenue Sharing Act of 1935, as amended	Provided for payments to counties in lieu of taxes from areas administered by the Fish and Wildlife Service. Counties are required to pass payments along to other units of local government within the county, which suffer losses in tax revenues due to the establishment of Service areas.

STATUTE	DESCRIPTION
Rehabilitation Act of 1973	Requires nondiscrimination in the employment practices of federal agencies of the executive branch and contractors. It also requires all federally assisted programs, services, and activities to be available to people with disabilities.
Rivers and Harbors Appropriations Act of 1899, as amended	Requires the authorization by the U.S. Army Corps of Engineers prior to any work in, on, over, or under a navigable water of the United States. The Fish and Wildlife Coordination Act provides authority for the Service to review and comment on the effects on fish and wildlife activities proposed to be undertaken or permitted by the Corps of Engineers. Service concerns include contaminated sediments associated with dredge or fill projects in navigable waters.
Sikes Act (1960), as amended	Provides for the cooperation by the Departments of Interior and Defense with state agencies in planning, development, and maintenance of fish and wildlife resources and outdoor recreation facilities on military reservations throughout the United States. It requires the Secretary of each military department to use trained professionals to manage the wildlife and fishery resource under his jurisdiction, and requires that federal and state fish and wildlife agencies be given priority in management of fish and wildlife activities on military reservations.
Transfer of Certain Real Property for Wildlife Conservation Purposes Act of 1948	This Act provides that upon determination by the Administrator of the General Services Administration, real property no longer needed by a federal agency can be transferred, without reimbursement, to the Secretary of the Interior if the land has particular value for migratory birds, or to a state agency for other wildlife conservation purposes.
Transportation Equity Act for the 21st Century (1998)	Established the Refuge Roads Program, requires transportation planning that includes public involvement, and provides funding for approved public use roads and trails and associated parking lots, comfort stations, and bicycle/pedestrian facilities.
Uniform Relocation and Assistance and Real Property Acquisition Policies Act (1970), as amended	Provides for uniform and equitable treatment of persons who sell their homes, businesses, or farms to the Service. The Act requires that any purchase offer be no less than the fair market value of the property.
Water Resources Planning Act of 1965	Established Water Resources Council to be composed of Cabinet representatives including the Secretary of the Interior. The Council reviews river basin plans with respect to agricultural, urban, energy, industrial, recreational and fish and wildlife needs. The Act also established a grant program to assist States in participating in the development of related comprehensive water and land use plans.
Wild and Scenic Rivers Act of 1968, as amended	This Act selects certain rivers of the nation possessing remarkable scenic, recreational, geologic, fish and wildlife, historic, cultural, or other similar values; preserves them in a free-flowing condition; and protects their local environments.

STATUTE	DESCRIPTION
Wilderness Act of 1964, as amended	This Act directs the Secretary of the Interior to review every roadless area of 5,000 acres or more and every roadless island regardless of size within the National Wildlife Refuge System and to recommend suitability of each such area. The Act permits certain activities within designated wilderness areas that do not alter natural processes. Wilderness values are preserved through a "minimum tool" management approach, which requires refuge managers to use the least intrusive methods, equipment, and facilities necessary for administering the areas.
Youth Conservation Corps Act of 1970	Established a permanent Youth Conservation Corps (YCC) program within the Departments of Interior and Agriculture. Within the Service, YCC participants perform many tasks on refuges, fish hatcheries, and research stations.

EXECUTIVE ORDERS	DESCRIPTIONS
EO 11593, Protection and Enhancement of the Cultural Environment (1971)	States that if the Service proposes any development activities that may affect the archaeological or historic sites, the Service will consult with Federal and State Historic Preservation Officers to comply with Section 106 of the National Historic Preservation Act of 1966, as amended.
EO 11644, Use of Off-road Vehicles on Public Land (1972)	Established policies and procedures to ensure that the use of off-road vehicles on public lands will be controlled and directed so as to protect the resources of those lands, to promote the safety of all users of those lands, and to minimize conflicts among the various uses of those lands.
EO 11988, Floodplain Management (1977)	The purpose of this Executive Order is to prevent federal agencies from contributing to the "adverse impacts associated with occupancy and modification of floodplains" and the "direct or indirect support of floodplain development." In the course of fulfilling their respective authorities, federal agencies "shall take action to reduce the risk of flood loss, to minimize the impact of floods on human safety, health and welfare, and to restore and preserve the natural and beneficial values served by floodplains."
EO 11989 (1977), Amends Section 2 of EO 11644	Directs agencies to close areas negatively impacted by off-road vehicles.

EXECUTIVE ORDERS	DESCRIPTIONS
EO 11990, Protection of Wetlands (1977)	Federal agencies are directed to provide leadership and take action to minimize the destruction, loss of degradation of wetlands, and to preserve and enhance the natural and beneficial values of wetlands.
EO 12372, Intergovernmental Review of Federal Programs (1982)	Seeks to foster intergovernmental partnerships by requiring federal agencies to use the state process to determine and address concerns of state and local elected officials with proposed federal assistance and development programs.
EO 12898, Environmental Justice (1994)	Requires federal agencies to identify and address disproportionately high and adverse effects of its programs, policies, and activities on minority and low-income populations.
EO 12906, Coordinating Geographical Data Acquisition and Access (1994), Amended by EO 13286 (2003). Amendment of EOs and other actions in connection with transfer of certain functions to Secretary of DHS.	Recommended that the executive branch develop, in cooperation with state, local, and tribal governments, and the private sector, a coordinated National Spatial Data Infrastructure to support public and private sector applications of geospatial data. Of particular importance to comprehensive conservation planning is the National Vegetation Classification System (NVCS), which is the adopted standard for vegetation mapping. Using NVCS facilitates the compilation of regional and national summaries, which in turn, can provide an ecosystem context for individual refuges.
EO 12962, Recreational Fisheries (1995)	Federal agencies are directed to improve the quantity, function, sustainable productivity, and distribution of U.S. aquatic resources for increased recreational fishing opportunities in cooperation with states and tribes.
EO 13007, Native American Religious Practices (1996)	Provides for access to, and ceremonial use of, Indian sacred sites on federal lands used by Indian religious practitioners and direction to avoid adversely affecting the physical integrity of such sites.
EO 13061, Federal Support of Community Efforts Along American Heritage Rivers (1997)	Established the American Heritage Rivers initiative for the purpose of natural resource and environmental protection, economic revitalization, and historic and cultural preservation. The Act directs Federal agencies to preserve, protect, and restore rivers and their associated resources important to our history, culture, and natural heritage.
EO 13084, Consultation and Coordination With Indian Tribal Governments (2000)	Provides a mechanism for establishing regular and meaningful consultation and collaboration with tribal officials in the development of federal policies that have tribal implications.

EXECUTIVE ORDERS	DESCRIPTIONS
EO 13112, Invasive Species (1999)	Federal agencies are directed to prevent the introduction of invasive species, detect and respond rapidly to and control populations of such species in a cost effective and environmentally sound manner, accurately monitor invasive species, provide for restoration of native species and habitat conditions, conduct research to prevent introductions and to control invasive species, and promote public education on invasive species and the means to address them. This EO replaces and rescinds EO 11987, Exotic Organisms (1977).
EO 13186, Responsibilities of Federal Agencies to Protect Migratory Birds. (2001)	Instructs federal agencies to conserve migratory birds by several means, including the incorporation of strategies and recommendations found in Partners in Flight Bird Conservation plans, the North American Waterfowl Plan, the North American Waterbird Conservation Plan, and the United States Shorebird Conservation Plan, into agency management plans and guidance documents.
Executive Order 13443, Facilitation of Hunting Heritage and Wildlife Conservation (August 20, 2007)	Instructs federal agencies to implement actions that expand and enhance hunting opportunities for the public; consider hunting in agency actions; manage wildlife and wildlife habitats on public lands in a manner that expands and enhances opportunities for the use of hunting in wildlife management planning and; and establish short- and long-term goals to foster opportunities for the public to hunt.

Appendix D. Public Involvement

Public involvement is a very important part of the development of all Comprehensive Conservation Plans (CCPs), and every effort was made to assure that public comments were solicited throughout the development of this plan. A notice of intent to prepare the CCP was published in the *Federal Register* on May 8, 2008. The public was notified in the local newspapers and media of public scoping meetings to be held on May 22, 2008. Approximately 10 members of the public attended the public scoping meeting. Six members of the public offered their comments at the public meeting. In addition, two other comments were returned from the general public and one comment from the State.

Major Issues Identified During Scoping and Internal Review:

- *Internally*: With regard to wildlife and habitat management, the most significant issues identified internally were managing for invasive species, species of special concern, such as the alligator snapping turtle, mixed pine upland hardwood forest management, land protection, urban development and wildlife management issues, maintaining the excellent environmental education and interpretation programs, and increasing permanent staff.

- *State*: The Louisiana Department of Wildlife and Fisheries was initially contacted during November 2007 (the preplanning stage of the process) and supports the efforts of refuge management. The state had chosen to participate actively in the CCP process by appointing two employees to the core planning team. The State believes an aggressive alligator monitoring and control program should be incorporated into the CCP due to the extensive amount of alligator habitat and capacity for increased human-wildlife conflict as urban growth continues to expand around the refuge. The State also believes continued and heightened efforts must be put forth to enlighten all refuge users of the important role hunting has and continues to play in conservation on the refuge and across the nation. The State also noted that zebra mussel occurance in the State of Lousiana was verified in the 1990's. These comments were addressed in the draft CCP/EA by: adding a strategy to work with the State to monitor alligator populations and implement control efforts where appropriate; continue to support educational programs supporting hunting; and corrected the text to indicate the occurance of zebra mussels in the State of Louisiana.

- *Tribes*: Letters were provided to representatives of Tunica-Biloxi Indians of Louisiana, Caddo Nation of Oklahoma, and the Quapaw Tribe requesting issues they would like to see addressed in the CCP and inviting them to participate in the process. No responses were received.

- *Public*: The following comments were received from the public either at the public forums or in correspondence are noted below:

Fish and Wildlife Population Management

- Need a complete inventory of invertebrates prior to habitat management.
- Concerned about the encroachment of black bears into the area, how to encourage the increase of bears and also how to plan for public safety.
- Concerned about too much public access which violates the "wildlife first" mandate; suggests a moratorium on increased infrastructure.
- Concerned that there is a fine line between education, public assess and wildlife.

Habitat Management

- Concerned about the algae growth on the lake.
- Want to manage water levels on the lake to mimic the historic and natural hydrological regime.
- Wants to purchase land within acquisition area but only from willing land owners.
- Would like to see cooperative agreements with adjacent landowners regarding water quality and other ecological integrity issues.
- Concerned that over the next 15 years with the increased suburbanization of the surrounding area, the priority public uses will need to be re-evaluated, especially with hunting (gun safety issues).
- Would like to see that emphasis is given to birds and bird habitat.
- Would like to see certain areas always managed for early successional habitat particularly for birds.

Visitor Services

- Would like to see the refuge continue to be a place for people to meet and discuss refuge issues, host groups that are concerned with environmental issues and use existing facilities.
- Make the refuge a focal point for conservationists to meet and also a place to focus on education; make it a pilot for public education and awareness.
- Does not want increased access to the refuge; wants to maintain present access levels. Don't want it to become a "park."
- Concerned with litter problem on the refuge.
- Concerned with littering; need law enforcement; not enough personnel to pick up litter.
- Increase signage to discourage littering; ensure that school groups are educated on littering problem.
- Increase signage—lake high priority area.
- Does not want the refuge open to nighttime use.
- Want to use yo-yos, juglines, and trotlines.
- May be some need for security cameras or other type of surveillance.
- Need more staff, another public use person, more maintenance staff, need to educate the public about cultural resources on the refuge.
- Need more law enforcement; another law enforcement officer.
- Need the existing employees to have more law enforcement authority.
- Have signs that say "if you see someone littering, call this number;" use existing Parish laws to enforce littering regulations.
- Think the refuge has a superior staff and is managed well; the community has a lot of respect for the way the refuge is managed and how much has been accomplished.
- Continue and build partnerships with the community.
- Fishing is one of the major public uses on the refuge; wants to increase partnerships with anglers on the refuge.
- Use the "free fishing" days to host an event or focus on the anglers in the community.
- Need to partner with anglers regarding subsistence fishing.
- Would like to see "clean-up" days maybe associated with Earth Day.
- Continue to educate on environmental issues that are not just refuge-specific.
- Focus education towards seniors.

Refuge Administration

- Concerned that in the next 15 years, the refuge may not be able to support financially or logistically the existing facilities. Concerned that the refuge will "overdo" the public access.
- Want to keep in mind that the USFWS budget keeps getting slashed. When new facilities or uses are created, they have to be maintained and/or staffed so the refuge needs to be realistic about future capability to upkeep public use programs.
- Concerned that the refuge will have the budget necessary to maintain programs in the future.
- Concerned that the refuge somehow encourage a building of the budget to help with educational and maintenance needs. Concerned that the refuge staff is reduced—need more staff.

SUMMARY OF PUBLIC DRAFT CCP COMMENTS

Public involvement in the development of the Comprehensive Conservation Plan and Environment Assessment for Black Bayou Lake National Wildlife Refuge, Ouachita Parish, Louisiana, was sought throughout the planning process.

The issues and alternatives generated from the scoping meeting, coupled with the input of the planning team, are summarized in Chapters III of the Plan. Within 1 year a draft plan was developed for the Refuge, which will direct management over the next 15 years.

The draft CCP/EA was made available for public review, beginning September 30, 2009, and ended October 30, 2009 (74 FR 6053). Copies of the plan were posted at refuge headquarters and area locations and over 100 copies of the draft comprehensive conservation plan and environmental assessment were distributed to local landowners, the public, and local, state, and federal agencies. Five respondents consisting of the Service and local citizens submitted written comments by mail or email. Draft plan comments and the Service response to those comments are summarized below.

DRAFT PLAN COMMENTS AND SERVICE RESPONSE

Three respondents provided general editorial comments.

Service Response: The Service incorporated these changes where appropriate.

One respondent requested the title Herptile List be changed to Amphibian and Reptile List.

Service Response: The Service incorporated this change.

One respondent requested hunting, trapping and prescribed fires be banned from the refuge.

Service Response: Hunting is one of the six priority public uses identified in the 1997 Refuge Improvement Act, and hunting has been found to be compatible with the purposes for which Black Bayou Lake Refuge was established.

On Black Bayou Lake Refuge, beavers cause an unacceptable degree of damage to the bottomland hardwood forest and habitat on adjacent lands. On a landscape scale, considering the historical forest as greatly diminished in size, the percent of remaining forest impacted by beavers is much greater than would have occurred naturally in an undisturbed setting. Although some beaver-driven habitat is desirable, the current level is disproportionate for a diverse, healthy forest.

Beaver damage on Black Bayou Lake Refuge is mitigated by (1) removing dams manually, with explosives, and/or heavy equipment; (2) installing excluder devices on water control structures; and (3) shooting/trapping by Service employees. The extent of beaver damage is too vast and widespread for techniques, such as fencing, tree wrapping, and repellents, to be cost effective when considering the amount of required labor and materials. Lethal control is site-specific and intended to remove those individuals causing the most serious problems.

Raccoons and opossums depredate bird, mammal, and reptile nests at much higher rates than occurred historically, directly causing population threats to some species, such as Neotropical migratory birds. The extirpation of natural predators in Louisiana, such as wolves and cougars, has led to overpopulation of some species. Public hunting instead of trapping of these species is encouraged in order to maintain healthy population levels.

A great deal of scientific research proves that certain ecosystems are fire-evolved and maintained. Two habitats that are present on Black Bayou Lake NWR are the prairie habitat and native canebrakes. Without fire, these habitat types decline and then are completely lost due to invasion by woody plant species. All prescribed burning is conducted according to the approved Fire Management Plan and fire prescriptions that have strict parameters guiding the use of fire. All employees involved in burning are highly trained and re-certified annually.

Appendix E. Appropriate Use Determinations

BLACK BAYOU LAKE NATIONAL WILDLIFE REFUGE APPROPRIATE USE DETERMINATIONS

An appropriate use determination is the initial decision process a refuge manager follows when first considering whether or not to allow a proposed use on a refuge. The refuge manager must find that a use is appropriate before undertaking a compatibility review of the use. This process clarifies and expands on the compatibility determination process by describing when refuge managers should deny a proposed use without determining compatibility. If a proposed use is not appropriate, it will not be allowed and a compatibility determination will not be undertaken.

Except for the uses noted below, the refuge manager must decide if a new or existing use is an appropriate refuge use. If an existing use is not appropriate, the refuge manager will eliminate or modify the use as expeditiously as practicable. If a new use is not appropriate, the refuge manager will deny the use without determining compatibility. Uses that have been administratively determined to be appropriate are:

- Six wildlife-dependent recreational uses - As defined by the National Wildlife Refuge System Improvement Act of 1997, the six wildlife-dependent recreational uses (hunting, fishing, wildlife observation, wildlife photography, and environmental education and interpretation) are determined to be appropriate. However, the refuge manager must still determine if these uses are compatible.

- Take of fish and wildlife under state regulations - States have regulations concerning take of wildlife that includes hunting, fishing, and trapping. The Service considers take of wildlife under such regulations appropriate. However, the refuge manager must determine if the activity is compatible before allowing it on a refuge.

Statutory Authorities for this policy:

National Wildlife Refuge System Administration Act of 1966, as amended by the National Wildlife Refuge System Improvement Act of 1997, 16 U.S.C. 668dd-668ee. This law provides the authority for establishing policies and regulations governing refuge uses, including the authority to prohibit certain harmful activities. The Act does not authorize any particular use, but rather authorizes the Secretary of the Interior to allow uses only when they are compatible and "under such regulations as he may prescribe." This law specifically identifies certain public uses that, when compatible, are legitimate and appropriate uses within the Refuge System. The law states ". . . it is the policy of the United States that . . .compatible wildlife-dependent recreation is a legitimate and appropriate general public use of the System . . .compatible wildlife-dependent recreational uses are the priority general public uses of the System and shall receive priority consideration in refuge planning and management; and . . . when the Secretary determines that a proposed wildlife-dependent recreational use is a compatible use within a refuge, that activity should be facilitated . . . the Secretary shall . . . ensure that priority general public uses of the System receive enhanced consideration over other general public uses in planning and management within the System . . . ." The law also states "in administering the System, the Secretary is authorized to take the following actions: . . . issue regulations to carry out this Act." This policy implements the standards set in the Act by providing enhanced consideration of priority general public uses and ensuring other public uses do not interfere with our ability to provide quality, wildlife-dependent recreational uses.

Refuge Recreation Act of 1962, 16 U.S.C. 460k. The Act authorizes the Secretary of the Interior to administer refuges, hatcheries, and other conservation areas for recreational use, when such uses do not interfere with the area's primary purposes. It authorizes construction and maintenance of recreational facilities and the acquisition of land for incidental fish and wildlife oriented recreational development or protection of natural resources. It also authorizes the charging of fees for public uses.

Other Statutes that Establish Refuges, including the Alaska National Interest Lands Conservation Act of 1980 (ANILCA) (16 U.S.C. 410hh - 410hh-5, 460 mm - 460mm-4, 539-539e, and 3101 - 3233; 43 U.S.C. 1631 et seq.).

Executive Orders. The Service must comply with Executive Order 11644 when allowing use of off-highway vehicles on refuges. This order requires the Service to designate areas as open or closed to off-highway vehicles in order to protect refuge resources, promote safety, and minimize conflict among the various refuge users; monitor the effects of these uses once they are allowed; and amend or rescind any area designation as necessary based on the information gathered. Furthermore, Executive Order 11989 requires the Service to close areas to off-highway vehicles when it is determined that the use causes or will cause considerable adverse effects on the soil, vegetation, wildlife, habitat, or cultural or historic resources. Statutes, such as ANILCA, take precedence over executive orders.

Definitions:

Appropriate Use. A proposed or existing use on a refuge that meets at least one of the following four conditions:

1) The use is a wildlife-dependent recreational use as identified in the Improvement Act.
2) The use contributes to fulfilling the refuge purpose(s), the Refuge System mission, or goals or objectives described in a refuge management plan approved after October 9, 1997, the date the Improvement Act was signed into law.
3) The use involves the take of fish and wildlife under state regulations.
4) The use has been found to be appropriate as specified in section 1.11.

Native American. American Indians in the conterminous United States and Alaska Natives (including Aleuts, Eskimos, and Indians) who are members of federally recognized tribes.

Priority General Public Use. A compatible wildlife-dependent recreational use of a refuge involving hunting, fishing, wildlife observation, wildlife photography, and environmental education and interpretation.

Quality. The criteria used to determine a quality recreational experience include:

- Promotes safety of participants, other visitors, and facilities.
- Promotes compliance with applicable laws and regulations and responsible behavior.
- Minimizes or eliminates conflicts with fish and wildlife population or habitat goals or objectives in a plan approved after 1997.
- Minimizes or eliminates conflicts with other compatible wildlife-dependent recreation.
- Minimizes conflicts with neighboring landowners.
- Promotes accessibility and availability to a broad spectrum of the American people.
- Promotes resource stewardship and conservation.
- Promotes public understanding and increases public appreciation of America's natural resources and the Service's role in managing and protecting these resources.

- Provides reliable/reasonable opportunities to experience wildlife.
- Uses facilities that are accessible and blend into the natural setting.
- Uses visitor satisfaction to help define and evaluate programs.

Wildlife-Dependent Recreational Use. As defined by the Improvement Act, a use of a refuge involving hunting, fishing, wildlife observation, wildlife photography, and environmental education and interpretation.

FINDING OF APPROPRIATENESS OF A REFUGE USE

Refuge Name: Black Bayou Lake NWR

Use: Walking, Hiking, and Jogging

This form is not required for wildlife-dependent recreational uses, take regulated by the State, or uses already described in a refuge CCP or step-down management plan approved after October 9, 1997.

Decision Criteria:	YES	NO
(a) Do we have jurisdiction over the use?	x	
(b) Does the use comply with applicable laws and regulations (Federal, State, Tribal, and local)?	x	
(c) Is the use consistent with applicable Executive orders and Department and Service policies?	x	
(d) Is the use consistent with public safety?	x	
(e) Is the use consistent with goals and objectives in an approved management plan or other document?	x	
(f) Has an earlier documented analysis not denied the use or is this the first time the use has been proposed?	x	
(g) Is the use manageable within available budget and staff?	x	
(h) Will this be manageable in the future within existing resources?	x	
(i) Does the use contribute to the public's understanding and appreciation of the refuge's natural or cultural resources, or is the use beneficial to the refuge's natural or cultural resources?	x	
(j) Can the use be accommodated without impairing existing wildlife-dependent recreational uses or reducing the potential to provide quality (see section 1.6D, 603 FW 1, for description), compatible, wildlife-dependent recreation into the future?	x	

Where we do not have jurisdiction over the use ["no" to (a)], there is no need to evaluate it further as we cannot control the use. Uses that are illegal, inconsistent with existing policy, or unsafe ["no" to (b), (c), or (d)] may not be found appropriate. If the answer is "no" to any of the other questions above, we will **generally** not allow the use.

If indicated, the refuge manager has consulted with State fish and wildlife agencies.   **Yes _X_ No ___**

When the refuge manager finds the use appropriate based on sound professional judgment, the refuge manager must justify the use in writing on an attached sheet and obtain the refuge supervisor's concurrence.

Based on an overall assessment of these factors, my summary conclusion is that the proposed use is:
              Not Appropriate_____   Appropriate __X__

Refuge Manager: _____*Signed*_____
        Date: __1-14-10_____

If found to be **Not Appropriate**, the refuge supervisor does not need to sign concurrence if the use is a new use. If an existing use is found **Not Appropriate** outside the CCP process, the refuge supervisor must sign concurrence. If found to be **Appropriate**, the refuge supervisor must sign concurrence.

Refuge Supervisor: ____*Signed*___am_____
        Date: __2/11/10_____

A compatibility determination is required before the use may be allowed.

FINDING OF APPROPRIATENESS OF A REFUGE USE

Refuge Name: Black Bayou Lake NWR

Use: All-terrain Vehicles

This form is not required for wildlife-dependent recreational uses, take regulated by the State, or uses already described in a refuge CCP or step-down management plan approved after October 9, 1997.

Decision Criteria:	YES	NO
(a) Do we have jurisdiction over the use?	x	
(b) Does the use comply with applicable laws and regulations (Federal, State, Tribal, and local)?	x	
(c) Is the use consistent with applicable Executive orders and Department and Service policies?	x	
(d) Is the use consistent with public safety?	x	
(e) Is the use consistent with goals and objectives in an approved management plan or other document?	x	
(f) Has an earlier documented analysis not denied the use or is this the first time the use has been proposed?	x	
(g) Is the use manageable within available budget and staff?	x	
(h) Will this be manageable in the future within existing resources?	x	
(i) Does the use contribute to the public's understanding and appreciation of the refuge's natural or cultural resources, or is the use beneficial to the refuge's natural or cultural resources?	x	
(j) Can the use be accommodated without impairing existing wildlife-dependent recreational uses or reducing the potential to provide quality (see section 1.6D, 603 FW 1, for description), compatible, wildlife-dependent recreation into the future?	x	

Where we do not have jurisdiction over the use ["no" to (a)], there is no need to evaluate it further as we cannot control the use. Uses that are illegal, inconsistent with existing policy, or unsafe ["no" to (b), (c), or (d)] may not be found appropriate. If the answer is "no" to any of the other questions above, we will **generally** not allow the use.

If indicated, the refuge manager has consulted with State fish and wildlife agencies.   Yes _X_ No ___

When the refuge manager finds the use appropriate based on sound professional judgment, the refuge manager must justify the use in writing on an attached sheet and obtain the refuge supervisor's concurrence.

Based on an overall assessment of these factors, my summary conclusion is that the proposed use is:

         Not Appropriate_____   **Appropriate__ X __**

Refuge Manager:___/____*Signed*_____
       Date:___1-14-10_____

If found to be **Not Appropriate**, the refuge supervisor does not need to sign concurrence if the use is a new use. If an existing use is found **Not Appropriate** outside the CCP process, the refuge supervisor must sign concurrence. If found to be **Appropriate**, the refuge supervisor must sign concurrence.

Refuge Supervisor:___*Signed*_____
       Date:__2/11/10_____

A compatibility determination is required before the use may be allowed.

FINDING OF APPROPRIATENESS OF A REFUGE USE

Refuge Name: Black Bayou Lake NWR

Use: Boating

This form is not required for wildlife-dependent recreational uses, take regulated by the State, or uses already described in a refuge CCP or step-down management plan approved after October 9, 1997.

Decision Criteria:	YES	NO
(a) Do we have jurisdiction over the use?	x	
(b) Does the use comply with applicable laws and regulations (Federal, State, Tribal, and local)?	x	
(c) Is the use consistent with applicable Executive orders and Department and Service policies?	x	
(d) Is the use consistent with public safety?	x	
(e) Is the use consistent with goals and objectives in an approved management plan or other document?	x	
(f) Has an earlier documented analysis not denied the use or is this the first time the use has been proposed?	x	
(g) Is the use manageable within available budget and staff?	x	
(h) Will this be manageable in the future within existing resources?	x	
(i) Does the use contribute to the public's understanding and appreciation of the refuge's natural or cultural resources, or is the use beneficial to the refuge's natural or cultural resources?	x	
(j) Can the use be accommodated without impairing existing wildlife-dependent recreational uses or reducing the potential to provide quality (see section 1.6D, 603 FW 1, for description), compatible, wildlife-dependent recreation into the future?	x	

Where we do not have jurisdiction over the use ["no" to (a)], there is no need to evaluate it further as we cannot control the use. Uses that are illegal, inconsistent with existing policy, or unsafe ["no" to (b), (c), or (d)] may not be found appropriate. If the answer is "no" to any of the other questions above, we will **generally** not allow the use.

If indicated, the refuge manager has consulted with State fish and wildlife agencies.   Yes _X_ No ___

When the refuge manager finds the use appropriate based on sound professional judgment, the refuge manager must justify the use in writing on an attached sheet and obtain the refuge supervisor's concurrence.

Based on an overall assessment of these factors, my summary conclusion is that the proposed use is:

Not Appropriate _____   Appropriate __X__

Refuge Manager: ___ *Signed* ___
      Date: __1-14-10__

If found to be **Not Appropriate**, the refuge supervisor does not need to sign concurrence if the use is a new use. If an existing use is found **Not Appropriate** outside the CCP process, the refuge supervisor must sign concurrence. If found to be **Appropriate**, the refuge supervisor must sign concurrence.

Refuge Supervisor: ___ *Signed* ___
      Date: __2/11/10__

A compatibility determination is required before the use may be allowed.

FINDING OF APPROPRIATENESS OF A REFUGE USE

Refuge Name: Black Bayou Lake NWR

Use: Bicycling

This form is not required for wildlife-dependent recreational uses, take regulated by the State, or uses already described in a refuge CCP or step-down management plan approved after October 9, 1997.

Decision Criteria:	YES	NO
(a) Do we have jurisdiction over the use?	x	
(b) Does the use comply with applicable laws and regulations (Federal, State, Tribal, and local)?	x	
(c) Is the use consistent with applicable Executive orders and Department and Service policies?	x	
(d) Is the use consistent with public safety?	x	
(e) Is the use consistent with goals and objectives in an approved management plan or other document?	x	
(f) Has an earlier documented analysis not denied the use or is this the first time the use has been proposed?	x	
(g) Is the use manageable within available budget and staff?	x	
(h) Will this be manageable in the future within existing resources?	x	
(i) Does the use contribute to the public's understanding and appreciation of the refuge's natural or cultural resources, or is the use beneficial to the refuge's natural or cultural resources?	x	
(j) Can the use be accommodated without impairing existing wildlife-dependent recreational uses or reducing the potential to provide quality (see section 1.6D, 603 FW 1, for description), compatible, wildlife-dependent recreation into the future?	x	

Where we do not have jurisdiction over the use ["no" to (a)], there is no need to evaluate it further as we cannot control the use. Uses that are illegal, inconsistent with existing policy, or unsafe ["no" to (b), (c), or (d)] may not be found appropriate. If the answer is "no" to any of the other questions above, we will **generally** not allow the use.

If indicated, the refuge manager has consulted with State fish and wildlife agencies.   Yes _X_ No ___

When the refuge manager finds the use appropriate based on sound professional judgment, the refuge manager must justify the use in writing on an attached sheet and obtain the refuge supervisor's concurrence.

Based on an overall assessment of these factors, my summary conclusion is that the proposed use is:

Not Appropriate_____   Appropriate__X__

Refuge Manager:___*Signed*_____
          Date:__1-14-10_____

If found to be **Not Appropriate**, the refuge supervisor does not need to sign concurrence if the use is a new use. If an existing use is found **Not Appropriate** outside the CCP process, the refuge supervisor must sign concurrence. If found to be **Appropriate**, the refuge supervisor must sign concurrence.

Refuge Supervisor:___*Signed*_____
          Date:__2/11/10_____

A compatibility determination is required before the use may be allowed.

FINDING OF APPROPRIATENESS OF A REFUGE USE

Refuge Name: Black Bayou Lake NWR

Use: Forest Management – Timber Harvest

This form is not required for wildlife-dependent recreational uses, take regulated by the State, or uses already described in a refuge CCP or step-down management plan approved after October 9, 1997.

Decision Criteria:	YES	NO
(a) Do we have jurisdiction over the use?	x	
(b) Does the use comply with applicable laws and regulations (Federal, State, Tribal, and local)?	x	
(c) Is the use consistent with applicable Executive orders and Department and Service policies?	x	
(d) Is the use consistent with public safety?	x	
(e) Is the use consistent with goals and objectives in an approved management plan or other document?	x	
(f) Has an earlier documented analysis not denied the use or is this the first time the use has been proposed?	x	
(g) Is the use manageable within available budget and staff?	x	
(h) Will this be manageable in the future within existing resources?	x	
(i) Does the use contribute to the public's understanding and appreciation of the refuge's natural or cultural resources, or is the use beneficial to the refuge's natural or cultural resources?	x	
(j) Can the use be accommodated without impairing existing wildlife-dependent recreational uses or reducing the potential to provide quality (see section 1.6D, 603 FW 1, for description), compatible, wildlife-dependent recreation into the future?	x	

Where we do not have jurisdiction over the use ("no" to (a)), there is no need to evaluate it further as we cannot control the use. Uses that are illegal, inconsistent with existing policy, or unsafe ("no" to (b), (c), or (d)) may not be found appropriate. If the answer is "no" to any of the other questions above, we will **generally** not allow the use.

If indicated, the refuge manager has consulted with State fish and wildlife agencies.　　　Yes _X_ No ___

When the refuge manager finds the use appropriate based on sound professional judgment, the refuge manager must justify the use in writing on an attached sheet and obtain the refuge supervisor's concurrence.

Based on an overall assessment of these factors, my summary conclusion is that the proposed use is:

Not Appropriate_____　　　　　　　　Appropriate__X__

Refuge Manager: _____Signed_____
　　　Date: __1-14-10____

If found to be **Not Appropriate**, the refuge supervisor does not need to sign concurrence if the use is a new use. If an existing use is found **Not Appropriate** outside the CCP process, the refuge supervisor must sign concurrence. If found to be **Appropriate**, the refuge supervisor must sign concurrence.

Refuge Supervisor: ___Signed_____
　　　Date: _2/11/10_____

A compatibility determination is required before the use may be allowed.

FINDING OF APPROPRIATENESS OF A REFUGE USE

Refuge Name: Black Bayou Lake NWR

Use: Plant Gathering

This form is not required for wildlife-dependent recreational uses, take regulated by the State, or uses already described in a refuge CCP or step-down management plan approved after October 9, 1997.

Decision Criteria:	YES	NO
(a) Do we have jurisdiction over the use?	x	
(b) Does the use comply with applicable laws and regulations (Federal, State, Tribal, and local)?	x	
(c) Is the use consistent with applicable Executive orders and Department and Service policies?	x	
(d) Is the use consistent with public safety?	x	
(e) Is the use consistent with goals and objectives in an approved management plan or other document?	x	
(f) Has an earlier documented analysis not denied the use or is this the first time the use has been proposed?	x	
(g) Is the use manageable within available budget and staff?	x	
(h) Will this be manageable in the future within existing resources?	x	
(i) Does the use contribute to the public's understanding and appreciation of the refuge's natural or cultural resources, or is the use beneficial to the refuge's natural or cultural resources?	x	
(j) Can the use be accommodated without impairing existing wildlife-dependent recreational uses or reducing the potential to provide quality (see section 1.6D, 603 FW 1, for description), compatible, wildlife-dependent recreation into the future?	x	

Where we do not have jurisdiction over the use ("no" to (a)), there is no need to evaluate it further as we cannot control the use. Uses that are illegal, inconsistent with existing policy, or unsafe ("no" to (b), (c), or (d)) may not be found appropriate. If the answer is "no" to any of the other questions above, we will **generally** not allow the use.

If indicated, the refuge manager has consulted with State fish and wildlife agencies.   Yes _X_ No ___

When the refuge manager finds the use appropriate based on sound professional judgment, the refuge manager must justify the use in writing on an attached sheet and obtain the refuge supervisor's concurrence.

Based on an overall assessment of these factors, my summary conclusion is that the proposed use is:

Not Appropriate_____   Appropriate__X__

Refuge Manager: _____Signed_____
        Date: _1-14-10_____

If found to be **Not Appropriate**, the refuge supervisor does not need to sign concurrence if the use is a new use. If an existing use is found **Not Appropriate** outside the CCP process, the refuge supervisor must sign concurrence. If found to be **Appropriate**, the refuge supervisor must sign concurrence.

Refuge Supervisor: ____Signed_____
        Date: _2/11/10_____

A compatibility determination is required before the use may be allowed.

Appendix F. Compatibility Determinations

BLACK BAYOU LAKE NATIONAL WILDLIFE REFUGE COMPATIBILITY DETERMINATIONS

Introduction: The Fish and Wildlife Service reviewed several uses for compatibility during the comprehensive conservation planning process for Black Bayou Lake NWR. Descriptions and anticipated impacts of each of these uses are addressed separately. However, the Uses through National Wildlife Refuge System Mission and the Approval of Compatibility Determinations section apply to each use. If one of these uses is considered outside of the Comprehensive Conservation Plan, then those sections become part of that compatibility determination.

Uses: Several uses were evaluated to determine their compatibility with the Refuge System and mission and purposes of the refuge: (1) wildlife observation and photography; (2) environmental education and interpretation; (3) big game hunting; (4) small game hunting; (5) migratory bird hunting; (6) fishing; (7) hiking, jogging, and walking; (8) boating; (9) all-terrain vehicles; (10) plant gathering; (11) bicycling; and (12) forest management - timber harvest.

Refuge Name: Black Bayou Lake National Wildlife Refuge

County: Ouachita Parish, Louisiana

Establishing and Acquisition Authority: Emergency Wetlands Resources Act of 1986

Refuge Purpose(s): "... the conservation of the wetlands of the Nation in order to maintain the public benefits they provide and to help fulfill international obligations contained in various migratory bird treaties and conventions ..."
16 U.S.C. 3901(b), 100 Stat. 3583.

National Wildlife Refuge System Mission: "The mission of the National Wildlife Refuge System is to administer a national network of lands and waters for the conservation, management, and where appropriate, restoration of the fish, wildlife, and plant resources and their habitats within the United States for the benefit of present and future generations of Americans" (National Wildlife Refuge System Administration Act of 1966, as amended) [16 U.S.C. 668dd-668ee].

Description of Use:
Wildlife Observation and Photography

Wildlife observation and photography have been identified in the National Wildlife Refuge System Improvement Act of 1997 as priority wildlife-dependent recreational uses provided they are compatible with the purpose for which the refuge was established.

Wildlife photography, including other image-capturing activities such as videography, has occurred on the refuge since its inception. A wildlife photography blind, a birdwatching blind, an observation platform, and a wildlife pier exist on the refuge. Many thousands of people use these structures each year to observe and photograph nature and wildlife.

Wildlife observation and photography could occur anywhere on the refuge throughout the year during daylight hours only. These activities can be accomplished while driving, boating, or walking on the refuge according to refuge regulations.

Availability of Resources:

Resources involved in the administration and management of the use:

Minor amounts of personnel time associated with administration, management, and law enforcement.

Special equipment, facilities, or improvements necessary to support the use:

Observation platform, wildlife pier, blinds, access roads, parking lots, kiosks, trails, and brochures.

Maintenance costs:

$10,000/year

Monitoring costs:

$5,000/year

Offsetting revenues:

None

Anticipated Impacts of the Use:

Short-term impacts:

The refuge provides habitat for resident and migratory wildlife. As a result of these activities, individual animals may be disturbed by human contact to varying degrees. Examples of potential disturbance include flushing of birds from feeding, resting, or nesting areas and trampling of plants by observers and photographers; however, disturbance to trust species are expected to be minimal. Hiking trails are established throughout most of the refuge, reducing impacts to vegetation. Short-term impacts to facilities, such as roads and trails, can be avoided by special closures due to unsafe or wet conditions.

Long-term impacts:

Current utilization of these uses is incidental to overall refuge programs and no long-term adverse impacts have been experienced.

Cumulative impacts:

No cumulative impacts are anticipated.

Public Review and Comment:

This compatibility determination was part of the Draft Comprehensive Conservation Plan and Environmental Assessment (Draft CCP/EA) for Black Bayou Lake National Wildlife Refuge. The availability of the Draft CCP/EA was announced in the *Federal Register* on September 30, 2009, for a 30-day comment period. Copies of the Draft CCP/EA were posted at refuge headquarters and area locations and over 150 copies were distributed to local landowners; the public; and local, state, and federal agencies.

Determination (check one below):

_____ Use is Not Compatible

___X___Use is Compatible with Following Stipulations

Stipulations Necessary to Ensure Compatibility:

Visitors are required to abide by all refuge regulations that limit impacts on plant and wildlife populations. If evidence of unacceptable adverse impacts begins to appear, it may be necessary to make changes to the visitor use program.

Justification:

Visitors have the opportunity to view and photograph many species of wildlife with relative ease at many places on the refuge. Opportunities exist for these activities by boating, by walking, or by driving the public roads. During summer, wading birds are easily viewed from the wildlife pier and photography blind. Hikes on nature trails produce sightings of snakes, turtles, and birds. Approximately 38,000 people visit the refuge each year from every state. The refuge has had visitors from 36 different countries. Black Bayou Lake NWR is located partially within the city limits of Monroe, Louisiana, making it easily assessable by visitors that otherwise would probably not be introduced to the outdoors or a national wildlife refuge. Black Bayou Lake NWR may be many of these visitors' first experience with nature and provides quality wildlife-dependent outdoor experiences.

Mandatory 15-Year Re-evaluation Date: **March 10, 2025**

Description of Use:
Environmental Education and Interpretation

Environmental education and interpretation activities include traditional environmental education, such as teacher- or staff-led on-site field trips, off-site programs in classrooms, and interpretation of wildlife resources on the refuge. These activities are largely conducted at Black Bayou Lake NWR for the North Louisiana NWR Complex. The environmental education and interpretation activities teach citizens of all ages good land ethic, foster public support, increase visibility, and improve the image of the Service. More than 8,000 individuals participated in environmental education and interpretation programs conducted in 2007. Partnerships exist between the refuge and local school districts.

Environmental education and interpretation have been identified in the National Wildlife Refuge System Improvement Act of 1997 as priority public uses provided they are compatible with the purpose for which the refuge was established.

Environmental education and interpretation could occur throughout the refuge year-round as requested by the public. Although the activities do not require special use permits, they are most often closely coordinated and led by refuge public use specialists.

Availability of Resources:

Resources involved in the administration and management of the use:

One public use specialist and one refuge operating specialist work full time to offer the environmental education and interpretation program to the public. Volunteers help with the program when available and needed.

Special equipment, facilities, or improvements necessary to support the use:

Observation platform, wildlife pier, blinds, access roads, parking lots, kiosks, brochures, interpretive panels and exhibits, conservation learning center, visitor's center, arboretum, prairie demonstration area, trails, and environmental education materials.

Maintenance costs:

$100,000/year

Monitoring costs:

None

Offsetting revenues:

None

Anticipated Impacts of the Use:

Short-term impacts:

The use of on-site, hands-on, action-oriented activities by groups of teachers/students to accomplish environmental education objectives may impose a low-level impact on the sites used for these activities. Impacts may include trampling of vegetation and temporary disturbance to wildlife species in the immediate vicinity during the activities. Since activities take place on existing roads, trails, and other facilities, impacts will be minimal.

Long-term impacts:

Current utilization of these uses is incidental to overall refuge programs and no long-term adverse impacts have been experienced. Long-term beneficial impacts include the furthering of the refuge mission through the education of the general public.

Cumulative impacts:

No cumulative impacts are anticipated.

Public Review and Comment:

This compatibility determination was part of the Draft Comprehensive Conservation Plan and Environmental Assessment (Draft CCP/EA) for Black Bayou Lake National Wildlife Refuge. The availability of the Draft CCP/EA was announced in the *Federal Register* on September 30, 2009, for a 30-day comment period. Copies of the Draft CCP/EA were posted at refuge headquarters and area locations and over 150 copies were distributed to local landowners; the public; and local, state, and federal agencies.

Determination (check one below):

_____ Use is Not Compatible

___X___ Use is Compatible with Following Stipulations

Stipulations Necessary to Ensure Compatibility:

On-site activities will be held where minimal impacts occur. Evaluations of sites and programs will be conducted periodically to assess if objectives are being met and to ensure that the natural resources are not being degraded. If evidence of unacceptable adverse impacts begins to appear, it may be necessary to change the location of the outdoor activities.

Justification:

Environmental education and interpretation are used to encourage citizens of all ages to act responsibly in protecting a healthy ecosystem. They are tools to use in building land ethic, developing public support, and decreasing wildlife violations. They constitute one method of increasing visibility in the community and improving the image of the Service. The refuge is partially within the city limits of Monroe, Louisiana, and is highly used by the local school districts. Thousands of children visit the refuge to participate in its educational programs. Many inner-city children are being introduced to the outdoors at Black Bayou Lake NWR for the first time.

Mandatory 15-Year Re-evaluation Date: March 10, 2025

Description of Use:
Big Game Hunting

Big game hunting on Black Bayou Lake NWR consists of archery white-tailed deer hunting. Hunting activities are permitted with a valid refuge hunt permit and appropriate state licenses. The refuge hunt program is an excellent wildlife management and public relations tool, which provides quality recreational opportunities for the public while regulating specific animal populations at desired levels. The refuge hunt plan was developed to ensure that associated public recreation and wildlife management objectives are met in a responsible and consistent manner.

Hunting, a wildlife-dependent recreation, has been identified in the National Wildlife Refuge System Improvement Act of 1997 as a priority public use provided it is compatible with the purpose for which the refuge was established.

Hunting can occur on 2,475 acres (55 percent) of the refuge. All hunting seasons are established annually through coordination with the Louisiana Department of Wildlife and Fisheries. Archery only hunting is permitted on the refuge. One deer of either sex can be harvested per day. All regulations and annual changes are published in the Code of Federal Regulations (50 CFR).

Hunters access the refuge on open roads, by foot, and by all-terrain vehicles (ATVs) limited to designated trails.

Public hunting opportunities are limited in north Louisiana. Hunting opportunities on private land are virtually non-existent unless a person is willing and able to purchase hunting rights through hunting leases.

Availability of Resources:

Resources involved in the administration and management of the use:

Personnel time associated with administration and law enforcement.

Special equipment, facilities, or improvements necessary to support the use:

Access roads, ATV trails, parking lots, gates, brochures, kiosks, and law enforcement equipment.

Maintenance costs:

$15,000/year

Monitoring costs:

$5,000/year

Offsetting revenues:

None

Anticipated Impacts of the Use:

Short-term impacts:

National wildlife refuges administered by the North Louisiana NWR Complex have been open to hunting since 1975, with no documented disturbance to refuge habitats and no noticeable adverse impact on the population of species hunted or other associated wildlife. While managed hunting opportunities may result in localized disruption of individual animals' daily routines, no negative effects on populations have been documented.

Long-term impacts:

To date, there is no indication of adverse biological impacts associated with the Complex's hunting program. Harvest rates are low when only archery hunting occurs; for example, approximately 10 deer are harvested annually on the refuge. However, should it become necessary, the refuge has the latitude to adjust hunting seasons and bag limits annually, or to close the refuge entirely if there are safety issues or other concerns. This latitude, coupled with monitoring of wildlife populations and habitat conditions by the Service and the Louisiana Department of Wildlife and Fisheries, will ensure that long-term negative impacts to either wildlife populations and/or habitats on the refuge are unlikely. Should hunting pressure increase on the refuge, alternatives such as quota hunts, a reduction in the number of days of hunting, or restrictions on that part of the refuge open to hunting can be utilized to limit impacts.

Cumulative impacts:

Deer gun hunting has been occurring on lands adjacent to the refuge for many years. Data from the Louisiana Department of Wildlife and Fisheries indicate stable populations of deer. Therefore, archery only hunting on Black Bayou Lake NWR should not have negative cumulative impacts on deer populations.

Public Review and Comment:

This compatibility determination was part of the Draft Comprehensive Conservation Plan and Environmental Assessment (Draft CCP/EA) for Black Bayou Lake National Wildlife Refuge. The availability of the Draft CCP/EA was announced in the *Federal Register* on September 30, 2009, for a 30-day comment period. Copies of the Draft CCP/EA were posted at refuge headquarters and area locations and over 150 copies were distributed to local landowners; the public; and local, state, and federal agencies.

Determination (check one below):

_____ Use is Not Compatible

__X__ Use is Compatible with Following Stipulations

Stipulations Necessary to Ensure Compatibility:

Hunting seasons and bag limits are established annually as agreed upon during the annual hunt coordination meeting with state personnel. These generally fall within the state framework. The refuge can, and has, established more restrictive seasons and bag limits to prevent over-harvest of individual species or disturbance to trust species. All hunters are required to possess a refuge hunting permit while participating in refuge hunts. This permit, which augments the state hunting regulations, explains both the general hunt regulations and the refuge-specific regulations. Law enforcement patrols are frequently conducted throughout the hunting season to ensure compliance with refuge laws and regulations. The refuge has included a Refuge Operating Needs System project for a full-time officer to ensure compatibility over the long term.

Justification:

Deer hunts have proven to be compatible with refuge objectives. White-tailed deer hunting is a very popular wildlife-dependent use by the public. Deer hunting provides wildlife-dependent recreation to the public in a region where these opportunities are vanishing. The vast majority of private land is leased for hunting, often costing a person $300-$2000/year for membership. The refuge often attracts those hunters who cannot afford to join a hunting club.

Mandatory 15-Year Re-evaluation Date: March 10, 2025

Description of Use:

Small Game Hunting

Small game hunting consists of squirrels, rabbits, raccoons, opossum, and quail. Hunting activities are permitted with a valid refuge hunt permit and appropriate state licenses. The refuge hunt program is an excellent public relations tool, which provides quality recreational opportunities for the public while promoting national wildlife refuges. The refuge hunt plan was developed to ensure that associated public recreation and wildlife management objectives are met in a responsible and consistent manner.

Hunting, a wildlife-dependent recreation, has been identified in the National Wildlife Refuge System Improvement Act of 1997 as a priority public use provided it is compatible with the purpose for which the refuge was established.

Hunting can occur on 2,475 acres (55 percent) of the refuge. Small game hunting seasons on the refuge follow the state regulated seasons, which usually are from October through February. All hunting seasons are established annually through coordination with the Louisiana Department of Wildlife and Fisheries. All regulations and annual changes are published in the Code of Federal Regulations (50 CFR).

Hunters access the refuge on open roads, by foot, and by all-terrain vehicles (ATVs) limited to designated trails.

Public hunting opportunities are limited in north Louisiana. Hunting opportunities on private land are virtually non-existent unless a person is willing and able to purchase hunting rights through hunting leases.

Availability of Resources:

Resources involved in the administration and management of the use:

Personnel time associated with administration and law enforcement.

Special equipment, facilities, or improvements necessary to support the use:

Access roads, ATV trails, gates, parking lots, brochures, kiosks, and law enforcement equipment.

Maintenance costs:

$5,000/year

Monitoring costs:

$1,000/year

Offsetting revenues:

None

Anticipated Impacts of the Use:

Short-term impacts:

National wildlife refuges administered by the North Louisiana NWR Complex have been open to hunting since 1975, with no documented disturbance to refuge habitats and no noticeable adverse impact on the population of species hunted or other associated wildlife. While managed hunting opportunities may result in localized disruption of individual animals' daily routines, no noticeable adverse effects on populations have been documented.

Long-term impacts:

To date, there is no indication of adverse biological impacts associated with the Complex's hunting program. However, should it become necessary, the refuge has the latitude to adjust hunting seasons and bag limits annually or to close the refuge entirely if there are safety issues or other concerns. This latitude, coupled with monitoring of wildlife populations and habitat conditions by the Service and the Louisiana Department of Wildlife and Fisheries, will ensure that long-term negative impacts to either wildlife populations and/or habitats on the refuge are unlikely.

Should hunting pressure increase on the refuge, alternatives such as quota hunts, a reduction in the number of days of hunting, or restrictions on that part of the refuge open to hunting can be utilized to limit impacts.

Cumulative impacts:

Negative cumulative impacts on small game are unlikely. Consultation with the Louisiana Department of Wildlife and Fisheries during the development of this determination concluded that small game can sustain long-term regulated hunting at local and state levels. State regulations are drafted annually, taking into consideration population trends and sustainability of small game.

Public Review and Comment:

This compatibility determination was part of the Draft Comprehensive Conservation Plan and Environmental Assessment (Draft CCP/EA) for Black Bayou Lake National Wildlife Refuge. The availability of the Draft CCP/EA was announced in the *Federal Register* on September 30, 2009, for a 30-day comment period. Copies of the Draft CCP/EA were posted at refuge headquarters and area locations and over 150 copies were distributed to local landowners; the public; and local, state, and federal agencies.

Determination (check one below):

_____ Use is Not Compatible

___X___Use is Compatible with Following Stipulations

Stipulations Necessary to Ensure Compatibility:

Hunting seasons and bag limits are established annually as agreed upon during the annual hunt coordination meeting with state personnel. These generally fall within the state framework. The refuge can establish more restrictive seasons and bag limits to prevent over-harvest of individual species or disturbance to trust species. All hunters are required to possess a refuge hunting permit while participating in refuge hunts. This permit, which augments the state hunting regulations, explains both the general hunt regulations and the refuge-specific regulations. Law enforcement patrols are frequently conducted throughout the hunting season to ensure compliance with refuge laws and regulations. The refuge has included a Refuge Operating Needs System project for a full-time officer to ensure compatibility over the long term.

Justification:

Overpopulation of raccoons and opossum causes abnormally high rates of depredation on turtle, turkey, and songbird nests. Research on Black Bayou Lake NWR indicates extremely high depredation rates (over 90 percent) of alligator snapping turtle nests by raccoons. Hunting of these two species would help reduce raccoon and opossum numbers. Studies have consistently shown that small game, such as rabbits and squirrels, are not affected by hunting, but rather are limited by food resources. Gray squirrels, fox squirrels, and eastern cottontail and swamp rabbits are prolific breeders and their populations have never been threatened by hunting in Louisiana, even prior to the passing of modern hunting regulations. Coyotes and beavers are overpopulated and can have adverse effects on their habitats. Coyotes depredate small mammals, songbirds and their nests, turkey and quail nests, and any other animal they opportunistically encounter. When coyote numbers are high, local wildlife populations can be negatively affected. Beavers being overpopulated can kill thousands of acres of bottomland hardwood trees by damming sloughs and brakes. Forests inundated into the growing season quickly show signs of stress and trees eventually die. Hunting of both coyotes and beaver is beneficial in helping meet refuge objectives. Hunting of small game is a priority public use, offering the public an inexpensive wildlife-dependent recreational opportunity that is popular with the local community and is compatible with refuge purposes.

Mandatory 15-Year Re-evaluation Date: March 10, 2025

Description of Use:
Migratory Bird Hunting

Migratory bird hunting on Black Bayou Lake NWR consists of ducks, woodcock, coots, and geese. Hunting activities are permitted with a valid refuge hunt permit and appropriate state licenses. The refuge hunt program is an excellent public relations tool, which provides quality recreational opportunities for the public while promoting national wildlife refuges. The refuge hunt plan was developed to ensure that associated public recreation and wildlife management objectives were being met in a responsible and consistent manner.

Hunting, a wildlife-dependent recreation, has been identified in the National Wildlife Refuge System Improvement Act of 1997 as a priority public use provided it is compatible with the purpose for which the refuge was established.

Hunting can occur on 2,475 acres (55 percent) of the refuge. Migratory bird hunting seasons on the refuge follow the state regulated seasons, except waterfowl can only be hunted until noon each day. All hunting seasons are established annually through coordination with the Louisiana Department of Wildlife and Fisheries. All regulations and annual changes are published in the Code of Federal Regulations (50 CFR).

Hunters access the refuge on open roads, by foot, and by all-terrain vehicles (ATVs) limited to designated trails.

Public hunting opportunities are limited in north Louisiana. Hunting opportunities on private land are virtually non-existent unless a person is willing and able to purchase hunting rights through hunting leases.

Availability of Resources:

Resources involved in the administration and management of the use:

Personnel time associated with administration and law enforcement

Special equipment, facilities, or improvements necessary to support the use:

Access roads, ATV trails, gates, parking lots, brochures, kiosks, and law enforcement equipment.

Maintenance costs:

$5,000/year

Monitoring costs:

$1,000/year

Offsetting revenues:

None

Anticipated Impacts of the Use:

Short-term impacts:

National wildlife refuges administered by the North Louisiana NWR Complex have been open to hunting since 1975, with no documented disturbance to refuge habitats and no noticeable adverse impact on the population of species hunted or other associated wildlife. While managed hunting opportunities may result in localized disruption of individual animals' daily routines, no noticeable adverse effects on populations have been documented.

Long-term impacts:

To date, there is no indication of adverse biological impacts associated with the Complex's hunting program. However, should it become necessary, the refuge has the latitude to adjust hunting seasons and bag limits annually or to close the refuge entirely if there are safety issues or other concerns. This latitude, coupled with monitoring of wildlife populations and habitat conditions by the Service and the Louisiana Department of Wildlife and Fisheries, will ensure that long-term negative impacts to either wildlife populations and/or habitats on the refuge are unlikely.

Should hunting pressure increase on the refuge, alternatives such as quota hunts, a reduction in the number of days of hunting, or restrictions on that part of the refuge open to hunting can be utilized to limit impacts.

Cumulative impacts:

Migratory bird hunting regulations, including seasons and bag limits, are set annually by the Service using survey, production, harvest, and hunter participation data to ensure that cumulative adverse impacts do not occur to migratory bird populations. These regulations are then adopted by the state. State regulations can never be more liberal, only more conservative, than federal regulations. Negative cumulative impacts to migratory birds should be minimal on the refuge, especially since the refuge will have a more restricted (hunting until noon only) season.

Public Review and Comment:

This compatibility determination was part of the Draft Comprehensive Conservation Plan and Environmental Assessment (Draft CCP/EA) for Black Bayou Lake National Wildlife Refuge. The availability of the Draft CCP/EA was announced in the *Federal Register* on September 30, 2009, for a 30-day comment period. Copies of the Draft CCP/EA were posted at refuge headquarters and area locations and over 150 copies were distributed to local landowners; the public; and local, state, and federal agencies.

Determination (check one below):

_____ Use is Not Compatible

__X__ Use is Compatible with Following Stipulations

Stipulations Necessary to Ensure Compatibility:

Hunting seasons and bag limits are established annually as agreed upon during the annual hunt coordination meeting with state personnel. These generally fall within the state framework. The refuge can, and has, established more restrictive seasons and bag limits to prevent over-harvest of individual species or disturbance to trust species. All hunters are required to possess a refuge hunting permit while participating in refuge hunts. This permit, which augments the state hunting regulations, explains both the general hunt regulations and the refuge-specific regulations. Law enforcement patrols are frequently conducted throughout the hunting season to ensure compliance with refuge laws and regulations. The refuge has included a Refuge Operating Needs System project for a full-time officer to ensure compatibility over the long term.

Justification:

Regulated hunting does not have an adverse impact on populations of migratory birds. Hunting is a priority public use and offers the public an inexpensive wildlife-dependent recreational opportunity that is popular in the community.

Mandatory 15-Year Re-evaluation Date: March 10, 2025

Description of Use:
Fishing

Fishing was a traditional recreational use of the area that is now Black Bayou Lake NWR prior to its inclusion into the National Wildlife Refuge System and continues to be a recreational pursuit with the public. It is one of the more popular wildlife-dependent uses on the refuge. Fish populations currently support a sustainable harvest under a regulated fishing program.

Fishing, a wildlife-dependent recreation, has been identified in the National Wildlife Refuge System Improvement Act of 1997 as a priority public use, provided it is compatible with the purpose for which the refuge was established.

Fishing is permitted in the entire refuge. The use is conducted year-round during daylight hours only. Fishing is conducted subject to regulations established by the Louisiana Department of Wildlife and Fisheries. Fishing is further restricted on the refuge by regulations which prohibit commercial fishing on the refuge and prohibit the use of certain fishing methods.

Availability of Resources:

Resources involved in the administration and management of the use:

Personnel time associated with administration and law enforcement.

Special equipment, facilities, or improvements necessary to support the use:

Boat ramps, kiosks, brochures, parking lots, law enforcement equipment, and access roads.

Maintenance costs:

$10,000/year

Monitoring costs:

$5,000/year

Offsetting revenues:

None

Anticipated Impacts of the Use:

Short-term impacts:

Minor impacts, such as litter and gasoline contamination, could occur but not at a level that would cause serious concern. There could be some erosion from outboard wakes. The possibility exists that aquatic invasive plants could be introduced to the lake from boats and their trailers. Weekly monitoring of the boat ramp area is conducted by refuge staff for new invaders and signs are present at the boat ramp informing the public about invasive plants and the precautionary measures that should be taken to prevent new invasions from occurring.

Long-term impacts:

Fishing, as regulated, should not have any long-term negative impacts on the refuge.

Cumulative impacts:

No cumulative impacts are known to occur.

Public Review and Comment:

This compatibility determination was part of the Draft Comprehensive Conservation Plan and Environmental Assessment (Draft CCP/EA) for Black Bayou Lake National Wildlife Refuge. The availability of the Draft CCP/EA was announced in the *Federal Register* on September 30, 2009, for a 30-day comment period. Copies of the Draft CCP/EA were posted at refuge headquarters and area locations and over 150 copies were distributed to local landowners; the public; and local, state, and federal agencies.

Determination (check one below):

_____ Use is Not Compatible

__X__ Use is Compatible with Following Stipulations

Stipulations Necessary to Ensure Compatibility:

Commercial fishing is prohibited. Trotlines, yo-yos, and recreational fishing with commercial gear are prohibited. The taking of turtles is not permitted. Fishing is permitted during daylight hours only.

Justification:

Fishing is probably one of the most popular forms of outdoor recreation in the state, and the refuge has the opportunity to provide quality fishing to the public, which is a priority public use. Current state and refuge regulations limit impacts to fish and wildlife populations on the refuge, while providing a safe and rewarding experience for the refuge visitor. In 2002, the University of Louisiana at Monroe and the Louisiana Department of Wildlife and Fisheries conducted research on the sport fisheries of Black Bayou Lake. They found that the overall stock density of game fish contained balanced populations and should result in high angler satisfaction (Aku and Wood 2002).

Aku, P.K. and M. Wood. 2002. Evaluation of the status of sport fishes of the Black Bayou Lake National Refuge. Final Report of Challenge Cost-share Agreement Number: 42651, 20 pp.

Mandatory 15-Year Re-evaluation Date: March 10, 2025

Description of Use:
Hiking, Jogging, and Walking

Hiking, jogging, and walking facilitate travel and access for the priority public uses. Priority public uses as defined in the National Wildlife Refuge System Improvement Act of 1997 include hunting, fishing, wildlife observation, wildlife photography, and environmental education and interpretation.

The primary areas of these uses occur along refuge roads and trails which are maintained for priority public uses. At times, individuals will walk along rights-of-way or across country throughout the refuge scouting for hunting areas. Individuals accessing the refuge for hunting will need to possess a valid hunting permit and follow all refuge regulations. Access to the refuge is open every day during daylight hours. Entry on all or portions of individual areas may be temporarily suspended by posting upon occasions of unusual or critical conditions affecting land, water, vegetation, wildlife populations, or public safety.

Hiking, jogging, or walking can facilitate non-consumptive priority public uses by allowing observation of the natural landscape and wildlife viewing. Individuals stop to observe associated animals and plant communities. The uses mainly occur in very small groups or by individuals. Regarding consumptive uses, anglers and hunters can access refuge lands by walking anywhere on the refuge.

Access to the refuge is necessary for desirable use and management of the refuge. Foot traffic on the refuge provides increased access and opportunities to participate in priority public uses such as hunting, fishing, wildlife observation, and wildlife photography. Hiking, jogging, and walking can also be a form of exercise while enjoying the outdoors that coincides with former Secretary Norton's 2004 America's Public Lands get Fit with US initiative; this initiative is part of a larger partnership initiated by President George W. Bush to promote trails and refuges for health and recreation. The initiative is a direct result of President Bush's executive order, which was issued for the purpose of improving the health of all Americans. It is designed to promote a healthy lifestyle alliance between public health and recreation.

Availability of Resources:

Resources involved in the administration and management of the use:

Personnel time associated with administration and law enforcement.

Special equipment, facilities, or improvements necessary to support the use:

None

Maintenance costs:

Maintenance costs are not directly attributable to these incidental uses on the refuge.

Monitoring costs:

Minimal costs are associated with these uses to monitor consequences of public having access to the refuge, such as degree of littering and vandalism. Plants and wildlife will be monitored to determine any impacts as a result of public use.

Offsetting revenues:

None

Anticipated Impacts of the Use:

Short-term Impacts:

Hiking, jogging, and walking access is typically by single individuals or small groups on improved refuge roads or the 9 miles of hiking trails available. Damage to habitat is negligible. Foot traffic off of designated roads and trails is sporadic and dispersed for minimal disturbance.

Some temporary disturbance does occur to wildlife due to human activity on the land, as with any level of public use. Use is sporadic though and limited. Any unreasonable harassment will be grounds for the refuge manager to close the area to these uses or restrict the uses to minimize harm.

Disturbance to trust species is minimal due to the locations of the designated gravel roads and trails. Short-term impacts to facilities, such as roads and trails, are not expected.

Long-term Impacts:

Long-term impacts are not anticipated; however, plants and wildlife will be monitored.

Cumulative Impacts:

No cumulative impacts are anticipated; however, the program can be modified in the future to mitigate unforeseen impacts.

Public Review and Comment:

This compatibility determination was part of the Draft Comprehensive Conservation Plan and Environmental Assessment (Draft CCP/EA) for Black Bayou Lake National Wildlife Refuge. The availability of the Draft CCP/EA was announced in the *Federal Register* on September 30, 2009, for a 30-day comment period. Copies of the Draft CCP/EA were posted at refuge headquarters and area locations and over 150 copies were distributed to local landowners; the public; and local, state, and federal agencies.

Determination (check one below):

_____ Use is Not Compatible

___X___Use is Compatible with Following Stipulations

Stipulations Necessary to Ensure Compatibility:

Camping and fires are prohibited, and personal belongings may not be left on the refuge overnight. Harassment of wildlife is prohibited, as well as the taking of any plant, animal, or artifact from the refuge. If any adverse impacts occur from any aspect of public access, then further restrictions may be imposed to protect the plant and animal resources of the refuge. Any group associated with a commercial operator (e.g., birding tour) will need to request permission from the refuge manager.

Individuals walking or hiking to support hunting opportunities will follow all refuge regulations and possess a valid hunting permit. Road races/fun runs are generally not allowed if off-refuge sites are available, but permission may be requested from the refuge manager through the special use permit process.

Justification:

Hiking, walking, and jogging, as identified in this determination, are not expected to materially interfere with or detract from the mission of the National Wildlife Refuge System or from the purposes for which the refuge was established. The associated disturbance to wildlife and habitat is temporary and minor. Monitoring will be conducted to ensure that these uses remain compatible. If uses increase and impacts are suspected, a re-evaluation will be conducted and corrective actions taken to protect refuge resources. These uses provide opportunities to participate in wildlife observation and photography. Outdoor recreational activities provide individuals with quality wildlife-dependent experiences, educational opportunities, and allow them to utilize a natural environment. This activity also supports our initiative to promote physical fitness opportunities on public lands.

Mandatory 10-Year Re-evaluation Date: March 10, 2020

Description of Use:
Boating – Motorized and Human-powered

Black Bayou Lake, consisting of approximately 1,500 acres, is open to boating. Outboard motors greater than 50 horsepower are prohibited on the lake. Boating facilitates fishing and wildlife observation and photography. Access to the lake is from a boat ramp located on the refuge. The refuge is open during daylight hours only. Entry on all or portions of the lake may be temporarily suspended by posting upon occasions of unusual or critical conditions affecting land, water, vegetation, wildlife populations, or public safety.

Boating provides access to fishing, wildlife observation, and wildlife photography, which are all priority public uses under the National Wildlife Refuge System Improvement Act of 1997.

Availability of Resources:

Resources involved in the administration and management of the use:

Personnel time associated with administration and law enforcement;

Special equipment, facilities, or improvements necessary to support the use:

Boat ramp, brochures, parking lot, and access roads;

Maintenance costs:

Every 3 to 5 years the annual maintenance costs may increase in order to provide gravel for parking lots and roads and to replace signs.

Monitoring costs:

Minimal costs are associated with monitoring the consequences of the public having access to the refuge, such as degree of littering and vandalism.

Offsetting revenues:

None

Anticipated Impacts of the Use:

Boating is restricted to the lake which is not directly connected to any other water body or tributary. Disturbance by boats may affect wildlife, but it is expected to be minimal, especially since boat motor size is restricted. One small rookery exists on the lake but is inaccessible by boat due to emergent vegetation and shallow water. Continued monitoring for significant disturbance to wildlife, in particular birds, will allow the refuge to determine if additional regulations are needed if use increases. Any unreasonable harassment will be grounds for the manager to close the area to boating or restrict the use to minimize harm. The possibility exists that aquatic invasive plants could be introduced to the lake from boats and their trailers. Weekly monitoring of the boat ramp area is conducted by refuge staff for new invaders and signs are present at the boat ramp informing the public about invasive plants and the precautionary measures that should be taken to prevent new invasions from occurring.

Public Review and Comment:

This compatibility determination was part of the Draft Comprehensive Conservation Plan and Environmental Assessment (Draft CCP/EA) for Black Bayou Lake National Wildlife Refuge. The availability of the Draft CCP/EA was announced in the *Federal Register* on September 30, 2009, for a 30-day comment period. Copies of the Draft CCP/EA were posted at refuge headquarters and area locations and over 150 copies were distributed to local landowners; the public; and local, state, and federal agencies.

Determination (check one below):

_____ Use is Not Compatible

__X__ Use is Compatible with Following Stipulations

Stipulations Necessary to Ensure Compatibility:

Motorized land vehicles are required to remain on designated roads only. Boats and other personal belongings are not allowed to be left on the refuge overnight. Harassment of wildlife is prohibited. Outboard motors greater than 50 horsepower are prohibited. Boating is allowed during daylight hours only. If any adverse impacts occur from any aspect of boating, then further restrictions may be imposed to protect the plant and animal resources of the refuge.

Justification:

Outdoor recreational activities provide individuals with quality wildlife-dependent experiences and educational opportunities, and allow them to utilize a natural environment. Motorized and human-powered boating for fishing and wildlife observation is a low-impact and low-cost activity on Black

Bayou Lake NWR. Boating is considered a wildlife-oriented activity and does not materially detract from or interfere with the purposes of the refuge or mission of the National Wildlife Refuge System.

Mandatory 10-Year Re-evaluation Date: March 10, 2020

Description of Use:
All-terrain Vehicles

All-terrain vehicles (ATVs) are generally defined as 3-, 4-, or 6-wheeled vehicles that are equipped with low pressure tires designed primarily for off-road use. The use of ATVs is strictly in support of the priority public use of hunting. The refuge has a very limited system of roads and only two ATV trails exist on the refuge. All ATV use is restricted to 4.4-miles of marked trails. ATVs are prohibited from one hour after legal shooting hours end until 4:00 a.m. Trails are marked with signs and are closed from March 1 through August 31. ATV access is by the general public for access to hunting areas. ATV tires are restricted to those no larger than 25x12, with a maximum 1" lug height and a maximum allowable tire pressure of 7 lbs. psi, as indicated on the tire by the manufacturer. ATVs are usually trailored to a parking lot and ridden on the trail to access remote areas within the refuge prior to walking to hunting areas. The existing designated trail system is close to optimum for the public use program. Minor additions/deletions, re-routing or seasonal opening date changes may be implemented from time-to-time to address needs as they occur. No major changes/modifications are foreseen.

Availability of Resources:

Resources involved in the administration and management of the use:

Personnel time associated with administration and law enforcement.

Special equipment, facilities, or improvements necessary to support the use:

Access roads, parking lots, trails, brochures.

Maintenance costs:

Maintenance costs are already considered in the cost of maintaining a hunting program.

Monitoring costs:

None

Offsetting revenues:

None

Anticipated Impacts of the Use:

Use of ATVs does result in some minor disturbance to wildlife as with any use. Restricting use to designated trails routed to avoid sensitive areas, such as major stream crossings or archaeological areas, and opening trails only to seasonal use minimizes overall potential impacts. The primary compatibility issue of concern is with disturbance to migratory waterfowl. However, migratory waterfowl are not significantly impacted by ATV use due to trails being limited to areas where migratory birds do not congregate.

Public Review and Comment:

This compatibility determination was part of the Draft Comprehensive Conservation Plan and Environmental Assessment (Draft CCP/EA) for Black Bayou Lake National Wildlife Refuge. The availability of the Draft CCP/EA was announced in the *Federal Register* on September 30, 2009, for a 30-day comment period. Copies of the Draft CCP/EA were posted at refuge headquarters and area locations and over 150 copies were distributed to local landowners; the public; and local, state, and federal agencies.

Determination (check one below):

　　Use is Not Compatible

　X　Use is Compatible with Following Stipulations

Stipulations Necessary to Ensure Compatibility:

ATVs trails are open only from September 1 through February 28. Restrictions apply to tire size and ATVs can only be used on the designated trails. ATVs and other personal belongings are not allowed to be left on the refuge overnight. Harassment of wildlife is prohibited. If adverse impacts occur from any aspect of this limited public use, then further restrictions may be imposed to protect the plant and animal resources of the refuge.

Justification:

Use of ATVs is an access concession strictly in support of the priority public use of hunting. ATVs cause much less damage to trails than do conventional and 4-wheel drive vehicles. Use of ATVs helps distribute hunters, thereby facilitating a balanced harvest and reducing hunter crowding. This access enhances the pursuit of wildlife-dependent recreation in this resource-rich area. Providing such recreation is a refuge objective, and demand for this access is high among users.

Mandatory 10-Year Re-evaluation Date:　March 10, 2020

Description of Use:
Plant gathering

Berry picking is not one of the six priority public wildlife-dependent uses of the National Wildlife Refuge System but it is a historical use of the land before the refuge was established. The collection of native fruit on the refuge is for personal (non-commercial) use.

Mayhaw fruit ripens in late April-May, with collection being very time consuming and quite difficult, with further complication of the refuge being flooded in some years. No more than a few individuals make an effort to gather mayhaws, resulting in very little quantity of fruit actually removed, and therefore no restriction is made on the number of individuals allowed for this use. Blackberries/dewberries grow in thickets in the understory along trails and in the upland forest.

Sweet pecans are collected in the autumn off of the ground. Most pecan gathering occurs in and around the visitor's center and maintenance shop where several old pecan trees stand.

Seldom has the refuge received a request for acorn collection. These will be evaluated on a case-by-case basis to determine if the cause is for reforestation and whether productivity of the tree species is available. Stipulations for area and methods of collection will be issued with a special use permit. No commercial operations will be allowed.

Berry-picking, pecan, and acorn collections will be allowed on the entire refuge. Mayhaws occur in the bottomland hardwoods, and blackberries/dewberries are in most any of the areas on the refuge. Picking would most likely occur in the mornings of late spring for mayhaws and late summer for blackberries/dewberries. No commercial equipment will be used. Mayhaw pickers may use cherry picking ladders to get in the tops of trees but will have to carry the ladder in and out on each trip. Mayhaws will primarily be picked in areas adjacent to roads or in water by boat.

This was an existing use prior to refuge establishment, and the general public still requests access for the activity as it is a traditional use. The demand for this use is very light, but the refuge wants the public to feel free to pick a handful of blackberries, mayhaws, or pecans to eat while walking the refuge.

Availability of Resources:

Resources involved in the administration and management of the use:

Staff will not be involved in the collection of berries and pecans. Acorn collection proposals will be evaluated on a case-by-case basis within existing resources.

Special equipment, facilities, or improvements necessary to support the use:

None

Maintenance costs:

None

Monitoring costs:

Monitoring and compliance will be handled within existing resources, programs, and staff time.

Offsetting revenues:

None

Anticipated Impacts of the Use:

Short-term Impacts:

Collection of fruits and berries for personal use will have a negligible impact on forest and wildlife resources. Some habitat trampling or disturbance may occur with foot-traffic to berry-picking areas, but no more than other uses such as wildlife observation while hiking. Short-term impacts are minimal and not significant due to the current, small number of users.

No significant increase in the magnitude of this use is expected over the next 10 years. In fact, there may be a decrease based on change in demographics. If for some unanticipated reason this use increases a significant degree, a new compatibility determination will be required and regulating measures (e.g., special use permit and quantity restrictions) could be evaluated with subsequent public comment.

Long-term Impacts:

Direct impact is a small amount of plant resources taken from individual trees or shrubs, but is extremely insignificant on the scale of habitat acres available over the long-term for mayhaw and blackberry/dewberry seeding. Little concern exists for removing too many mayhaws since the amount is insignificant and it has been noted by Martin et al. (1961) that "the small apple-like fruits are not used by wildlife to nearly so great an extent as might be anticipated." Most of the pecans are near refuge facilities and will rot on the ground. Blackberries/dewberries are ubiquitous in range and so numerous that wildlife will not be impacted by the small amount removed for human consumption.

Cumulative Impacts:

No negative cumulative impacts are expected. As stated earlier, it is expected the use will decline in the future as demographics change. No conflict of users occurs since berry picking takes place outside of the hunting season, except for pecan gathering, which is primarily conducted in the non-hunting zone of the refuge.

Public Review and Comment:

This compatibility determination was part of the Draft Comprehensive Conservation Plan and Environmental Assessment (Draft CCP/EA) for Black Bayou Lake National Wildlife Refuge. The availability of the Draft CCP/EA was announced in the *Federal Register* on September 30, 2009, for a 30-day comment period. Copies of the Draft CCP/EA were posted at refuge headquarters and area locations and over 150 copies were distributed to local landowners; the public; and local, state, and federal agencies.

Determination (check one below):

    Use is Not Compatible

  X   Use is Compatible with Following Stipulations

Stipulations Necessary to Ensure Compatibility:

Berry pickers may not sell berries or otherwise engage in commercial activities associated with berry picking. Cherry picking ladders can be used but must be carried in and out on each trip. No personal belongings may be left on the refuge overnight. All refuge regulations are applicable, including vehicle use.

Justification:

Picking wild berries for personal consumption is not an economic use and does not materially interfere with or detract from the fulfillment of the National Wildlife Refuge System mission or the purpose of the refuge. No significant wildlife or habitat disturbance occurs from the light demand, and accessibility is limited to roads and trails. No refuge support is needed for implementation of this use. Picking wild berries fosters wildlife observation on the refuge and illustrates the advantage of certain plants and a healthy environment to the public.

Martin, Zim and Nelson. 1961. "American Wildlife and Plants—A Guide to Wildlife Food Habits"

Mandatory 10-Year Re-evaluation Date: March 10, 2020

Description of Use:
Bicycling

Bicycling facilitates travel and access for the priority public uses on Black Bayou Lake NWR. Priority public uses as defined in the National Wildlife Refuge System Improvement Act of 1997 include hunting, fishing, wildlife observation, wildlife photography, and environmental education and interpretation.

Bicycles are considered legal modes of transportation on most state and parish roads. Therefore, in most cases where refuge roads are open to vehicles, they are open to bicycles. Bicycles will not be allowed if there are safety issues or wildlife disturbance issues. Secondary roads that are closed to vehicles are open to bicycles since they support the wildlife-dependent recreational activities. Bicycle races or other organized group events are not allowed.

The refuge is open during daylight areas only. Bicycling will only be allowed in areas open to the public. Cyclists accessing the refuge for hunting will need to possess a valid hunting permit and follow all refuge regulations. Access to the refuge is open every day. Entry on all or portions of individual areas may be temporarily suspended by posting upon occasions of unusual or critical conditions affecting land, water, vegetation, wildlife populations, or public safety.

Bicycling to facilitate non-consumptive priority public uses involves observing the natural landscape from a bicycle. Riders stop to observe associated animals and plant communities. The use mainly occurs by individual users rather than groups.

Bicycle travel is conducted in accordance with stipulations necessary to ensure compatibility. Access to the refuge is necessary for desirable use and management of the refuge. Bicycle travel on the refuge provides increased access and opportunities to participate in priority public uses such as hunting, fishing, wildlife observation, and wildlife photography. It is an alternative means of travel to view the refuge's diverse biological assets and can be less physically demanding than pedestrian travel for some users. It can also be a form of exercise while enjoying the outdoors that coincides with the Federal Government's initiative, "America's Public Lands Get Fit with US" to promote physical fitness activities on public lands.

Availability of Resources:

Resources involved in the administration and management of the use:

Personnel time associated with administration and law enforcement.

Special equipment, facilities, or improvements necessary to support the use:

None

Maintenance costs:

None

Monitoring costs:

Monitoring and compliance will be handled within existing resources, programs, and staff time.

Offsetting revenues:

None

Anticipated Impacts of the Use:

Short-term Impacts:

Bicycle access is typically by single individuals on improved refuge roads. Damage to habitat is negligible. Access by bicycle during the hunting season is often used to retrieve game or to access remote areas of the refuge to hunt. Use is sporadic and dispersed for minimal disturbance.

Some temporary disturbance can occur to wildlife due to human activity on the land, but no more so than any other use, and actually probably less. Disturbance to wildlife is temporary and minor but will be monitored. Any unreasonable harassment will be grounds for the refuge manager to close the area to bicycling or restrict the use to minimize harm.

Long-term Impacts:

No long-term impacts are anticipated; however, the program can be modified in the future to mitigate unforeseen impacts.

Cumulative Impacts:

No cumulative impacts are anticipated; however, the program can be modified in the future to mitigate unforeseen impacts.

Public Review and Comment:

This compatibility determination was part of the Draft Comprehensive Conservation Plan and Environmental Assessment (Draft CCP/EA) for Black Bayou Lake National Wildlife Refuge. The availability of the Draft CCP/EA was announced in the *Federal Register* on September 30, 2009, for a 30-day comment period. Copies of the Draft CCP/EA were posted at refuge headquarters and area locations and over 150 copies were distributed to local landowners; the public; and local, state, and federal agencies.

Determination (check one below):

Use is Not Compatible

__X__ Use is Compatible with Following Stipulations

Stipulations Necessary to Ensure Compatibility:

No equipment may be left on the refuge overnight. Harassment of wildlife is prohibited. If any adverse impacts occur from any aspect of this use, then further restrictions may be imposed to protect the plant and animal resources on the refuge. Individuals using bicycles to support hunting will follow all refuge regulations and will posses a valid hunting permit.

Justification:

Bicycle use, as identified in this determination, is not expected to materially interfere with or detract from the mission of the National Wildlife Refuge System or from the purposes for which the refuge was established. The associated disturbance to wildlife and habitat is temporary and minor. Monitoring will be conducted to ensure that this use remains compatible. If use increases and impacts are suspected, a re-evaluation will be conducted and corrective actions taken to protect refuge resources. Bicycles are used to facilitate priority public uses as a reasonable mode of access. Outdoor recreational activities provide individuals with quality wildlife-dependent experiences, educational opportunities, and allow them to utilize a natural environment. This activity also supports our initiative to promote physical fitness on public lands.

Mandatory 10-Year Re-evaluation Date: March 10, 2020

Description of Use:

Forest Management – Timber Harvest

Forest management, per timber harvest sales, is the only realistic tool that is available to enable the refuge to achieve wildlife habitat objectives. The forests of the southeast often require significant disturbance at a level of acreage that cannot be achieved without commercial operations. Therefore, forest management packages are offered for bid, with those trees in excess of management needs offered for harvest. The excess value of the trees in relation to the cost of the entire management package will be the amount paid to the government and placed in the general fund. Forest management is conducted to benefit wildlife and further the refuge purpose. It is not based on current or future economic gain from timber harvest.

Refuge foresters, biologists, and managers decide where forest management is needed. Designated areas are marked with blue paint and on a map. Timber harvest sales occur when forest management is needed, soil conditions are appropriate for the least impact, and when the bidding process is complete.

Active forest management consists of mechanical removal of commercial and non-commercial forest products by refuge personnel or contractors utilizing conventional logging equipment. The refuge is sub-divided into manageable sized compartments that are selected for forest management activities based on the greatest need for wildlife habitat improvement, tempered with considerations for spatial, temporal, and area constraints. Once selected, vegetative/wildlife data are collected and analyzed to determine the extent of treatment needed, then expressed in a document that details the specific silvicultural strategies necessary to obtain specific wildlife habitat objectives. Only those trees marked with two spots of blue paint could be cut. Stumps are cut as low as possible to the ground as long as some portion of the paint remains visible on the stump. Special use permits detailing specific environmental, fiscal, physical, and administrative constraints are issued to contractors that have bid the highest for the forest products or through the negotiation process, if applicable. All state and federal permits, clearances, and consultations, such as State Historic Preservation Office cultural resource clearance, permits associated with the Clean Water Act, and Intra-Service Section 7 consultation, are obtained prior to implementing the special use permit. Timber harvest sales require a pre-entry conference between a refuge forester and permittee before starting logging operations.

Forest management is often needed to improve the general health, productivity, diversity, and quality of the bottomland and upland forests. Forest stands often need to be gradually thinned to reduce competition, to increase diversity, to lessen the chance for epidemics of damaging insects, and to remove diseased trees. Accomplishment of habitat improvement targets heavily utilize the commercial sale of refuge forest products (timber sales) to accomplish needed habitat improvements since funding and staffing never has, and never will be, at a level to achieve force account (refuge staff) conducted actions only.

The comprehensive conservation plan calls for a forest management plan to be written for Black Bayou Lake NWR. This plan will incorporate all of the objectives written in the comprehensive conservation plan, as well as the operating parameters to execute a timber harvest.

Availability of Resources:

Resources involved in the administration and management of the use:

Forest management activities are administered by refuge staff and do not exceed the general operational costs of the refuge. Recent management staff losses due to inadequate operational funding is and will continue to impact the refuge's ability to implement habitat management actions at a level needed to maintain and improve habitat conditions. This activity is perhaps the single highest priority for the refuge due to its critical nature in achieving wildlife objectives (LMVJV 2007) and staff will continue to make every effort to address forest stand improvements needed.

Special equipment, facilities, or improvements necessary to support the use:

None

Maintenance costs:

None

Monitoring Costs:

Refuge staff will conduct monitoring protocols in line with adaptive management, the comprehensive conservation plan, and the future forest management plan to determine when habitat condition targets are met signaling treatment and to monitor achievement of habitat condition objectives post treatment.

Offsetting Revenues:

Utilizing contract loggers to achieve forest habitat management goals is the only way to achieve improvement given the lack of staff to implement force account harvest activities. Receipts generated from the sale of forest products removed from the refuge are deposited into the Refuge Revenue Sharing Account. The funds collected annually from all refuges are distributed to the parishes on a prorated basis (acreage of refuge land within each parish and appraised value of this land) as an "in-lieu-taxes payment" as directed by the Refuge Revenue Sharing Act.

Anticipated Impacts of the Use:

Short-term Impacts

Logging activities result in some soil disturbance which causes minor soil compaction and erosion. Minor siltation and turbidity of streams may occur. Most streams on the refuge are intermittent and are mostly dry during normal logging seasons. Best management practices are implemented; thereby, buffer zones are placed along bayous, rivers, and creeks. Besides the removal of some trees on sales, minor damage of some residual trees and other vegetation will occur.

Long-term Impacts

No adverse long-term impacts are anticipated. On the contrary, the refuge expects positive long-term impacts such as increased forest health, diversity, species composition, and vertical structure. These forest characteristics will lead to better habitat for resident wildlife, such as squirrels and deer, waterfowl, and nesting songbirds, such as hooded, Kentucky, and Swainson's warblers.

Cumulative Impacts

No adverse cumulative impacts are anticipated. The refuge forest management program implemented according to the comprehensive conservation plan will promote a healthy, native forest for generations to come.

Public Review and Comment:

This compatibility determination was part of the Draft Comprehensive Conservation Plan and Environmental Assessment (Draft CCP/EA) for Black Bayou Lake National Wildlife Refuge. The availability of the Draft CCP/EA was announced in the *Federal Register* on September 30, 2009, for a 30-day comment period. Copies of the Draft CCP/EA were posted at refuge headquarters and area locations and over 150 copies were distributed to local landowners; the public; and local, state, and federal agencies.

Determination (check one below):

    Use is Not Compatible

X   Use is Compatible with Following Stipulations

Stipulations Necessary to Ensure Compatibility:

- Ensure adherence to the future forest management plan.
- Sale of forest products is utilized only when it is the most efficient and cost effective method of managing refuge forests.
- Harvested trees are sold under fair trade principles, and in a manner in which the government will be compensated at a fair market value.
- All roads, pipelines, and ditches must be kept clear of brush and debris.
- All tops falling into rights-of-way must be immediately cleared.
- To prevent rutting on access roads, entry is prohibited during periods of wet ground conditions.
- No littering or fires.
- No firearms or archery equipment may be transported in vehicles.
- Unmarked trees less than 3 inches diameter may be cut to provide access to marked trees.
- Personal protective equipment (e.g., glasses, gloves, chaps) are strongly recommended.
- Best Management Practices will be implemented.

Justification:

The refuge forest needs a variety of treatments to enhance habitat conditions for all migratory and resident wildlife species. Bottomland forests must have openings created to keep adequate understory and midstory for a variety of songbirds, white-tailed deer, turkey, and other wildlife (LMVJV 2007). Thinning bottomland forests will create better conditions for remaining trees to grow larger and create better mast crop for wood ducks and other game species. Timber harvest in upland pine and hardwood forests is directed towards increasing tree species diversity and vertical structure. Forest management, per timber harvest, is compatible with the purposes for which the refuge was established and is the single most effective tool enabling the refuge to meet wildlife habitat objectives.

LMVJV Forest Resource Conservation Working Group. 2007. Restoration, Management and Monitoring of Forest Resources in the Mississippi Alluvial Valley: Recommendations for Enhancing Wildlife Habitat. Edited by R. Wilson, K. Ribbeck, S. King, and D. Twedt

Mandatory 10-Year Re-evaluation Date: March 10, 2020

Approval of Compatibility Determinations

The signature of approval is for all compatibility determinations considered within the comprehensive conservation plan for Black Bayou Lake National Wildlife Refuge. If one of the descriptive uses is considered for compatibility outside of the comprehensive conservation plan, the approval signature becomes part of that determination.

Refuge Manager: _____ *Signed* / 1/14/10
(Signature/Date)

Regional Compatibility
Coordinator: _____ *Signed* 2/16/18
(Signature/Date)

Refuge Supervisor: _____ *Signed* 2/22/10
(Signature/Date)

Regional Chief, National
Wildlife Refuge System,
Southeast Region: _____ *Signed* 2-23-10
Jon Andrew (Signature/Date)

Appendix G. Intra-Service Section 7 Biological Evaluation

Originating Person: Gypsy Hanks
Telephone Number: 318-726-4222   **E-Mail:** gypsy_hanks@fws.gov
Date: 03-10-09

PROJECT NAME (Grant Title/Number): Comprehensive Conservation Plan for Black Bayou Lake NWR

I.   **Service Program:**
___ **Ecological Services**
___ **Federal Aid**
    ___ **Clean Vessel Act**
    ___ **Coastal Wetlands**
    ___ **Endangered Species Section 6**
    ___ **Partners for Fish and Wildlife**
    ___ **Sport Fish Restoration**
    ___ **Wildlife Restoration**
___ **Fisheries**
  X **Refuges/Wildlife**

II.   **State/Agency:** Louisiana/USFWS

III.   **Station Name:** Black Bayou Lake NWR

IV.   **Description of Proposed Action (attach additional pages as needed):**
Implement the Comprehensive Conservation Plan for Black Bayou Lake NWR by adopting the proposed alternative. This plan directs the management of the refuge for the next 15 years.

V.   **Pertinent Species and Habitat:**

A.   Include species/habitat occurrence map: No known endangered or threatened species utilize the refuge. There is the small possibility of a Louisiana black bear passing through the refuge. However, due to the small acreage of available habitat and the location of the refuge in the city limits of Monroe, a black bear would be unlikely to take up residence on the refuge.

B.   Complete the following table:

Table 1. Listed/proposed species/critical habitat that occur or may occur within the project area:

SPECIES/CRITICAL HABITAT	STATUS[1]
Louisiana Black Bear	T

[1]STATUS: E=endangered, T=threatened, PE=proposed endangered, PT=proposed threatened, CH=critical habitat, PCH=proposed critical habitat, C=candidate species

VI.   **Location (attach map):**

A.   **Ecoregion Number and Name:** Mississippi Alluvial Valley

B.   **County and State:** Ouachita Parish, Louisiana

C.   **Section, township, and range (or latitude and longitude):** See Figure 1.

D.   **Distance (miles) and direction to nearest town:** ~2 miles north of Monroe, Louisiana on east side of U.S. Highway 165.

E.   **Species/habitat occurrence:**

Not applicable.

VII.   **Determination of Effects:**

A. **Explanation of effects of the action on species and critical habitats in item V. B (attach additional pages as needed):**

Table 2. Project impacts to listed/proposed species/critical habitat.

SPECIES/ CRITICAL HABITAT	IMPACTS TO SPECIES/CRITICAL HABITAT
Louisiana black bear	None

There is no critical habitat designation for Louisiana black bears on Black Bayou Lake NWR. The refuge consists of approximately 4,500 acres, with 1,600 acres open water. The refuge is surrounded by suburban and urban sprawl. The refuge would not be able to sustain a bear population. In the unlikely event that a black bear would take up residence on the refuge, nothing in the preferred alternative would adversely impact black bears.

B.   Explanation of actions to be implemented to reduce adverse effects:

Table 3. Conservation measures proposed to minimize or eliminate adverse impacts to proposed/listed species, critical habitat.

SPECIES/ CRITICAL HABITAT	ACTIONS TO MINIMIZE IMPACTS
Louisiana black bear	None

As stated above, nothing in the preferred alternative would negatively affect black bears. All habitat management, including forest treatments, would be beneficial to most wildlife, including bears, by providing more structure, food, and possible den trees. Big game hunting on the refuge is limited to "archery only" deer hunting; therefore, the possibility of a bear being mistakenly shot is minuscule.

VIII.   Effect Determination and Response Requested:

Table 4. The effect determination and response requested for impacts to each proposed/listed species/critical habitat.

SPECIES/ CRITICAL HABITAT	DETERMINATION[1]			RESPONSE[1] REQUESTED
	NE	NA	AA	
Louisiana black bear	X			Concurrence

[1]DETERMINATION/RESPONSE REQUESTED:

   NE = no effect. This determination is appropriate when the proposed action will not directly, indirectly, or cumulatively impact, either positively or negatively, any listed, proposed, candidate species or designated/proposed critical habitat. Response Requested is optional but a Concurrence is recommended for a complete Administrative Record.

   NA = not likely to adversely affect. This determination is appropriate when the proposed action is not likely to adversely impact any listed, proposed, candidate species or designated/proposed critical habitat or there may be beneficial effects to these resources. Response Requested is a Concurrence.

   AA = likely to adversely affect. This determination is appropriate when the proposed action is likely to adversely impact any listed, proposed, candidate species or designated/proposed critical habitat. Response Requested for listed species is Formal Consultation. Response Requested for proposed or candidate species is Conference.

Signed   4-6-09

Signature (originating station)   date

Wildlife Biologist

Title

If the project description changes or incidental take exceeds that which has been exempted under section 9 of the Act, then the Ecological Services Field Office must be contacted.

IX. Reviewing Ecological Services Office Evaluation:

A. Concurrence _____ Non-concurrence _____

B. Formal consultation required _____

C. Conference required _____

D. Informal conference required _____

E. Remarks (attach additional pages as needed):

Signed

4/30/09

_____   _____
Signature   Date

Field Supervisor
_____
Title/Office

Lafayette ES FO
_____

Figure 11. Location of Black Bayou Lake

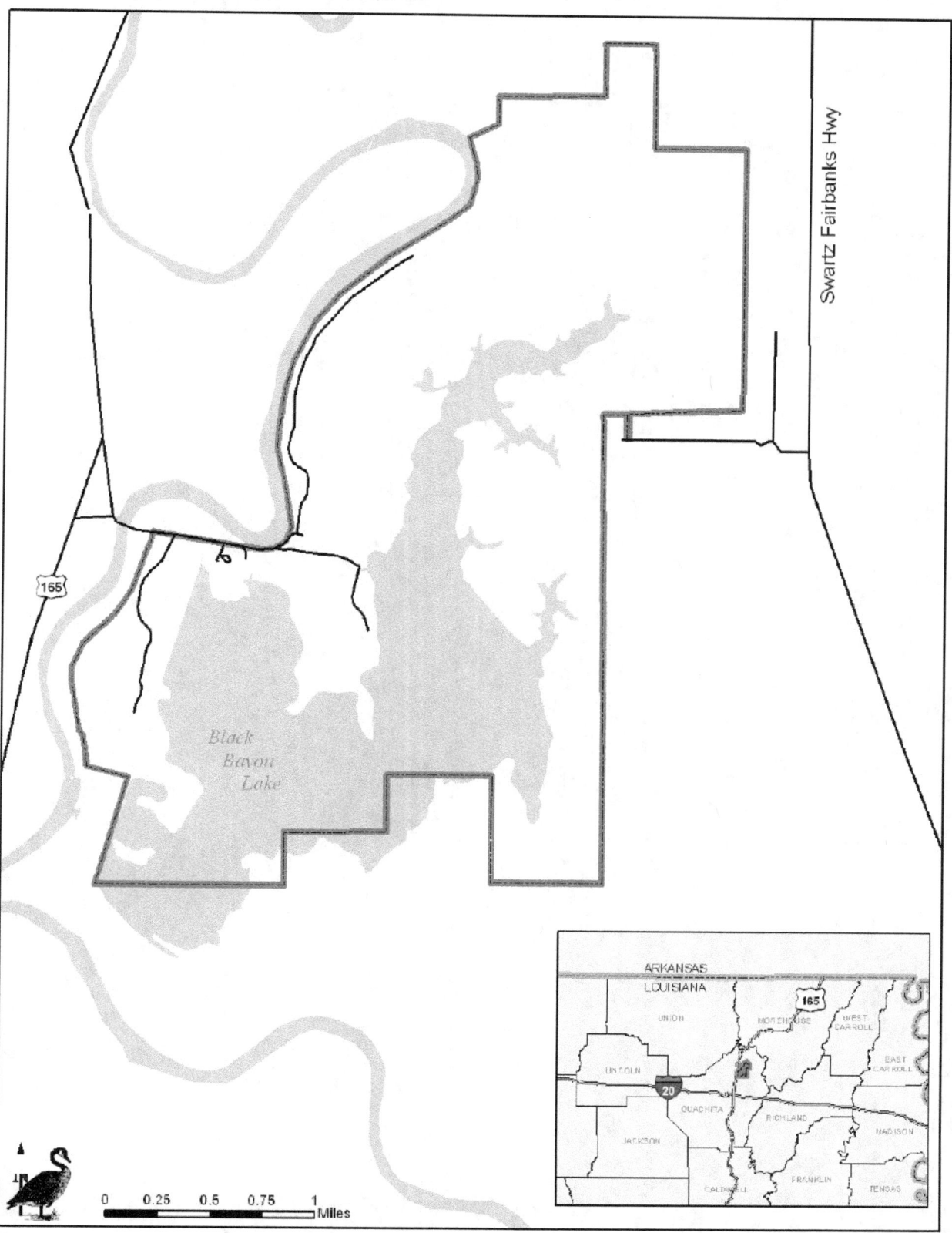

Appendix H. Wilderness Review

The Wilderness Act of 1964 defines a wilderness area as an area of federal land that retains its primeval character and influence, without permanent improvements or human inhabitation, and is managed so as to preserve its natural conditions and which:

1. generally appears to have been influenced primarily by the forces of nature, with the imprint of man's work substantially unnoticeable;

2. has outstanding opportunities for solitude or primitive and unconfined types of recreation;

3. has at least 5,000 contiguous roadless acres or is of sufficient size to make practicable its preservation and use in an unimpeded condition; or is a roadless island, regardless of size;

4. does not substantially exhibit the effects of logging, farming, grazing, or other extensive development or alteration of the landscape, or its wilderness character could be restored through appropriate management at the time of review; and

5. may contain ecological, geological, or other features of scientific, educational, scenic, or historic value.

The lands within Black Bayou Lake NWR were reviewed for their suitability in meeting the criteria for wilderness, as defined by the Wilderness Act of 1964. No lands in the refuge were found to meet these criteria. Therefore, the suitability of refuge lands for wilderness designation in not further analyzed in this plan.

Appendix I. Refuge Biota

North Louisiana NWR Complex
Bird List

This list contains those species of birds thought to occur on lands owned by the North Louisiana NWR Complex according to various literature sources, surveys, and observations.

Grebes
Pied-billed Grebe (*Podilymbus podiceps*)
Horned Grebe (*Podiceps auritus*)

Pelicans, Cormorants, and Darters
American White Pelican (*Pelecanus erythrorhynchos*)
Double-crested Cormorant (*Phalacrocorax auritus*)
Anhinga (*Anhinga anhinga*)

Bitterns, Herons, and Egrets
American Bittern (*Botaurus lentiginosus*)
Least Bittern (*Ixobrychus exilis*)
Great Blue Heron (*Ardea herodias*)
Great Egret (*Ardea alba*)
Snowy Egret (*Egretta thula*)
Little Blue Heron (*Efretta caerulea*)
Tricolored Heron (*Egretta tricolor*)
Cattle Egret (*Bubulcus ibis*)
Green Heron (*Butoroides virescens*)
Black-crowned Night-heron (*Nycticorax nycticorax*)
Yellow-crowned Night-heron (*Nyctanassa violacea*)

Ibises, Spoonbills, Storks, and New World Vultures
White Ibis (*Eudocimis albus*)
Roseate Spoonbill (*Ajaia ajaia*)
Wood Stork (*Mycteria americana*)
Black Vulture (*Coragyps atratus*)
Turkey Vulture (*Cathartes aura*)

Waterfowl
Greater White-fronted Goose (*Anser albifrons*)
Snow Goose (*Chen caerulescens*)
Ross's Goose (*Chen rossi*)
Canada Goose (*Branta canadensis*)
Black-bellied Whistling Duck (*Dendrocygna autumnalis*)
Wood Duck (*Aix sponsa*)
Gadwall (*Anas strepera*)
American Wigeon (*Anas americana*)
American Black Duck (*Anas rubripes*)
Mallard (*Anas platyrhynchos*)

Waterfowl

Mottled Duck (*Anas fulvigula*)
Blue-winged Teal (*Anas discors*)
Northern Shoveler (*Anas clypeata*)
Northern Pintail (*Anas acuta*)
Green-winged Teal (*Anas crecca*)
Canvasback (*Aythya valisineria*)
Redhead (*Aythya americana*)
Ring-necked Duck (*Aythya collaris*)
Greater Scaup (*Aythya marila*)
Lesser Scaup (*Aythya affinis*)
Bufflehead (*Bucephala albeola*)
Hooded Merganser (*Lophodytes cucullatus*)
Common Merganser (*Mergus merganser*)
Red-breasted Merganser (*Mergus serrator*)
Ruddy Duck (*Oxyura jamaicensis*)

Hawks, Eagles, and Kites

Osprey (*Pandion haliaetus*)
Mississippi Kite (*Ictinia mississippiensis*)
Bald Eagle (*Haliaeetus leucocephalus*)
Northern Harrier (*Circus cyaneus*)
Sharp-shinned Hawk (*Accipiter striatus*)
Cooper's Hawk (*Accipiter cooperii*)
Red-shouldered Hawk (*Buteo lineatus*)
Broad-winged Hawk (*Buteo platypterus*)
Red-tailed Hawk (*Buteo jamaicensis*)
Golden Eagle (*Aquila chrysaetos*)

True Falcons

American Kestrel (*Falco sparverius*)
Merlin (*Falco columbarius*)
Peregrine Falcon (*Falco peregrinus*)

Gallinaceous Birds (Quail, Turkey, and Allies)

Wild Turkey (*Meleagris gallopavo*)
Northern Bobwhite (*Colinus virginianus*)

Rails, Gallinules, Coots, and Cranes

King Rail (*Rallus elegans*)
Virginia Rail (*Rallus limicola*)
Sora)*Porzana carolina*)
Purple Gallinule (*Porphyrula martinica*)
Common Moorhen (*Gallinula chloropus*)
American Coot (*Fulica americana*)

Plovers

American Golden-Plover (*Pluvialis dominica*)
Black-bellied Plover (*Pluvialis squatarola*)
Semipalmated Plover (*Charadrius semipalmatus*)
Piping Plover (*Charadrius melodus*)

Plovers

    Snowy Plover (*Charadrius alexandrinus*)
    Killdeer (*Charadrius vociferous*)

Avocets and Sandpipers

    Black-necked Stilt (*Himantopus mexicanus*)
    American Avocet (*Recurvirostra americana*)
    Greater Yellowlegs (*Tringa melanoleuca*)
    Lesser Yellowlegs (*Tringa flavipes*)
    Solitary Sandpiper (*Tringa solitaria*)
    Spotted Sandpiper (*Actitis macularia*)
    Upland Sandpiper (*Bartramia longicauda*)
    Whimbrel (*Numenius phaeopus*)
    Willet (*Catoptrophorus semipalmatus*)
    Dunlin (*Calidris alpine*)
    Semipalmated Sandpiper (*Calidris pusilla*)
    Western Sandpiper (*Calidris mauri*)
    Least Sandpiper (*Calidris minutilla*)
    Pectoral Sandpiper (*Caladris melanotos*)
    Stilt Sandpiper (*Calidris himantopus*)
    Wilson's Phalarope
    Short-billed Dowitcher (*Limnodromus griseus*)
    Long-billed Dowitcher (*Limnodromus scolopaceus*)
    Wilson's Snipe (*Gallinago gallinago*)
    American Woodcock (*Scolopax minor*)

Gulls, Terns, and Skimmers

    Bonaparte's Gull (*Larus philadelphia*)
    Ring-billed Gull (*Larus delawarensis*)
    Herring Gull (*Larus argentatus*)
    Caspian Tern (*Sterna caspia*)
    Forster's tern (*Sterna forsteri*)
    Least Tern (*Sterna antillarum*)
    Black Tern (*Chlidonias niger*)

Pigeons and Doves

    Rock Dove (*Columba livia*)
    Mourning Dove (*Zenaida macroura*)
    Common Ground Dove (*Columbina passerine*)
    Eurasian Collared Dove (*Streptopelia decaocto*)

Cuckoos

    Black-billed Cuckoo (*Coccyzus erythropthalmus*)
    Yellow-billed Cuckoo (*Coccyzus americanus*)
    Greater Roadrunner (*Geococcyx californianus*)

Owls

    Barn Owl (*Tyto alba*)
    Eastern Screech-Owl (*Otus asio*)
    Great Horned Owl (*Bubo virginianus*)
    Barred Owl (*Strix varia*)

Owls
Short-eared owl (*Asio flammeus*)

Nightjars
Common Nighthawk (*Chordeiles minor*)
Chuck-will's-widow (*Caprimulgus carolinensis*)
Whip-poor-will (*Caprimulgus vociferous*)

Swifts and Hummingbirds
Chimney Swift (*Chaeura pelagica*)
Ruby-throated hummingbird (*Archilochus colubris*)

Kingfishers
Belted Kingfisher (*Ceryle alcyon*)

Woodpeckers
Red-headed Woodpecker (*Melanerpes erythrocephalus*)
Red-bellied Woodpecker (*Melanerpes carolinus*)
Yellow-bellied Sapsucker (*Sphyrapicus varius*)
Downy Woodpecker (*Picoides pubescens*)
Hairy Woodpecker (*Picoides villosus*)
Red-cockaded Woodpecker (*Picoides borealis*)
Northern Flicker (*Colaptes auratus*)
Pileated Woodpecker (*Dryocopus pileatus*)

Shrikes
Loggerhead Shrike (*Lanius ludovicianus*)

Vireos
White-eyed Vireo (*Vireo griseus*)
Yellow-throated Vireo (*Vireo flavifrons*)
Blue-headed Vireo (*Vireo solitarius*)
Warbling Vireo (*Vireo gilvus*)
Philadelphia Vireo (*Vireo philadephicus*)
Red-eyed Vireo (*Vireo olivaceus*)

Jays and Crows
Blue Jay (*Cyanocitta cristata*)
American Crow (*Corvus brachyrhynchos*)
Fish Crow (*Corvus ossigragus*)

Larks
Horned Lark (*Eremophila alpestris*)

Martins and Swallows
Purple Martin (*Progne subis*)
Tree Swallow (*Tachycineta bicolor*)
N. Rough-winged Swallow (*Stelgidopteryx serripennis*)
Bank Swallow (*Riparia riparia*)
Barn Swallow (*Hirundia rustica*)

Chickadees and Titmice

       Carolina Chickadee (*Poecile carolinensis*)
       Tufted Titmouse (*Baeolophus bicolor*)

Nuthatches

       Red-breasted Nuthatch (*Sitta canadensis*)
       White-breasted Nuthatch (*Sitta carolinensis*)
       Brown-headed Nuthatch (*Sitta pusilla*)

Creepers

       Brown Creeper (*Certhia americana*)

Wrens

       Carolina Wren (*Thryothorus ludovicianus*)
       Bewick's Wren (*Thryomanes bewickii*)
       House Wren (*Troglodytes aedon*)
       Winter Wren (*Troglodytes troglodytes*)
       Sedge Wren (*Cistothorus platensis*)

Kinglets and Gnatcatchers

       Golden-crowned Kinglet (*Regulus satrapa*)
       Ruby-crowned Kinglet (*Regulus calendula*)
       Blue-gray Gnatcatcher (*Polioptila caerulea*)

Thrushes

       Eastern Bluebird (*Sialia sialis*)
       Veery (*Catharus fuscescens*)
       Gray-cheeked thrush (*Catharus minimus*)
       Swainson's Thrush (*Catharus ustulatus*)
       Hermit Thrush (*Catharus guttatus*)
       Wood Thrush (*Hylocichla mustelina*)
       American Robin (*Turdus migratorius*)

Mockingbirds and Thrashers

       Gray Catbird (*Dumetella carolinensis*)
       Northern Mockingbird (*Mimus polyglottos*)
       Brown Thrasher (*Toxostoma rufum*)

Starlings

       European Starling (*Sturnus vulgaris*)

Pipits

       American Pipit (*Anthus rubescens*)

Waxwings

       Cedar Waxwing (*Bombycilla garrulous*)

Wood Warblers

       Blue-winged warbler (*Vermivora pinus*)
       Golden-winged Warbler (*Vermivora chrysoptera*)
       Tennessee Warbler (*Vermivora peregrine*)

Wood Warblers
Orange-crowned Warbler (*Vermivora celata*)
Nashville Warbler (*Vermivora ruficapilla*)
Northern Parula (*Parula americana*)
Yellow Warbler (*Dendroica petechia*)
Chestnut-sided Warbler (*Dendroica pensylvanica*)
Magnolia Warbler (*Dendroica magnolia*)
Black-throated Blue Warbler (*Dendroica caerulescens*)
Yellow-rumped Warbler (*Dendroica coronata*)
Black-throated Green Warbler (*Dendroica virens*)
Blackburnian Warbler (*Dendroica fusca*)
Yellow-throated Warbler (*Dendroica dominica*)
Pine Warbler (*Dendroica pinus*)
Prairie Warbler (*Dendroica discolor*)
Palm Warbler (*Dendroica palmarum*)
Bay-breasted Warbler (*Dendroica castanea*)
Blackpoll Warbler (*Dendroica striata*)
Cerulean Warbler (*Dendroica cerulean*)
Black-and-white Warbler (*Mniotilta varia*)
American redstart (*Setophaga ruticilla*)
Prothonotary Warbler (*Protonotaria citrea*)
Worm-eating Warbler (*Helmitheros vermivorus*)
Swainson's warbler (*Limnothlypsis swainsonii*)
Ovenbird (*Seiurus aurocapillus*)
Northern Waterthrush (*Seiurus noveboracensis*)
Louisiana Waterthrush (*Seiurus motacilla*)
Kentucky Warbler (*Oporornis formosus*)
Mourning Warbler (*Oporornis philadelphia*)
Common Yellowthroat (*Geothlypis trichas*)
Hooded Warbler (*Wilsonia citrine*)
Wilson's Warbler (*Wilsonia pusilla*)
Canada Warbler (*Wilsonia canadensis*)
Yellow-breasted Chat (*Icteria virens*)

Tanagers
Summer Tanager (*Piranga rubra*)
Scarlet Tanager (*Piranga olivacea*)

Sparrows
Eastern Towhee (*Pipilo erythrophthalmus*)
Bachman's Sparrow (*Aimophila aestivalis*)
Chipping Sparrow (*Spizella passerine*)
Field Sparrow (*Spizella pusilla*)
Vesper Sparrow (*Pooecetes gramineus*)
Savannah Sparrow (*Passerculus sandwichensis*)
Grasshopper Sparrow (*Ammodramus savannarum*)
Henslow's Sparrow (*Ammodramus henslowii*)
Le Conte's Sparrow (*Ammodramus leconteii*)
Fox Sparrow (*Passerella iliaca*)
Song Sparrow (*Melospiza melodia*)
Lincoln's Sparrow (*Melospiza lincolnii*)

Sparrows
> Swamp Sparrow (*Melospiza georgiana*)
> White-throated Sparrow (*Zonotrichia albicollis*)
> White-crowned Sparrow (*Zonotrichia leucophrys*)
> Dark-eyed Junco (*Junco hyemalis*)
> Lapland Longspur (*Calcarius lapponicus*)

New World Finches
> Northern Cardinal (*Cardinalis cardinalis*)
> Rose-breasted Grosbeak (*Pheuticus ludovicianus*)
> Blue Grosbeak (*Passerina caerulea*)
> Indigo Bunting (*Passerina cyanea*)
> Painted Bunting (*Passerina ciris*)
> Dickcissel (*Spiza americana*)

Blackbirds
> Red-winged Blackbird (*Agelaius phoeniceus*)
> Eastern Meadowlark (*Sturnella magna*)
> Rusty Blackbird (*Euphagus carolinus*)
> Brewer's Blackbird (*Euphagus cyanocephalus*)
> Common Grackle (*Quiscalus quiscula*)
> Brown-headed Cowbird (*Molothrus ater*)
> Orchard Oriole (*Icterus spurious*)
> Baltimore Oriole (*Icterus galbula*)

Old World Finches
> Purple Finch (*Carpodacus purpureus*)
> Pine Siskin (*Carduelis pinus*)
> American Goldfinch (*Carduelis tristis*)
> Evening Grosbeak (*Coccothraustes vespertinus*)

North Louisiana NWR Complex
Mammal List

This list contains those species of mammals thought to occur on lands owned by the North Louisiana NWR Complex according to various literature sources. Those species marked with an asterisk (*) have been documented on the specified refuge by sightings or specimens. The abbreviations are as follows: BBL – Black Bayou Lake NWR, UO – Upper Ouachita NWR, DB – D'Arbonne NWR, FSA tracts – Farm Services Agency. This list is largely based on information from The Mammals of Louisiana and Its Adjacent Waters by Lowery (1974).

Didelphiidae (Opossums)
*Opossum (*Dedelphis marsupialis*)—BBL, UO, DB

Soricidae (Shrews)
*Short-tailed Shrew (*Blarina brevicauda*)—DB
Least Shrew (*Cryptotis parva*)

Talpidae (Moles)
*Eastern Mole (*Scalopus aquaticus*)—DB

Bats (Chiroptera)
*Southeastern Myotis (*Myotis austroriparius*)—DB
Eastern Pipistrel (*Pipistrellus subflavus*)
*Big Brown Bat (*Eptesicus fuscus*)—DB, UO
*Red Bat (*Lasiurus borealis*)—DB, UO
*Seminole Bat (*Lasiurus seminolus*)—DB
Hoary Bat (*Lasiurus cinereus*)
*Evening Bat (*Nycticeius humeralis*)—DB
*Rafinesque's Big-eared Bat (*Coryrhincus rafinesquii*)—DB, UO
Brazilian Free-tailed Bat (*Tadarida brasiliensis*)

Dasypodidae (Armadillos)
*Nine-banded Armadillo (*Dasypus novemcinctus*)—DB, UO, BBL

Leporidae (Hares, Rabbits)
*Eastern Cottontail (*Sylvilagus floridanus*)—DB, UO, BBL
*Swamp Rabbit (*Sylvilagus aquaticus*)—DB, UO, BBL

Sciuridae (Squirrels)
*Eastern Gray Squirrel (*Sciurus carolinensis*)—DB, BBL, UO
*Fox Squirrel (*Sciurus niger*)—DB, BBL, UO
*Southern Flying Squirrel (*Glaucomys volans*)—DB, UO, BBL

Geomyidae (Pocket Gophers)
*Plains Pocket Gopher (*Geomys bursarius*)—DB

Castoridae (Beaver)
*Beaver (*Castor canadensis*)—DB, BBL, UO

Cricetidae (Mice, Rats, Lemmings, Voles)

Marsh Rice Rat (*Oryzomys palustris*)
Fulvous Harvest Mouse (*Reithrodontomys fulvescens*)
*White-footed Mouse (*Peromyscus luecopus*)—DB
*Cotton Mouse (*Peromyscus gossypinus*)—DB
*Golden Mouse (*Peromyscus nuttalli*)—DB
*Hispid Cotton Rat (*Sigmodon hispidus*)
*Eastern Woodrat (*Neotoma floridana*)—BBL
Pine Vole (*Pitymys pinetorum*)
*Muskrat (*Ondatra zibethica*)—DB, UO, BBL

Muridae (Old World Rats and Mice)
Roof Rat (*Rattus rattus*)
Norway Rat (*Rattus norvegicus*)
House Mouse (*Mus musculus*)

Capromyidae (Nutria)
*Nutria (*Myocastor coypus*)—DB, UO, BBL

Canidae (Dogs, Wolves, Foxes)
Red Wolf (*Canis rufus*) (extirpated)
*Coyote (*Canis latrans*)—DB, UO, BBL
*Red Fox (*Vulpes fulva*)—DB, UO, BBL
*Gray Fox (*Urocyon cinereoargenteus*)—DB, UO, BBL

Ursidae (Bears)
*Black Bear (*Ursus americanus*)—DB, UO, FSA TRACTS

Procyonidae (Racoons)
*Raccoon (*Procyon lotor*)—DB, BBL, UO

Mustelidae (Weasels, Skunks)
Long-tailed Weasel (*Mustela frenata*)
*Mink (*Mustela vison*)
*Striped Skunk (*Mephitis mephitis*)—DB, UO, BBL
*River Otter (*Lutra canadensis*)—DB, BBL, UO

Felidae (Cats)
*Bobcat (*Lynx rufus*)—DB, UO
Mountain Lion (*Felix concolor*) (extirpated)

Suidae (Hogs)
*Feral Hog (*Sus scrofa*)—UO

Cervidae (Deer)
*White-tailed Deer (*Odocoileus virginianus*)—DB, UO, BBL

North Louisiana NWR Complex
Amphibians and Reptiles List

This list contains those species of reptiles and amphibians thought to occur on lands owned by the North Louisiana NWR Complex according to various literature sources. Those species marked with an asterisk (*) have been documented on the specified refuge by sightings or specimens. The abbreviations are as follows: BBL – Black Bayou Lake NWR, UO – Upper Ouachita NWR, DB – D'Arbonne NWR. Documentation of these species was compiled from surveys conducted by the refuge biologist and by herpetologists at the University of Louisiana in Monroe, namely Dr. Carr.

Alligatoridae (Alligators)
*American Alligator (*Alligator mississippiensis*) – BBL, DB, UO

Chelydridae (Snapping Turtles)
*Common Snapping Turtle (*Chelydra serpentina*) – BBL, UO, DB
*Alligator Snapping Turtle (*Macroclemys temminckii*) – BBL, UO, DB

Kinosternidae (Musk and Mud Turtles)
*Common Musk Turtle (*Sternotherus odoratus*) – BBL, UO
*Razorback Musk Turtle (*Sternotherus carinatus*) – BBL
*Mississippi Mud Turtle (*Kinosternon subrubrum hippocrepis*) – BBL

Emydidae (Box and Water Turtles)
*Three-toed Box Turtle (*Terrapene carolina triunguis*) – BBL, DB
*Mississippi Map Turtle (*Graptemys pseudogeographica kohnii*) – BBL, UO, DB
Ouachita Map Turtle (*Graptemys ouachitensis*)
*Red-eared Slider (*Trachemys scripta elegans*) – BBL, UO, DB
*River Cooter (*Pseudemys concinna*) – BBL
*Southern Painted Turtle (*Chrysemys picta dorsalis*) – BBL, UO, DB
*Western Chicken Turtle (*Deirochelys reticularia miaria*) – BBL, HB, UO

Trionychidae (Softshell Turtles)
*Smooth Softshell (*Apalone mutica*) – UO
*Spiny Softshell (*Apalone spinifera*) – BBL

Iguanidae (Anoles and Fence Lizards)
*Green Anole (*Anolis carolinensis*) – BBL, DB, UO, M
*Northern Fence Lizard (*Sceloporus undulatus hyacinthinus*) – DB

Teiidae (Racerunners)
*Six-lined Racerunner (*Cnemidophorus sexlineatus sexlineatus*) – DB

Scincidae (Skinks)
*Little Brown Skink (*Scincella lateralis*) – BBL, DB
*Five-lined Skink (*Eumeces fasciatus*) – BBL, DB
*Broad-headed Skink (*Eumeces laticeps*) – BBL, UO, DB
Southern Coal Skink (*Eumeces anthracinus pluvialis*)

Anguidae (Glass and Alligator Lizards)
Western Slender Glass Lizard (*Ophisaurus attenuatus attenuatus*)

Colubridae (Snakes)
*Mississippi Green Water Snake (*Nerodia cyclopion*) – BBL, DB
*Diamondback Water Snake (*Nerodia rhombifer rhombifer*) – BBL, DB, UO
*Yellowbelly Water Snake (*Nerodia erythrogaster flavigaster*) – BBL, DB
*Broadbanded Water Snake (*Nerodia fasciata confluens*) – BBL
Graham's Crayfish Snake (*Regina grahamii*) – BBL
*Gulf Glossy Crayfish Snake (*Regina rigida sinicola*) – BBL, DB
*Midland Brown Snake (*Storeria dekayi wrightorum*) – BBL
Florida Red-bellied Snake (*Storeria occipitomaculata obscura*) – BBL
Eastern Garter Snake (*Thamnophis sirtalis sirtalis*) – DB
*Western Ribbon Snake (*Thamnophis proximus proximus*) – BBL, DB
Western Smooth Earth Snake (*Virginia valeriae elegans*)
Rough Earth Snake (*Virginia striatula*)
*Eastern Hognose Snake (*Heterodon platirhinos*) – DB
Mississippi Ringneck Snake (*Diadophis punctatus stictogenys*) – DB
Western Worm Snake (*Carphophis vermis*)
*Western Mud Snake (*Farancia abacura reinwardtii*) – BBL, DB
*Racer (*Coluber constrictor anthicus* or *C. c. latrunculus* or intergrades) – BBL, DB
Eastern Coachwhip (*Masticophis flagellum flagellum*) – DB
*Rough Green Snake (*Opheodrys aestivus*) – BBL, DB
Corn Snake (*Elaphe guttata guttata X emoryi*)
*Black Rat Snake (*Elaphe obsoleta obsoleta*) – BBL, DB, UO
*Speckled King Snake (*Lampropeltis getula holbrooki*) – BBL, DB
*Louisiana Milksnake (*Lampropeltis triangulum amaura*) – DB
Prairie King Snake (*Lampropeltis calligaster calligaster*)
Northern Scarlet Snake (*Cemophora coccinea copei*)
Flathead Snake (*Tantilla gracilis*)

Elapidae (Coral Snakes)
*Texas Coral Snake (*Micrurus fulvius tener*) – DB

Viperidae (Vipers & Pit Vipers)
*Southern Copperhead (*Agkistrodon contortrix contortrix*) – BBL, UO, DB
*Western Cottonmouth (*Agkistrodon piscivorus leucostoma*) – BBL, UO, DB
Western Pygmy Rattlesnake (*Sistrurus miliarius streckeri*)
*Timber Rattlesnake (*Crotalus horridis*) – UO, BBL

Proteidae (Waterdogs and Mudpuppies)
Red River Mudpuppy (*Necturus maculosus louisianensis*)

Amphiumidae (Amphiumas)
*Three-toed Amphiuma (*Amphiuma tridactlyum*) – BBL, DB

Sirenidae (Sirens)
*Western Lesser Siren (*Siren intermedia nettingi*) – BBL

Ambystomatidae (Salamanders)
*Mole Salamander (*Ambystoma talpoideum*) – DB
*Marbled Salamander (*Ambystoma opacum*) – DB
Smallmouth Salamander (*Ambystoma texanum*)
*Spotted Salamander (*Ambystoma maculatum*) – DB

Salamandridae (Newts)
*Central Newt (*Notophthalmus viridescens*) – BBL

Plethodontidae (Lungless Salamanders)
Dusky Salamander (*Desmognathus fuscus* complex)
Dwarf Salamander (*Eurycea quadridigittata*)

Bufonidae (Toads)
*Fowler's Toad (*Bufo fowleri*) – BBL. DB
Gulf Coast Toad (*Bufo valliceps valliceps*)

Hylidae (Treefrogs and Their Allies)
*Northern Cricket Frog (*Acris crepitans crepitans*) – BBL, DB, UO
*Green Treefrog (*Hyla cinerea*) – BBL, DB, UO
*Gray Treefrog (*Hyla versicolor*) – BBL, DB
*Cope's Gray Treefrog (*Hyla chrysoscelis*) – BBL, DB, UO
*Squirrel Treefrog (*Hyla squirella*) – BBL
*Bird-voiced Treefrog (*Hyla avivoca*) – BBL
*Northern Spring Peeper (*Pseudacris crucifer*) – BBL, DB, UO
*Upland Chorus Frog (*Pseudacris feriarum*) – BBL, DB, UO

Microhylidae (Narrowmouth Toads)
*Eastern Narrowmouth Toad (*Gastrophryne carolinensis*) – BBL, DB

Ranidae (True Frogs)
*Bullfrog (*Rana catesbeiana*) – BBL, DB, UO
*Bronze Frog (*Rana clamitans clamitans*) – BBL, DB, UO
*Southern Leopard Frog (*Rana sphenocephala*) – BBL, DB, UO
*Pickerel Frog (*Rana palustris*) – DB

North Louisiana NWR Complex
Fish List

This list contains those species of fish thought to occur in waters administered by the North Louisiana NWR Complex according to various literature sources. Those species marked with an asterisk (*) have been documented on the specified refuge by sightings, fishing, and/or specimens. The abbreviations are as follows: BBL – Black Bayou Lake NWR, UO – Upper Ouachita NWR, DB – D'Arbonne NWR. Documentation of these species was compiled from surveys conducted by Service personnel, Dr. Aku at the University of Louisiana in Monroe, and Arkansas Game and Fish Commission personnel. Literature sources used include Dr. Douglas' Fishes of Louisiana and Mike Wood's M.S. Thesis entitled "A taxonomic survey of the fishes of Bayou D'Arbonne after impoundment."

Petromyzontidae---Lampreys

Chestnut Lamprey (*Ichthyomyzon castaneus*)
Southern Brook Lamprey (*Ichthyomyzon gagei*)

Polydontidae—Paddlefishes
*Paddlefish (*Polydon spathula*)—UO, DB

Lepisosteidae—Gars
*Spotted Gar (*Lepisosteus oculatus*)—BBL, UO
*Longnose Gar (*Lepisosteus osseus*)—BBL
*Shortnose Gar (*Lepisosteus platostomus*)—UO
Alligator Gar (*Lepisosteus spatula*)

Amiidae—Bowfin
*Bowfin (*Amia calva*)-BBL/s, UO/s, DB

Anguillladae—Eels
American eel (*Anguilla rostrata*)

Clupeidae—Shads
Skipjack Herring (*Alosa chrysochloris*)
*Gizzard Shad (*Dorosoma cepedianum*)—BBL, UO
*Threadfin Shad (*Dorosoma petenense*)—BBL, UO

Hiodontidae--Mooneyes
*Mooneye (*Hiodon alosoides*)—BBL/s
Goldeye (*Hiodon alosoides*)

Esocidae—Pikes
Grass Pickeral (*Esox americanus*)
*Chain Pickeral (*Esox niger*)—BBL, UO

Cyprinidae—Minnows
Goldfish
* Common Carp (*Cyprinus carpio*)—UO
*Cypress Minnow (*Hybognathus hayi*)—UO
*Silvery Minnow (*Hybognathus nuchalis*)—UO

Cyprinidae—Minnows
Speckled Chub (*Hybopsis aestivalis*)
Silver Chub (*Hybopsis storeriana*)
*Golden Shiner (*Notemigonus crysoleucas*)—BBL, UO
*Pallid Shiner (*Notropis amnis*)—UO
*Emerald Shiner (*Notropis atherinoides*)—UO
Bigeyed Shiner (*Notropis boops*)
Ghost Shiner (*Notropis buchanani*)
*Ironcolor Shiner (*Notropis chalybaeus*)—UO
Striped Shiner (*Luxilus chrysocephalus*)
*Ribbon Shiner (*Notropis fumeus*)—UO
Bluehead shiner (*Notropis hubbsi*)
*Taillight Shiner (*Notropis maculatus*)—UO
Weed Shiner (*Notropis texanus*)
Redfin Shiner (*Lythrurus umbratilis*)
*Blacktail Shiner (*Cyprinella venusta*)—UO
Mimic Shiner (*Notropis volucellus*)
Steelcolor Shiner (*Notropis whipplei*)
*Pugnose Minnow (*Opsopoeodus emiliae*)—UO
Bluntnose Minnow (*Pimephales notatus*)
Flathead Minnow (*Pimephales promelas*)
Bullhead Minnow (*Pimephales vigilax*)
Cheek Chub (*Semotilus atromaculatus*)

Catostomidae--Suckers
River Carpsucker (*Carpiodes carpio*)
Creek Chubsucker (*Erimyzon oblongus*)
*Lake Chubsucker (*Erimyzon sucetta*)—UO
*Smallmouth Buffalo (*Ictiobus bubalus*)—UO
*Bigmouth Buffalo (*Ictiobus cyprinellus*)—UO
Black Buffalo (*Ictiobus niger*)
*Spotted Sucker (*Minytrema melanops*)—UO
Blacktail Redhorse (*Moxostoma poecilurum*)
River Redhorse—UO

Ictaluridae—Catfishes
*Blue Catfish (*Ictalurus furcatus*)—UO
*Black Bullhead (*Ameiurus melas*)—UO
*Brown Bullhead (*Ameiurus nebulosus*)—BBL, UO
*Yellow Bullhead (*Ameiurus natalis*)—BBL, UO
*Channel Catfish (*Ictalurus punctatus*)—UO
*Tadpole Madtom (*Noturus gyrinus*)—UO
Brindled Madtom (*Noturus miurus*)
Freckled Madtom (*Noturus nocturnus*)
Brown Madtom (*Noturus phaeus*)
*Flathead Catfish (*Pylodictis olivaris*)—UO

Aphredoderidae—Pirate Perch
*Pirate Perch (*Aphredoderus sayanus*)—UO

Cyrinodontidae—Topminnows
*Golden Topminnow (*Fundulus chrysotus*)—UO
*Blackstripe Topminnow (*Fundulus notatus*)—UO
Starhead Topminnow (*Fundulus notti*) listed as N. starhead F. dispar
*Blackspotted Topminnow (*Fundulus olivaceus*)—UO

Peociliidae—Livebearers
*Mosquitofish (*Gambusia affinis*)—UO

Atherinidae—Silversides
*Brook Silverside (*Labidesthes sicculus*)—BBL, UO

Percicthyidae—Temperate Basses
*White Bass (*Morone chrysops*)—UO
*Yellow Bass (*Morone mississippiensis*)—UO
Striped Bass (*Morone saxatilis*)

Centrarchidae--Sunfishes
*Flier (*Centrarchus macropterus*)—UO
*Green Sunfish (*Lepomis cyanellus*)—BBL
*Warmouth (*Lepomis gulosus*)—UO
*Orangespotted Sunfish (*Lepomis humilis*)—UO
*Bluegill (*Lepomis macrochirus*)—BBL, UO
*Dollar Sunfish (*Lepomis marginatus*)—UO
Longear Sunfish (*Lepomis megalotis*)
*Redear Sunfish (*Lepomis microlophus*)—BBL, UO
*Spotted Sunfish (*Lepomis punctatus*)—UO
*Bantam Sunfish (*Lepomis symmetricus*)—BBL, UO
Spotted Bass (*Micropterus punctulatus*)
*Largemouth Bass (*Micropterus salmoides*)—BBL, UO
*White Crappie (*Pomoxis annularis*)—UO, BBL
*Black Crappie (*Pomoxis nigromaculatus*)—BBL, UO

Elassomatidae—Pygmy Sunfishes
*Banded Pygmy Sunfish (*Elassoma zonatum*)BBL/s

Percidae--Perches
Scaly Sand Darter (*Ammocrypta vivax*)
Western Scaly Sand Darter (*Ammocrypta clara*)
*Mud Darter (*Etheostoma asprigene*)—UO
*Bluntnose Darter (*Etheostoma chlorosomum*)—UO
Creole Darter (*Etheostoma collettei*)
Swamp Darter (*Etheostoma fusiforme*)
Slough Darter (*Etheostoma gracile*)
Harlequin Darter (*Etheostoma histrio*)
Goldstripe Darter (*Etheostoma parvipinne*)
Cypress Darter (*Etheostoma proeliare*)
Speckled Darter (*Etheostoma stigmaeum*)
Redfin Darter (*Etheostoma whipplei*)
*Logperch (*Percina caprodes*)—UO
Channel Darter (*Percina copelandi*)

Cyprinidae—Minnows
Blackside Darter (*Percina maculata*)
Ouachita Darter (*Percina ouachitae*)
Dusky Darter (*Percina sciera*)
River Darter (*Percina shumardi*)
Sauger (*Stizostedion canadense*)
Walleye (*Stizostedion vitreum*)

Sciaenidae-Drums
*Freshwater Drum (*Aplodinotus grunniens*)—UO

North Louisiana NWR Complex
Woody Plant List

This list contains those species of woody plants thought to occur on lands owned by the North Louisiana NWR Complex according to various literature sources, specimens, and sightings.

Aceraceae
oxelder (*Acer negundo*)
Red Maple (*Acer rubrum*)

Agavaceae
Adam's needle (*Yucca filamentosa*)

Anacardiaceae
Shiny Sumac (*Rhus copallinum*)
Smooth Sumac (*Rhus glabra*)
Chittimwood (*Sideroxylon lanuginosum*)
Poison Ivy (*Toxicodendron radicans*)

Annonaceae
Dwarf Pawpaw (*Asimina parviflora*)
Pawpaw (*Asimina triloba*)

Araliaceae
Devil's Walkingstick (*Aralia spinosa*)

Arecaceae
Palmetto (*Sabal minor*)

Aristolochiaceae
Dutchman's pipevine (*Aristolochia tomentosa*)

Asteraceae
Saltbush (*Baccharis halimifolia*)
New Jersey Tea (*Ceanothus americanus*)

Aquifoliaceae
Carolina Holly (*Ilex ambigua*)
Deciduous Holly (*Ilex deciduas*)
American Holly (*Ilex opaca*)
Youpan (*Ilex vomitoria*)

Betulaceae
Smooth Alder (*Alnus serrulata*)
River Birch (*Betula nigra*)
Ironwood (*Carpinus caroliniana*)
Blue beech (*Carpinus caroliniana*)
Eastern Hophornbeam (*Ostrya virginiana*)

Bignoniaceae
Cross Vine (*Bignonia capreolata*)
Trumpet Creeper (*Campsis radicans*)
Southern Catalpa (*Catalpa bignonioides*)

Caprifoliaceae
Buttonbush (*Cephalanthus occidentalis*)
Coral Honeysuckle (*Lonicera sempervirens*)
Japanese honeysuckle (*Lonicera japonica*)
Elderberry (*Sambucus canadensis*)
Arrowwood (*Viburnum dentatum*)
Rusty Blackhaw (*Viburnum rufidulum*)

Celastraceae
Strawberrybush (*Evonymus americana*)

Clusiaceae
St. Andrew's Cross (*Hypericum hypericoides*)
Broombush (*Hypericum prolificum*)

Cornaceae
Rough-leaf Dogwood (*Cornus drummondii*)
Flowering Dogwood (*Cornus florida*)
Swamp dogwood (*Cornus foemina*)

Cuppressaceae
Eastern Red-cedar (*Juniperus virginiana*)

Ebonaceae
Persimmon (*Diospyrus virginiana*)

Ericaceae
Sparkleberry (*Vaccinium arboretum*)
Elliot's Blueberry (*Vaccinium elliotti*)
Deerberry (*Vaccinium stamineum*)
Large Cluster Blueberry (*Vaccinium virgatum*)

Euphorbiaceae
Chinese Tallowtree (*Triadica sebiferum*)

Fabaceae
False Indigo (*Amorpha spp.*)
Mimosa (*Albizia julibrissin*)
Eastern Redbud (*Cercis canadensis*)
Coralbean (*Erythrina herbacea*)
Water Locust (*Gleditsia aquatica*)
Honey Locust (*Gleditsia triacanthos*)
Black Locust (*Robinia pseudoacacia*)
American Wisteria (*Wisteria frutescens*)

Fagaceae
Allegheny chinquapin (*Castanea pumila*)
American Beech (*Fagus grandifolia*)
White Oak (*Quercus alba*)
Southern Red Oak (*Quercus falcate*)
Laurel Oak (*Quercus laurifolia*)
Overcup Oak (*Quercus lyrata*)
Blackjack Oak (*Quercus marilandica*)
Swamp Chestnut Oak (*Quercus michauxii*)
Water Oak (*Quercus nigra*)
Post Oak (*Quercus stellata*)
Cherrybark Oak (*Quercus pagodafolia*)
Willow Oak (*Quercus phellos*)
Shumard Oak (*Quercus shumardii*)
Delta Post Oak (*Quercus similes*)
Nuttall Oak (*Quercus texana*)
Black Oak (*Quercus velutina*)

Grossulariaceae
Sweetspire (*Itea virginica*)

Hamamelidaceae
Witch hazel (*Hamamelis virginiana*)
Sweetgum (*Liquidambar styraciflua*)

Hippocastanaceae
Red Buckeye (*Aesculus pavia*)
*Hoary Azalea (*Rhododendron canescens)

Juglandaceae
Mockernut Hickory (*Carya alba (C. tomentosa*)
Bitter Pecan (*Carya aquatica*)
Bitternut Hickory (*Carya cordiformis*)
Pignut Hickory (*Carya glabra*)
Sweet Pecan (*Carya illinoiensis*)
Black Hickory (*Carya texana*)
Black Walnut (*Juglans nigra*)

Lauraceae
Sassafras (*Sassafras albidium*)
Spicebush (*Lindera benzoin*)

Loganiaceae
Carolina Jessemine (*Gelsemium sempervirens*)

Magnoliaceae
Sweetbay Magnolia (*Magnolia virginiana*)

Meliaceae
Chinaberry (*Melia azedarach*)

Moraceae
Osage-orange (*Maclura pumifera*)
Red Mulberry (*Morus rubra*)

Myricaceae
Waxmyrtle (*Myrica cerifica*)

Nyssaceae
Water Tupelo (*Nyssa aquatica*)
Blackgum (*Nyssa sylvatica*)

Oleaceae
Fringetree (*Chioanthus virginicus*)
Swamp Privet (*Forestiera acuminate*)
White Ash (*Fraxinus americana*)
Green Ash (*Fraxinus pennsylvanica*)
Chinese privet (*Ligustrum sinense*)

Pinaceae
Shortleaf Pine (*Pinus echinata*)
Loblolly Pine (*Pinus taeda*)

Platanaceae
American Sycamore (*Platanus occidentalis*)

Polygonaceae
Lady's eardrop vine (*Brunnichia ovata*)

Ranunculaceae
Virgin's bower (*Clemantis virginiana*)

Rhamnaceae
Rattan vine (*Berchemia scandens*)
Carolina Buckthorn (*Frangula caroliniana*) (*Rhamnus caroliniana*)

Rosaceae
Serviceberry (*Amelanchier arborea*)
Cockspur hawthorn (*Cretageous crus-galli*)
Parsleyhaw (*Cretageous marshallii*)
Mayhaw (*Cretageous opaca*)
Green Hawthorn (*Cretageous viridis*)
Chickasaw Plum (*Prunus angustifolia*)
Mexican Plum (*Prunus mexicana*)
Black Cherry (*Prunus serotina*)
Blackberry (*Rubus argutus*)

Rubiaceae
Buttonbush (*Cephalanthus occidentalis*)

Rutaceae
Toothache Tree (*Zanthoxylum clava-hercules*)
Trifoliate-orange (*Poncirus trifoliate*)

Salicaceae
Ea. Cottonwood (*Populus deltoids*)
Black Willow (*Salix nigra*)

Sapotaceae
Gum Bumelia (*Bumelia lanuginose*)

Schizaeaceae
Japanese Climbingfern (*Lygodium japonicum*)

Scrophulariaceae
Princesstree (*Paulownia tomentosa*)

Simarubaceae
Tree-of-heaven (*Ailanthus altissima*)

Smilacaceae
Fiddleleaf Greenbriar (*Smilax bona-nox*)
Sawbriar (*Smilax glauca*)
Common Greenbriar (*Smilax rotundifolia*)
Upland Bamboo Vine (*Smilax smallii*)
Red Berry Greenbriar (*Smilax walterii*)

Styracaceae
Two-winged Silverbell (*Halesia diptera*)
Large Snowbell (*Styrax americanum*)
Small Snowbell (*Styrax grandifolius*)

Symplocaceae
Sweetleaf (*Symplocos tinctoria*)

Taxodiaceae
Baldcypress (*Taxodium distichum*)

Ulmaceae
Southern Hackberry (*Celtis laevigata*)
Winged Elm (*Ulmus alata*)
American Elm (*Ulmus americana*)
Cedar Elm (*Ulmus crassifolia*)
Slippery Elm (*Ulmus rubra*)
Water Elm (*Planer aquatica*)

Verbenaceae
American beautyberry (*Callicarpa americana*)

Vitaceae
Peppervine (*Ampelopsis arborea*)
Heart-leaf Peppervine (*Ampeopsis cordata*)
Virginia Creeper (*Parthenocissus quinquefolia*)
Summer Grape (*Vitis aestivalis*)
Gray Grape (*Vitis cinerea*)
Muscadine Grapes (*Vitis rotundifolia*)

Appendix J. Consultation and Coordination

OVERVIEW

This appendix summarizes the consultation and coordination that has occurred to date in identifying the issues, alternatives, and preferred alternative that are presented in this CCP. It lists the meetings that have been held with the various agencies, organizations, and individuals who were consulted during its preparation.

The Black Bayou Lake NWR CCP was written with the participation and assistance of refuge, Service staff, LDWF, and the general public. The CCP planning process itself began in May 2008, with the formation of a planning team; a notice of intent to prepare a CCP had earlier been published in the *Federal Register.*

In February 2008, in preparation for the planning process, a team of biologists conducted a comprehensive biological review for the refuge. Participants in the biological review were drawn from the refuge and the Service, including Ecological Services, Realty, Migratory Birds, and Planning specialists; Louisiana State University; and LDWF.

Also in March 2008, refuge and Service personnel met to conduct a visitor services review. The information and recommendations in the reports of the biological and visitor services reviews proved a valuable "point of departure" for the authors of the CCP. Subsequently, the refuge hosted a public scoping meeting on May 22, 2008, and began an outreach campaign through various media to collect ideas and concerns from all stakeholders. Please see Chapter III of the CCP for more information on public scoping and overall consultation and coordination in plan development.

CORE PLANNING TEAM MEMBERS

The core planning team consisted of the listed individuals.

Kelby Ouchley – Deputy Project Leader (Former)
Brett Hortman – Refuge Manager
Tina Chouinard – Natural Resouces Planner
George Chandler – Project Leader
Gypsy Hanks – Wildlife Biologist
Chris Foster – Forester
Gay Brantley – Visitor Services
Sharon Fuller – Visitor Services (Former)

INTERDISCIPLINARY PLANNING TEAM MEMBERS

Several individuals supported the planning process with participation on the biological review team, visitor services review team, and additional special topic discussions. Their information provided additional biological support for developing objectives found in this plan. Some members are internal to the Service and provide additional policy guidance and support for objective development as well.

Biological Review Team

Tom Edwards – Wildlife Biologist, Migratory Birds
Randy Wilson – Wildlife Biologist, Migratory Birds
John Simpson – Administrative Forester, Bayou Cocodrie NWR
Cedric Doolittle – Fisheries Biologist
John Pitre – Wildlife Biologist, Natural Resources Conservation Service
Kirk Cormier – Regional Manager, Louisiana Department of Environmental Quality
Amanda Daniels – Louisiana Department of Environmental Quality
Ryan Daniels – Fisheries Biologist, Louisiana Department of Wildlife and Fisheries
Mike Wood – Fisheries Biologist, Louisiana Department of Wildlife and Fisheries
Jerald Owens – District Supervisor, Louisiana Department of Wildlife and Fisheries
John Carr – Herpetology Professor, University of Louisiana at Monroe
Joydeep Bhattacharjee – Associate Professor, University of Louisiana at Monroe
Anna Hill – Associate Professor, University of Louisiana at Monroe
Steve Pagans – Forester, D'Arbonne NWR
Kelby Ouchley – Refuge Manager, North Louisiana NWR Complex
Tina Chouinard – Natural Resource Planner, FWS
Gypsy Hanks – Wildlife Biologist, North Louisiana NWR Complex
Chris Foster – Administrative Forester, North Louisiana NWR Complex

Visitor Services Review Team

Deborah Jerome – Visitor Services and Outreach, FWS
Garry Tucker – Visitor Services and Outreach, FWS
Amanda Wilkinson – Tensas River NWR
Emily Neidigh – Gulf Coast NWR Complex

Other Contributors

In addition to the above-listed core and extended planning team members, a number of individuals and groups contributed to the CCP. These included local citizens and agencies as well as the Friends of Black Bayou Lake (a private citizen group organized to support the refuge). These contributors participated in the scoping meeting or provided input at various stages of the planning process.

Friends of Black Bayou Lake, Inc.
Rose Hopp – Regional Planning Chief, FWS
Evelyn Nelson – Regional Planning Editor, FWS
Randy Musgraves – Regional Formatting, FWS
Richard Kanaski – Regional Archaeologist, FWS

Appendix K. Budget Requests

The Refuge System currently faces a backlog of project, operational, maintenance, and equipment needs. The current Refuge Operations Needs System (RONS) and Service Asset Maintenance Management System (SAMMS) provide a list of proposed projects for the refuge, over and above the current base operating budget of the refuge. The refuge's RONS and SAMMS needs would continue under this Plan. Once the CCP is approved, the RONS and SAMMS databases will be updated to reflect the needs and proposed actions outlined in the Plan.

Refuge Operations Needs System (RONS) Fiscal Year (FY) 2008 Requested Projects

Org Code	Project Type	Project ID	Rank	Complete	Title	One-Time	Recurring Base	Total First Year Need
42652	Project	FY08-2458	1	Yes	Black Bayou Lake NWR Invasive Species control	$45,000	$35,000	$115,901
42652	Project*	FY08-2489	2	Yes	Black Bayou Lake NWR Refuge Specialist		$80,046	$80,046
42652	Project*	FY08-2452	3	Yes	Black Bayou Lake NWR Maintenance		$77,650	$77,650
42652	Project	FY08-2496	4	Yes	Black Bayou Lake NWR Informational Video	$40,000	$5,000	$45,000
42652	Project	FY08-2478	5	Yes	Black Bayou Lake NWR Forest Health	$40,000	$15,000	$55,000
42652	Project	FY08-2491	6	Yes	Black Bayou Lake NWR Cell Phone Tour	$10,000	$8,000	$18,000
42652	Project	FY08-2492	7	Yes	Black Bayou Lake NWR Podcast Tour and Virtual Geo-caching	$25,000	$8,000	$33,000

Org Code	Project Type	Project ID	Rank	Complete	Title	One-Time	Recurring Base	Total First Year Need
	Staffing Model Positions - Non LE Predicted / Currently Authorized / New 3 / 1 / 2 **RONS Project Positions - Non LE** Number / Cost 2 / $206,591				**Staffing Model Positions - LE** Predicted / Currently Authorized / New 1 / / 1 **RONS Project Positions - LE** Number / Cost 1 / $114,439			

SAMMS Projects Black Bayou Lake NWR

2007734498 Construct Additional Parking Lot

Construct additional 9000 square foot asphalt parking area with associated sidewalks and solar powered lighting at Black Bayou Lake National Wildlife Refuge's environmental education center. The existing parking area is inadequate for routine surges in visitation. The new parking area will allow the refuge to meet an existing and growing demand (30,000 + annual visits) for compatible environmental education and interpretation by school groups and the general public by providing safe, convenient parking.
Estimated Cost $110,000

00123178 Construct Kiosks

Construct kiosk to improve visitor needs capabilities. Construct 4 three-panel kiosks out of treated lumber and metal roofs. A standard FWS kiosk can be used. These panels must be weather resistant and accommodate interpretive signs and brochure dispensers. The project will provide informational services by installation of entrance signs and kiosks for refuge visitors to Black Bayou Lake National Wildlife Refuge. The semi-urban refuge is now serving 10,000 visitors annually with a potential to serve a local population, within 50 miles, of 100,000+ with many non-local visitors. Created in partnership with the city of Monroe, this new and expanding refuge has more than doubled in size in the last few years.
Estimated Cost $25,000

2009964117 Repaint Visitor Center

Repaint wooden planters house that is used for Visitor Center and Environmental Education Center. The Environmental Education Center serves 30,000 visitors annually. The building has historical significance to the refuge and the previous use of the land. It is important to maintain the exterior paint to protect from water damage and rot. The wood siding needs to be inspected for leaks and repaired. Water leaks promote mold and mildew inside the building, which are health and safety issues for the employees and the public.
Estimated Cost: $30,000

2009964197 Rehabilitate Metal Storage Building

Rehabilitate metal storage building used to store boats and chemicals. Storage of chemicals needs to be separated from boat storage for the health and safety of employees. The wooden supports in the building need to be replaced with metal and the walls need to be insulated. Lighting needs to be improved to support better working conditions.
Estimated Cost $100,000

2009964101 Rehabilitate Boat Ramp

Rehabilitate boat ramp and accommodate increase in use. The ramp is caving off at the end and is a health and safety issue to the public. During low water levels, the ramp is not long enough to launch boats safely. The ramp is used by 6,000 boaters annually and is one of the most highly used facilities on the refuge. The docking area needs to be improved to handle more than one or two boats at a time.
Estimated Cost $ 50,000

Appendix L. Finding of No Significant Impact

INTRODUCTION

The Fish and Wildlife Service (Service) proposes to protect and manage certain fish and wildlife resources in Ouachita Parish, Louisiana, through the Black Bayou Lake National Wildlife Refuge (NWR). An Environmental Assessment has been prepared to inform the public of the possible environmental consequences of implementing the Comprehensive Conservation Plan (CCP) for Black Bayou Lake NWR. A description of the alternatives, the rationale for selecting the preferred alternative, the environmental effects of the preferred alternative, the potential adverse effects of the action, and a declaration concerning the factors determining the significance of effects, in compliance with the National Environmental Policy Act of 1969, are outlined below. The supporting information can be found in the Environmental Assessment—Section B of the Draft Comprehensive Conservation Plan for Black Bayou Lake NWR.

ALTERNATIVES

In developing the Comprehensive Conservation Plan for Black Bayou Lake National Wildlife Refuge, the Fish and Wildlife Service evaluated three alternatives:

> Alternative A: Current Management Direction (No Action Alternative)
> Alternative B: Optimize Biological Program and Visitor Services (Preferred Action)
> Alternative C: Minimize Management and Public Use

Each alternative is summarized below.

ALTERNATIVE A – CURRENT MANAGEMENT DIRECTION (NO ACTION ALTERNATIVE)

Black Bayou Lake NWR is part of the Lower Mississippi River Ecosystem and is considered to be in the Mississippi Alluvial Valley Conservation Area. As such, Black Bayou Lake NWR is a component of many regional and ecosystem conservation-planning initiatives. Under Alternative A, the No Action Alternative, present management of the refuge would continue at its current level of participation in these initiatives through the 15-year duration of the CCP. Current approaches to managing wildlife and habitats, protecting resources, and allowing for public use would remain unchanged.

The main habitat the refuge strives to restore and manage is bottomland hardwood and upland pine hardwood forests. Under Alternative A, management would continue to work with partners to acquire lands within the current refuge boundary. The refuge would continue to furnish benefits for native wildlife species, and continue to provide habitat for thousands of wintering waterfowl and year-round habitat for nesting wood ducks. It would also maintain the current habitat mix for the benefit of other migratory birds, shorebirds, marsh birds, and landbirds. Staff would continue existing surveys to monitor long-term population trends and health of resident species.

Existing staff and volunteers would maintain the public use and environmental education programs at the refuge. The refuge would continue to serve the public without being guided by a Visitor Services Management Plan, relying instead on experience, general Service mandates and practices, and guidance and advice from recreation staff in the Service's Regional Office.

ALTERNATIVE B – OPTIMIZE BIOLOGICAL PROGRAM AND VISITOR SERVICES (PREFERRED ALTERNATIVE)

Under Alternative B, the refuge would strive to optimize both its biological program and visitor services program. The refuge would continue to furnish benefits to resident wildlife species in Alternative B and would aim to increase the its knowledge base about migratory birds by developing and implementing monitoring programs, while continuing to provide habitats for the benefit of waterfowl, nesting colonial waterbirds, and landbirds. The refuge would use its resources to create and/or maintain a variety of habitats compatible with historic habitat types. Efforts to control invasive species would increase from Alternative A.

Under Alternative B, land acquisition, bottomland hardwood management, and resource protection at Black Bayou Lake NWR would be intensified from the level now maintained in the No Action Alternative. In its Private Lands Program, staff would work with private landowners on adjacent tracts to manage and improve habitats.

Alternative B would provide a full-time law enforcement officer, refuge operations specialist, maintenance worker, and park ranger (visitor services). With regard to cultural resources, including those of an archaeological or historical nature, within 15 years of CCP approval, the refuge would develop and begin to implement a Cultural Resources Management Plan (CRMP). Until such time as the CRMP is completed and implemented, the refuge would follow standard Service protocol and procedures in conducting cultural resource surveys by qualified professionals, in consultation with the RHPO and the SHPO, prior to commencing projects that entail extensive excavation.

Public use and environmental education would increase from the No Action Alternative only slightly. The program would be enhanced and improved with the addition of two park rangers (visitor services and law enforcement). Within 3 years of of the date of the CCP, the refuge would develop a Visitor Services Plan to be used in maintaining quality public use facilities and opportunities. This step-down management plan would provide overall, long-term direction and guidance in developing and running one of the country's premier public use programs.

Over the 15-year life of the CCP, staff would increase emphasis on environmental education and interpretation to lead to a better understanding of the importance of refuge habitats and resources.

ALTERNATIVE C – MINIMIZE MANAGEMENT AND PUBLIC USE MANAGEMENT

This alternative is driven by minimizing wildlife and habitat management and the public use program. Baseline inventorying and monitoring programs would be eliminated; monitoring for changes in trends would not be necessary to achieve purposes of the refuge.

Public use would be maintained under this alternative and monitored for impacts to wildlife. An extensive survey for monitoring the deer population and its association with habitat conditions would be implemented. Fishing would continue as currently managed. Environmental education, wildlife observation, and wildlife photography would be accommodated at present levels; but access would be limited to July-October and February-April, to minimize disturbance to migratory birds. Staffing would remain as in the No Action Alternative.

Selection Rationale
Alternative B is selected for implementation because it directs the development of programs to best achieve the refuge purpose and goals. Implementing the preferred alternative will result in management based on sound science for the conservation of a structurally and species diverse

bottomland hardwood habitat for migratory birds and resident wildlife. A focused effort will be placed on reducing invasive species, which are threatening the biological integrity of the refuge. Baseline inventorying and monitoring of management actions will be completed to gain information on a variety of species, from reptiles and amphibians to butterflies and several species of concern. Several cooperative projects will be conducted with universities, Louisiana Department of Wildlife and Fisheries, and other agencies and individuals to provide biological information to be used in management decisions. When compatible, the wildlife-dependent recreational opportunities for hunting, fishing, wildlife observation, wildlife photography, and environmental education and interpretation will be provided and enhanced, while achieving the refuge purpose and remaining consistent with existing laws, Service policies, and sound biological principles.

Under this alternative, all lands under the management and direction of the refuge will be protected, maintained, and enhanced to best achieve national, ecosystem, and refuge-specific goals and objectives within anticipated funding and staffing levels. In addition, the action positively addresses significant issues and concerns expressed by the public.

Environmental Effects

Implementation of the Service's management action is expected to result in environmental, social, and economic effects as outlined in the CCP. Habitat management, wildlife population management, resource protection, and visitor service activities on Black Bayou Lake NWR would result in increased migratory bird utilization and production; increased protection for threatened and endangered species; enhanced wildlife populations; bottomland hardwood forest and upland forest management; and enhanced opportunities for wildlife-dependent recreation and environmental education. These effects are detailed as follows:

1. Duck and shorebird use of the refuge would improve as water management efforts would provide dependable flooded habitats to match the migration chronologies of these species. Forest breeding birds would benefit from refuge land acquisition, reforestation, and forest management actions. Woodcock population numbers and habitat use would be monitored and managed and woodcock use would be expected to increase.

2. Migratory bird production would increase by enhancing forest habitat quality for neotropical migratory birds, habitat and food availability for wintering waterfowl, and through hydrological restoration and reforestation. Forest management practices such as reforestation, selective harvests, and conservation of mature stand components would benefit nesting and feeding habitat for neotropical migratory birds.

3. Land acquisition, reforestation, management, and protection would benefit the recovery of threatened and endangered species. All habitat management and protection, including forest treatments, would be beneficial to most wildlife, including transient Louisiana black bears, by providing more structure, food, and possible den trees. Improved habitat would support the conservation efforts of species of special concern such as the alligator snapping turtle and Rafinesque's big-eared and southeastern Myotis bats.

4. The refuge's habitat mix of moist-soil, early successional reforestation areas, and bottomland hardwood and upland forests, as well as habitat management, would improve food and cover for resident wildlife species and enhance wetland communities within the refuge.

5. Habitat restoration and management, along with a focus on accessibility and facility maintenance, would result in improved wildlife-dependent recreational opportunities. While public use would result in some minimal, short-term adverse effects on wildlife, and user conflicts may occur at certain times of the year, these effects are minimized by site design, time zoning, and implementing refuge regulations. Anticipated long-term impacts to wildlife and wildlife habitats of implementing the management action are positive. In the long run, wildlife habitat and increased r wildlife-dependent recreation opportunities could result in an increase in economic benefits to the local community.

6. Implementing the CCP is not expected to have any significant adverse effects on wetlands and floodplains, pursuant to Executive Orders 11990 and 11988, as actions would not result in development of buildings and/or structures within floodplain areas, nor would they result in irrevocable, long-term adverse impacts. In fact, a major thrust of the management action would be to implement bottomland hardwood forest and open wetland restoration within the wildlife communities of the refuge that have been severely impacted by actions of previous landowners. Implementing the management action would result in substantial enhancement of forest and open wetland communities and net increases to the Nation's bottomland hardwood forests and open wetland acreage and quality.

Potential Adverse Effects and Mitigation Measures
Wildlife Disturbance
Disturbance to wildlife at some level is an unavoidable consequence of any public use program, regardless of the activity involved. Obviously, some activities innately have the potential to be more disturbing than others. The management actions to be implemented have been carefully planned to avoid unacceptable levels of impact.

As currently proposed, the known and anticipated levels of disturbance of the management action are considered minimal and well within the tolerance level of known wildlife species and populations present in the area. Carefully controlled time and space zoning, establishment of protection zones around key sites, closures of all-terrain vehicle trails when appropriate, and routing of roads and trails to avoid direct contact with sensitive areas, such as nesting bird habitat, etc., minimize effects of public use. All hunting activities (season lengths, number of hunters) would be conducted within the constraints of sound biological principles and refuge-specific regulations established to restrict illegal or non-conforming activities. Monitoring activities through wildlife inventories and assessments of public use levels and activities would be utilized, and public use programs would be adjusted as needed to limit disturbance.

User Group Conflicts
As public use levels expand across time, some conflicts between user groups may occur. Programs would be adjusted, as needed, to eliminate or minimize these problems and provide quality wildlife-dependent recreational opportunities. Experience has proven that time and space zonings, such as establishment of separate use areas, use periods, and restricting numbers of users, are effective tools in eliminating conflicts between user groups.

Effects on Adjacent Landowners
Implementation of the management action would not impact adjacent or in-holding landowners. Essential access to private property would be allowed through issuance of special use permits. Future land acquisition would occur on a willing-seller basis only, at fair market values within the approved acquisition boundary. Lands are acquired through a combination of fee title purchases and/or donations and less-than-fee title interests (e.g., conservation easements, cooperative agreements) from willing sellers. Funds for the acquisition of lands within the approved acquisition

boundary would likely come from the Land and Water Conservation Fund or the Migratory Bird Conservation Act. The management action contains neither provisions nor proposals to pursue off-refuge stream bank riparian zone protection measures (e.g., fencing) other than on a volunteer/partnership basis.

Land Ownership and Site Development
Proposed acquisition efforts by the Service would result in changes in land and recreational use patterns, since all uses on national wildlife refuges must meet compatibility standards. Land ownership by the Service also precludes any future economic development by the private sector. Potential development of access roads, dikes, control structures, and visitor parking areas could lead to minor short-term negative impacts on plants, soil, and some wildlife species. When site development activities are proposed, each activity would be given the appropriate National Environmental Policy Act consideration during pre-construction planning. At that time, any required mitigation activities would be incorporated into the specific project to reduce the level of impacts to the human environment and to protect fish and wildlife and their habitats.

As indicated earlier, one of the direct effects of site development is increased public use; this increased use may lead to littering, noise, and vehicle traffic. While funding and personnel resources would be allocated to minimize these effects, such allocations make these resources unavailable for other programs.

The management action is not expected to have significant adverse effects on wetlands and floodplains, pursuant to Executive Orders 11990 and 11988.

Coordination
The management action has been thoroughly coordinated with all interested and/or affected parties. Parties contacted include:

Congressional representatives
Governor of Louisiana
Louisiana Department of Wildlife and Fisheries
Louisiana State Historic Preservation Officer
Tunica-Biloxi Indians of Louisiana
Quapaw Tribe
Caddo Nation of Oklahoma
Local community officials
Interested citizens
Friends of Black Bayou Lake, Inc.

Findings
It is my determination that the management action does not constitute a major federal action significantly affecting the quality of the human environment under the meaning of Section 102(2)(c) of the National Environmental Policy Act of 1969 (as amended). As such, an environmental impact statement is not required. This determination is based on the following factors (40 C.F.R. 1508.27), as addressed in the Environmental Assessment for the Black Bayou Lake NWR:

1. Both beneficial and adverse effects have been considered and this action will not have a significant effect on the human environment. (Environmental Assessment, pages 109-122)

2. The actions will not have a significant effect on public health and safety. (Environmental Assessment, pages 109-122)

3. The project will not significantly affect any unique characteristics of the geographic area, such as proximity to historical or cultural resources, wild and scenic rivers, or ecologically critical areas. (Environmental Assessment, pages 109-122)

4. The effects on the quality of the human environment are not likely to be highly controversial. (Environmental Assessment, pages 109-122)

5. The actions do not involve highly uncertain, unique, or unknown environmental risks to the human environment. (Environmental Assessment, pages 109-122)

6. The actions will not establish a precedent for future actions with significant effects nor do they represent a decision in principle about a future consideration. (Environmental Assessment, pages 109-122)

7. There will be no cumulatively significant impacts on the environment. Cumulative impacts have been analyzed with consideration of other similar activities on adjacent lands, in past action, and in foreseeable future actions. (Environmental Assessment, pages 109-122)

8. The actions will not significantly affect any site listed in, or eligible for listing in, the National Register of Historic Places, nor will they cause loss or destruction of significant scientific, cultural, or historic resources. (Environmental Assessment, page 109-122)

9. The actions are not likely to adversely affect threatened or endangered species, or their habitats. (Environmental Assessment, pages 109-122)

10. The actions will not lead to a violation of federal, state, or local laws imposed for the protection of the environment. (Environmental Assessment, pages 109-122)

Supporting References
U.S. Fish and Wildlife Service. 2009. Draft Comprehensive Conservation Plan and Environmental Assessment for Black Bayou Lake National Wildlife Refuge, Ouachita Parish, Louisiana. U.S. Department of the Interior, Fish and Wildlife Service, Southeast Region.

Document Availability

The Environmental Assessment was Section B of the Draft Comprehensive Conservation Plan for Black Bayou Lake National Wildlife Refuge and was made available in September 2009, for public review and comment. Additional copies are available by writing: North Louisiana National Wildlife Refuge Complex, 11372 Highway 143, Farmerville, Louisiana, 71241.

Signed
_____
Cynthia Dohner
Regional Director

3/10/10
_____
Date